Central Government Silver Treasury

# Global Economic History Series

VOLUME 12

---

# The Quantitative Economic History of China



VOLUME 1

The titles published in this series are listed at *brill.com/qehc*

# Central Government Silver Treasury

*Revenue, Expenditure and Inventory Statistics, ca. 1667–1899*

*By*

SHI Zhihong

BRILL

LEIDEN | BOSTON

First published 2014, in Chinese 清代户部银库收支与库存研究 (ISBN 978-7-5097-5673-7) by Social Sciences Academic Press, Beijing, China.

Cover illustration: displayed is the utter left part of the eighteenth-century remake of the twelfth-century original painting *Along the River During the Qingming Festival* by Zhang Zeduan. The remake is created by five Qing dynasty court painters (Chen Mu, Sun Hu, Jin Kun, Dai Hong and Cheng Zhidao) and is currently in the National Palace Museum in Taipei. The painting captures the daily life of people and the landscape of the capital, Bianjing (today's Kaifeng) from the Northern Song period. Licensed under public domain, via Wikimedia Commons.

Library of Congress Cataloging-in-Publication Data

Names: Shi, Zhihong, 1949- author.
Title: Central government silver treasury : revenue, expenditure and inventory statistics, ca. 1667-1899 / by Shi Zhihong.
Other titles: Qing dai hu bu yin ku shou zhi he ku cun yan jiu. English Description: Leiden ; Boston : Brill, [2016] | Series: Global economic
history series ; volume 12 | Series: The quantitative economic history of China ; volume 1 | Includes bibliographical references and index. |
Description based on print version record and CIP data provided by publisher; resource not viewed.
Identifiers: LCCN 2015045070 (print) | LCCN 2015040102 (ebook) | ISBN 9789004307339 (E-book) | ISBN 9789004307322 (hardback : alk. paper) | ISBN 9789004307339 (e-book : alk. paper)
Subjects: LCSH: Finance, Public--China--History. | Monetary
policy--China--History. | China--Economic policy--1644-1912. |
China--Economic conditions--1644-1912.
Classification: LCC HJ1402 (print) | LCC HJ1402 .S54513 2016 (ebook) | DDC 336.5109/033--dc23
LC record available at http://lccn.loc.gov/2015045070



Typeface for the Latin, Greek, and Cyrillic scripts: "Brill". See and download: brill.com/brill-typeface.

ISSN 2405-870X
ISBN 978-90-04-30732-2 (hardback)
ISBN 978-90-04-30733-9 (e-book)



This book is printed on acid-free paper and produced in a sustainable manner.

Printed by Printforce, the Netherlands

# Contents

# Series Editors' Preface to the Quantitative Economic History of China Series

For a long time now, there has been a real lack of quantitative information on the economy of China. This lack odd in view of the vast size of this population-rich country, which is currently one of the world's biggest economies. Given recently revived interest in the quantification of historical economies, which has resulted in projects on, for example, Indonesia, the United States and the United Kingdom, it is only logical that attention should also be directed towards China.

At first sight, one might conclude that no quantitative information on China is available. This is in part due to a non-quantitative research paradigm that exists in China itself, and in part because of the nature of the Chinese data. These are spread over a variety of sources, and they have taken form against a very different social, cultural, and economic background than comparable data from the West. Yet, recently some source publications have appeared that deal with, for example, prices and education, as well as some other isolated topics. Still, many of these publications are unsuitable for an analysis of China's economy, partly because they are often written in Chinese and partly because they do not offer a systematic overview of long-run quantitative data. This is especially problematic since historical economic and social research is increasing relying on quantitative methods.

As a combined effort of several Western and Chinese scholars, this book series presents data that will enable the compilation of Chinese historical economic statistics. The main objective is to fill in gaps in the quantification of the historical economy of China and facilitate analysis of its long-term evolution. We hope, with this series, to promote both research into, and knowledge of, this important country.

*Bas van Leeuwen, Yi Xu and Peter Foldvari*
(Utrecht, The Netherlands), 20 July 2015

# List of Figures and Tables

## Figures



## Tables

# Emperors of the Qing Dynasty

| | |
|---|---|
| *Shunzhi* | 1644-1661 |
| *Kangxi* | 1662-1722 |
| *Yongzheng* | 1723-1735 |
| *Qianlong* | 1736-1795 |
| *Jiaqing* | 1796-1820 |
| *Daoguang* | 1821-1850 |
| *Xianfeng* | 1851-1861 |
| *Tongzhi* | 1862-1874 |
| *Guangxu* | 1875-1908 |
| *Xuantong* | 1909-1911 |

# Chinese Terms

Anchashi Si (按察使司), the Yamen of Anchashi. Commonly called Nietai (臬台), Anchashi is the provincial judge who is charged with the supervision over the criminal law. He acts as a final (provincial) court of appeal in criminal cases and has jurisdiction over offences committed by provincial officials.

Anliang jintie (按粮津贴), a surcharge on the land tax levied in Sichuan province in the late Qing.

Baoquan Ju (宝泉局), the Mint Bureau under the Ministry of Revenue.

Baoxiao (报效), (businessmen) contribute money to the government for public use.

Baoyuan Ju (宝源局), the Mint Bureau under the Ministry of Works.

Beihuang Jingfei (备荒经费), fund for disaster relief; one of the special funds submitted to the capital by the provinces in the late Qing.

Beiyang Dachen (北洋大臣), Northern Commissioner of Trade.

Bennian shoukuan (本年收款), the current year's receipts.

Bitieshi (笔帖式), an official title, no grade, handling documentary affairs in offices.

Buzhengshi Si (布政使司), Provincial Treasuries with the head called Buzhengshi (布政使, Provincial Treasurer). In a province, the Buzhengshi is the nominal head of the civil service and the treasurer of the provincial exchequer.

Caiban yin (采办银), silver for purchasing expenexpenditure.

Caomi zhejia (漕米折价), tribute rice levied in silver.

Caoxiang (漕项), additional taxes on the grain tribute, collected in silver.

Caoyun Zongdu (漕运总督), Governor of Water Transport.

Changli juanshu (常例捐输), also called changjuan (常捐) for short, a recurrent contribution.

Changli zhengshou (常例征收), routine revenues.

Changshui (常税), also called changguan shui (常关税), referring to the collection of Chinese Regional Customs.

Chaoshen (朝审), a system of joint review by the central government ministers of condemned prisoners held by the Ministry of Punishments.

Chengse yin (成色银), low purity silver.

Choubei Xiangxu (筹备饷需), fund for preparing soldiers' pay, one of the special funds allocated to the provinces in the late Qing.

Choubian Junxiang (筹边军饷), military fund for the southeast coastal defence.

Chuan (串), a string. One chuan of copper cash contained 1000 coins.

Chuan-Chu Shili (川楚事例), the Contribution for the Sichuan and Hubei Incident.

Chuan yun junliang shili (川运军粮事例), the contribution for the transportation of army provisions in Sichuan province.

Chunbo (春拨), spring allocation.

Dachu Ce (大出册), the aggregate expenditure register.
Dajin Ce (大进册), the aggregate revenue register.
Dangfang (档房), Office of Records.
Dang shi qian (当十钱), 10-cash, a copper coin issued in the late Qing.
Daqian (大钱), large coins/ token metal coins issued during *Xianfeng*.
Daqing Baochao (大清宝钞), also called Baochao for short; Precious Paper Notes of the Great Qing, issued during *Xianfeng*.
Dashi (大使), an official title. In the Three Stores, a Dashi was in charge of the incoming and outgoing official documentary affairs.
Dashiting (大使厅), the Dashi's Office.
Diding (地丁), an agricultural land tax collected in silver.
Dimin Jingxiang (抵闽京饷), substituted fund for taking the place of Jingxiang of Fujian province, one of the special funds submitted to the capital by provinces in the late Qing.
Dongbei Bianfang Jingfei (东北边防经费), fund for the northeast border defence, one of the special funds submitted to the capital by provinces in the late Qing.
Donggu (冬估), winter estimate.
Duanpi Ku (缎匹库), the Store of Silk Fabrics.
Duanpi-Pizhang Ku (缎匹皮张库), the Store of Silk Fabrics and Leathers.
Ducha Yuan (都察院), the Court of Censors, a central government organ of the Qing dynasty.
Ezheng shu (额征数), the regular quota of a tax.
Fangkuan jianping (放款减平), balancing surplus from payments.
Fangyong (防勇), provincial defence forces.
Fanku (藩库), also called Buzhengshisi Ku ( or Siku for short), the Provincial Treasury.
Fu fama (副砝码), a copy balance-scale.
Gaitu guiliu (改土归流), introducing regular government in tribal areas.
Gaohuoyin (膏火银) literally means lamp expenses, referring to a grant of financial aid to students studying in official schools.
Gengzi Incident (庚子事变), the Boxer Rebellion.
Guangchu Si (广储司), the Storage Office, a section under the Department of Internal Affairs.
Guanku Dachen (管库大臣), the Minister of Management of the Three Stores.
Guanli Hubu Sanku Yamen (管理户部三库衙门, Managing Office of the Three Stores of the Ministry of Revenue.
Guanpiao (官票), also called Hubu Guanpiao (户部官票), Official Notes issued by the Ministry of Revenue during *Xianfeng*.
Guan yinqianhao (官银钱号), official banking house, mainly dealing in money exchange.

Guben Bingxiang (固本兵饷), literally meaning "solidiers' pay for consolidating the basis", one of the special funds allocated by the Ministry of Revenue from 1863; it was renamed Guben Jingxiang (固本京饷) from 1866 onwards.
Guben Jingxiang (固本京饷), literally meaning "Jingxiang for consolidating the basis", one of the special funds submitted to the capital by provinces in the late Qing.
Guozi Jian (国子监), the Imperial Academy.
Gupin kouliang qian (孤贫口粮钱), grain rations for orphans and the poor.
Haifang Jingfei (海防经费), fund for coastal defence.
Haifang Shili (海防事例), contribution for coastal defence.
Haijun Yamen (海军衙门), Naval yamen.
Haoxian (耗羡), land-tax surcharge under the name of meltage fees.
Haoxian guigong (耗羡归公), transferring meltage fees into the public state.
Hou Ku (后库), the Back Store (the original name of the Silver Treasury before 1656).
Huang Ce (黄册), the Yellow Registers.
Huanjie xikuan (还借息款), repayment of interest and loan.
Hubu (户部), the Ministry of Revenue.
Hubu Sanku (户部三库), the Three Stores of the Ministry of Revenue.
Hubu Yinhang (户部银行), Bank of the Ministry of Revenue, the first national bank of the Qing dynasty, established in 1904 and renamed Da Qing Bank in 1908..
Huitong Guan (会同馆), guesthouse for tributary envoys.
Jiafang Fengxiang (加放俸饷), fund for increasing the payment of official salaries, one of the special funds submitted to the capital by provinces in the late Qing.
Jiafu Fengxiang (加复俸饷), fund for restoring official salaries, one of the special funds submitted to the capital by provinces in the late Qing.
Jiangnan Chouban Fangwu Li (江南筹办防务例), contribution for preparing the defence of the southern regions of the Yangtze River.
Jiansheng (监生), student of the Imperial Academy.
Jiaojin yin (交进银), silver handed in for the use of the imperial household.
Jiaping (加平), handling fee..
Jifu (畿辅), areas near the capital.
Jingcheng (经承), a kind of service official who runs errands in the office.
Jingguan Jintie (京官津贴), allowance of capital officials, one of the special funds submitted to the capital by provinces in the late Qing.
Jingpiao (京票), also called Jing Qianpiao (京钱票), means "Beijing Notes", a paper money issued during *Xianfeng*.
Jingping (京平), the capital-standard scale.
Jing xiang (京饷), Provisions to the capital (by provinces).
Jinji Fangxiang (近畿防饷), fund for defending the capital region, one of the special funds allocated to the provinces in the late Qing.
Jinyin Ku (金银库), the Gold and Silver Treasury.

Juanmian (蠲免), to remit levies.
Juanna (捐纳), contributions from selling official positions.
Juanna Fang (捐纳房), Donation Office, a section under the Ministry of Revenue.
Juanshu (捐输), also called Jjuanna (捐纳), contributions from selling official positions.
Junji Dachen (军机大臣), the Grand Minister of the Strategy Board.
Junxu xiexiang (军需协饷), inter-provincial military assistance.
Kubing (库兵), soldiers guarding stores.
Kucang Si (库藏司), the Department of Storage, a section under the Ministry of Finance set up in 1906.
Kuping (库平), the treasury-standard scale.
Kushi (库使), title of an official of stores, no grade, in charge of keeping records and tallies.
Langzhong (郎中), an official title of the first class of grade five of the nine civilian ranks (the head of a sub-ministerial department of the central government of the Qing dynasty).
Li (厘), a unit of weight (also that of length and area). One li = 1/1000 of a tael.
Liangtai (粮台), an office set up to supply provisions for moving troops during a war.
Liangzhe (粮折), grain tax levied in silver.
Likin (厘金), a business tax levied in the late Qing and early Republic of China.
Lingqin gongying (陵寝供应), Royal Mausoleum supplies.
Lishiguan (理事官), an official Manchu title established in the early Qing, equivalent to Langzhong in position and level of rank. After *Yongzheng*, only the Imperial Clan Court (Zongren Fu宗人府) had Lishiguan.
Luying (绿营), the green standard army.
Mizheyin (米折银), rice as paid salary, or living subsidies paid in silver.
Nanyang Dachen (南洋大臣), Southern Commissioner of Trade.
Neige daku (内阁大库), Archives of the Grand Secretariat.
Neige dianjiting (内阁典籍厅), Certification Office of the Grand Secretariat.
Nei Ku (内库), the inner treasury (part of the Silver Treasury).
Neiwu Fu (内务府), Department of Internal Affairs, an organ responsible for the affairs of the royal family.
Neiwufu jingfei (内务府经费), fund for the Department of Internal Affairs.
Nian'e jiekuan (年额解款), funds forwarded annually in fixed quotas.
Piaohao (票号), an exchange office in old China; a firm dealing in money exchange, deposits and loans.
Pingyu (平余), balancing surplus.
Qianliang (钱粮), money and grain.
Qianliang Shumu Ce (钱粮数目册), a register recording amounts of money and grain.
Qianpiao (钱票), cash notes.

Qianzhuang (钱庄), a banking house in old China.
Qing ce (青册), blue covered register (or book).
Qintian Jian (钦天监), the Bureau of Astronomy.
Qiubo (秋拨), autumn allocation.
Qiying Jiaxiang (旗营加饷), fund for increasing Eight-banner soldiers' pay, one of the special funds allocated to the provinces in the late Qing.
San Ku (Sanku) (三库), the Three Stores.
Sansui yinliang (散碎银两), small pieces of silver.
Shangjuan (商捐), a donation from businessmen.
Shenji Ying (神机营), one of the troops of the praetorian guard set up in 1861.
Shilang (侍郎), an official title of the first class of grade two in the nine civilian ranks, assistant minister of the Six Ministries of the central government (each ministry had two Zuo Shilang (左侍郎), meaning Left Shilang, and two You Shilang (右侍郎), meaning Right Shilang).
Shiping (市平), the market-standard scale.
Shiquanwugong (十全武功), ten military exploits of the *Qianlong* emperor.
Shixianshu yin (时宪书银), Almanac expenses.
Shizu wenyin (十足纹银), full silver ( the official standard purity of full silver was 93.5374% in the Qing dynasty).
Siku (司库), storekeeper, an official title of the first class of grade seven in the nine civilian ranks of the Qing dynasty.
Siku fengchu (司库封储), keeping reserves in Fanku.
Sizhu Ce (四柱册), four-column inventory.
Suishi jiekuan (随时解款), irregularly forwarded funds.
Tandingrudi (摊丁入地), merging the poll tax with land tax.
Tie daqian (铁大钱), iron tokens issued during *Xianfeng*.
Tielu Jingfei (铁路经费), Railway fund.
Tiexie (贴写), copyist.
Ting (厅), an administrative district in the Qing dynasty.
Tong daqian (铜大钱), copper tokens issued during *Xianfeng*.
Tong yuan (铜元), copper yuan.
Tunfu yin (屯赋银), silver of land tax on military land.
Tuyao shuili (土药税厘), tax and likin on domestic opium.
Wai Ku (外库), the outer treasury (part of the Silver Treasury).
Waixiao (外销), government revenues/expenditures that do not have to be reported to the throne for approval.
Wen (文), a unit of Chinese copper coins, refers to one coin.
Wucheng Qiliusuo (五城栖流所), refugee station of the Five Districts of the capital.
Xian (县), county, the lowest provincial administrative district of ancient China.

Xiangpiao (饷票), an alias for Jing Qianpiao, since it was mainly used for paying salaries of the soldiers.

Xiebo (协拨), inter-provincial assistance.

Xiexiang (协饷), inter-provincial soldier's pay assistance.

Xijie Shangkuan (息借商款), Business Loan with Interest, a government bond issued in 1894.

Xin Haifang Juanxiang Yin (新海防捐项银), silver of new contribution for coastal defence.

Xinjun (新军), the new army.

Xinzeng zhengshou (新增征收), new levies.

Xizheng yangkuan (西征洋款), fund allocated for repaying the foreign loans borrowed by Zuo Zongtang during his westward march.

Xubo Jingxiang (续拨京饷), additionally allocated provisions to the capital.

Xuwan (续完), arrears collected in the current year.

Yamen (衙门), government office.

Yangkuan (洋款), foreign loans.

Yanglian yin (养廉银), anti-corruption allowance.

Yangshui (洋税), maritime customs duties.

Yangyao likin (洋药厘金), likin levied on imported opium.

Yanjiang (验匠), craftsman in charge of checking the purity of silver.

Yanjin jiajia (盐斤加价), price markup on salt.

Yanli (盐厘), likin on salt.

Yanliao Ku (颜料库), the Store of Dyes.

Yanliao-Zhizhang Ku(颜料纸张库), the Store of Dyes and Paper.

Yinfu (印付), a document with an official seal issued by the Ministry of Revenue to inform the Silver Treasury to accept the delivered silver.

Yin Ku (Yinku) (银库), the Silver Treasury.

Yinpiao (银票), silver notes.

Yinzha (印札), a document with an official seal issued by the Ministry of Revenue to inform the Silver Treasury to pay out silver.

Yuanbao (元宝), shoe-shaped ingots.

Yuanbo Jingxiang (原拨京饷), originally allocated provisions to the capital.

Yuanwailang (员外郎), an official title of the second class of grade five in the nine civilian ranks, immediately subordinate to the Langzhong in a department of the central government of the Qing dynasty.

Yushi (御史), also called Jiancha Yushi (监察御史), an official title of the second class of grade five in the nine civilian ranks, a censor.

Zangfa yinliang (赃罚银两), silver from confiscations and fines.

Zanxing shili (暂行事例), provisional contributions for raising special funds.

Zhangyin Langzhong (掌印郎中), Langzhong who keeps the office seal.

Zhen (镇), a division, i.e. a military unit of the "new army" of the late Qing dynasty.
Zheng'e (正额), the regular amount (of government revenues/expenditures).
Zheng fama (正砝码), an original (Treasury-standard) balance scale used to weigh objects.
Zhenggong Juanshu (郑工捐输), the contribution for Yellow River works in Zhengzhou.
Zhiqian (制钱), official copper coins.
Zhizao yin (织造银), silver for weaving expenses.
Zhou (州), an administrative district of ancient China.
Zhushi (主事), an official title of the first class of grade six in the nine civilian ranks of the Qing dynasty.
Zong Dangfang (总档房), General Office of Records, the main administrative department under the Managing Office of the Three Stores.
Zouxiao (奏销), submitting financial reports to the throne for approval.
Zouxiao Ce (奏销册), a register attached to a financial report to the throne for approval.
Zouxiao huangce (奏销黄册), a Yellow Register attached to a financial report to the throne for approval.

# Currencies Used during the Qing dynasty

## Silver

Silver and copper coins were the main currencies used in the Qing dynasty. Silver circulated in the form of small pieces and ingots of various weights. The basic unit of weight to measure silver was the "tael" (*liang*两; 16 *liang* = 1 catty or *jin*斤), which had decimal subdivisions, each with its own name, but those in daily use were the *qian* (钱), *fen* (分) and the *li* (厘):

One tael = 10 qian = 100 fen = 1000 li.

When measured using different standard scales, the actual weights of one tael of silver varied slightly. Three main official standard scales were in use: the *Kuping* (库平, Treasury standard scale), the *Guanping* (关平, Customs standard scale) and the *Caoping* (漕平, Tribute standard scale). In addition, hundreds of market standard scales (*shiping*市平) were used at different places, and sometimes even in the same place. The weights of one tael of silver measured by the three main official standard scales were:

| | | | |
|---|---|---|---|
| 1 *Kuping* tael | = | 37.31 grams | (≈ 1.316 oz avdp); |
| 1 *Guanping* tael | = | 37.68 grams | (≈ 1.329 oz avdp); |
| 1 *Caoping* tael | = | 36.69 grams | (≈ 1.294 oz avdp). |

The shoe-shaped silver ingot of 50 taels was generally called *yuanbao* (元宝). The smaller ones were called *zhongding* (中锭, middle-sized ingot, 10 taels) and *xiaoding* (小锭, small ingots, weighing 1 to 5 taels). Small pieces of silver weighed less than one tael.

The purity of silver that circulated in the market also differed. The officially stipulated standard silver to be used in tax collection and Treasury records was called *shizuwenyin* (十足纹银) or *wenyin* (纹银) for short (meaning full silver or fine silver), the purity of which was 935.374‰.

In addition, various types of silver dollars (*yinyuan*银元) circulated in the late Qing. As well as foreign dollars (e.g. the Mexican dollar, called *Ying Yang* (鹰洋) because it carried an eagle, the British trade dollar, *Zhan Yang* (站洋) and the Japanese dollar, called *Long Yang* (龙洋)), a native dollar called *Long Yang* (龙洋, Dragon dollar) was cast and used during the *Guangxu* era; it equaled 0.72 tael of *Kuping* wenyin.

## Copper Coins

The smallest unit of official copper coins (*zhiqian*制钱) was the *wen* (文), one cash. *Diao* (吊) or *chuan* (串), strings, of one thousand coins, were used as large counting units.

The officially stipulated weight of one copper coin was 1 qian (钱, one-tenth of a Chinese ounce or liang) before 1657, but the coin's weight was changed to 1.4 qian between 1657 and 1684. From 1684 to 1702, the weight was changed back to 1 qian, only to revert once more back to 1.4 qian during the period 1702 to 1734. From 1734 onwards, the weight of one copper coin was fixed at 1.2 qian, which did not change until the early 1850s.

Official copper coins cast before 1684 contained 70% copper and 30% zinc. The ratio between the two metals changed to 6:4 in 1684 and 5:5 in 1727, respectively. From 1740 onwards, the composition of copper coins was set at 50% pure copper, 41.5% zinc, 6.5% lead and 2% tin. This new cash containing lead and tin was called *qingqian* (青钱, blue coin); previously cast cash was called *huangqian* (黄钱, yellow coin).

Although there was a short period in the early 1850s (1853-1855) when the Qing government issued various copper and iron tokens, the prevailing copper cash circulating in the late Qing were 10-cash and copper coins. From 1900 onwards, a new machine-made copper cash called *Tongyuan* (铜元, Copper yuan) was issued and gradually took the place of traditional copper coins.

## Exchange Rates of Silver and Copper Coins

The official exchange rate between the two currencies was 1:1000:

1 tael of silver = 1000 wen of copper coins.

In reality, various complex factors, such as price changes of silver and copper, the weight and use of copper coins cast at different times, and market supply and demand caused exchange rates to fluctuate. Ignoring short-term fluctuations, generally market exchange rates of silver and copper coins were:

1 tael of silver = 700-800 wen of copper coins during 1644 - 1735;
= 800 - 900 wen of copper coins from 1736 to the early 1800s;
= more than 1000 wen of copper coins from the 1810s to the 1820s;
= 1500 – 2000$^{+}$ wen of copper coins from the 1830s to the early 1850s;
= 1000 – 1500 wen of copper coins from 1857 to 1911.

In the late Qing, the actual value on the market of a 10-cash copper token was 2 copper coins.

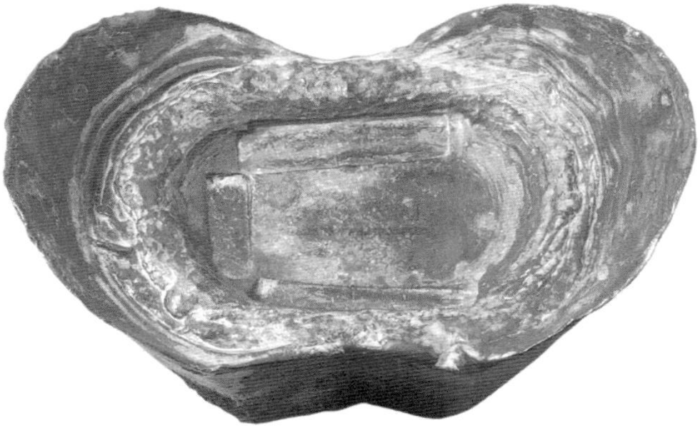

COIN 1 *Shoe Shaped Silver ingots in* Xianfeng *Period (1851–1861)*

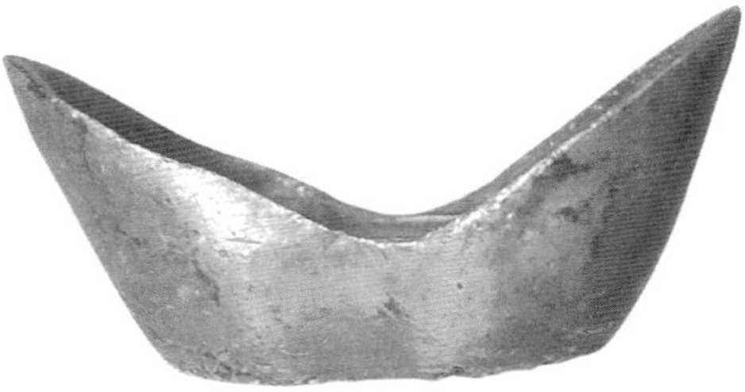

COIN 2 *Shoe Shaped Silver ingots in* Guangxu *Period (1875–1908)*

COIN 3 *Small silver ingots in* Guangxu *Period (1875–1908)*

COIN 4 *Copper coin in* Shunzhi *period* (*1644–1661*)

COIN 5 *Copper coin in* Kangxi *period* (*1662–1722*)

COIN 6 *Copper coin in* Yongzheng *period* (*1623–1735*)

COIN 7 *Copper coin in* Qianlong *period (1736–1795)*

COIN 8 *Copper coin in* Jiaqing *period (1796–1820)*

COIN 9 *Copper Coin in* Daoguang *period (1821–1850)*

COIN 10 *Large copper coin (1000-cash) in* Xianfeng *period (1851–1861)*

COIN 11 *Copper Yuan (20-cash) in* Guangxu *period (1875–1908)*

COIN 12 *Silver dollar issued in 1914* (Beiyang *Government Period*)

# Introduction

There were three major stores under the Ministry of Revenue in the Qing dynasty, which, together known as *Hubu Sanku* (户部三库) , were the Silver Treasury (*Yin Ku* 银库), the Store of Silk Fabrics (*Duanpi Ku* 缎匹库) and the Store of Dyes (*Yanliao Ku* 颜料库). Of these three stores, the Silver Treasury was the most important. As "the confluence of national tax receipts"[1], it kept all taxes on agricultural land, salt and customs, as well as miscellaneous levies submitted each year to the capital (i.e. Beijing) by provincial governments. It was responsible for the release of all central government expenditures, such as the stipends of Eight-Banner soldiers, princes, nobles and government officials, the expenses of government departments and offices in the capital, the costs of maintenance workers and servants, and so on. The importance of the Silver Treasury was to the Qing dynasty what national treasuries are to us today.

In fiscal matters, the Qing dynasty favored the capital above the provinces. During the early Qing period, all regular amounts (*zheng'e* 正额) of salt gabelle and customs duties collected within the country had to be sent to the capital and stored in the Silver Treasury, except for a small portion kept to meet necessary expenses of the tax authorities themselves. In addition, the provincial governments were also required to send a considerable portion of land taxes and various miscellaneous levies to the Silver Treasury as provisions to the capital (*jing xiang* 京饷), after deducting amounts needed to cover their own provincial budget. Up until the mid-nineteenth century, provincial contributions to the Silver Treasury at the disposal of the central government had been no less than one-quarter to one-third of national aggregate revenues. During the late Qing, due to increased fiscal autonomy and budgetary expenditure at the provincial level, a smaller proportion of the national aggregate revenue ended up in the Silver Treasury, but the absolute amount was still considerable.

Given the vast amount of money flowing through the Silver Treasury each year, any study on Qing finances would necessarily be incomplete if it did not discuss this particular aspect of the central government's revenues and expenditures. Thus far, however, there have been almost no in-depth writings on the Silver Treasury and its revenues and expenditures – the little literature there is on the subject is rather superficial.[2]. The main reason for this is the lack of

---

1 *Huidian Shili*, Volume 182.

2 As far as I know, the earliest introduction to the Silver Treasury and its evolution is a short essay entitled "Qingdai Hubu Sanku Shimo" (清代户部三库始末) by Zhao Quancheng

 | DOI 10.1163/9789004307339_002

relevant historical materials and reliable data covering extended periods. Neither official publications nor personal writings published during the Qing period contain any systematic records of the Silver Treasury.

There is, however, a considerable amount of surviving Qing archival materials pertaining to the Silver Treasury available. Among these, a great number of Yellow Registers (*Huangce* 黄册) containing aggregate revenues and expenditures (*Dajin Ce* 大进册 and *Dachu Ce* 大出册), as well as four-column inventories (*Sizhu* 四柱), are well preserved. As products of the system of *zouxiao* (奏销, submitting financial reports to the throne for approval), these registers contain detailed records of the revenues, expenditures and inventories of the Silver Treasury over consecutive years ranging from the early Qing to the late Qing, together forming a basically complete time series. In the 1930s, thanks to the efforts of Tao Menghe, head of the Peiping Institute of Social Survey[3], and Tang Xianglong, a member of the same institute, workers were dispatched to various places where the remaining Qing archives had been stored after 1911, including the Documentation Office of the Palace Museum

(赵泉澄) in the 53rd historical supplement to *Tienjin Yishi Bao* (天津益世报) May 2, 1937. After that, the main publications related to the subject are: Peng Zeyi (彭泽益), "Xianfengchao Yinku Shouzhi Pouxi" (咸丰朝银库收支剖析), in *Shijiu Shiji Houbanqi de Zhongguo Caizheng yu Jingji* (十九世纪后半期的中国财政与经济); "Kang Yong Qian Hubu Yinku Linian Cunyinshu" (康雍乾户部银库历年存银数), in *Lishi Dang'an* (历史档案), 4(1984); Sun Xiao (孙小), "Daoguang Hubu Yinku Shiqie'an Suolun" (道光户部银库失窃案琐论), in *Zhongguo Shehui Jingjishi Yanjiu* (中国社会经济史研究), 4 (1985)；岸本美绪 (Kishimoto Mio), 清代户部黄册について, in 石桥秀雄ed., 清代中国の诸问题；and Ren Zhiyong (任智勇), "Shishu Wanqing Hubu Yinku Zhidu yu Gengzi Zhihou de Biange" (试述晚清户部银库制度与庚子之后的变革), in *Qingshi Yanjiu* (清史研究), 2 (2005). In addition, Luo Yudong (罗玉东), Tang Xianglong (汤象龙) and Zhou Yumin (周育民) have also used parts of the Silver Treasury archives in their works; see Luo's *Zhongguo Likin Shi* (中国厘金史), Tang's *Zhongguo Jindai Haiguan Shuishou he Fenpei Tongji* (中国近代海关税收和分配统计) and Zhou's *Wanqing Caizheng yu Shehui Bianqian* (晚清财政与社会变迁). The articles and books mentioned above, except for the ones by Zhao, Kishimoto and Ren, discuss the Silver Treasury only briefly, besides quoting some data recorded in the Yellow Registers. Zhao and Ren's articles are only very brief introductions to the Silver Treasury and its evolution. Kishimoto's work is by far the most comprehensive of the writings published on the subject: it not only introduces the Silver Treasury of the Ministry of Revenue, but also contains a concise discussion on the Treasury's Yellow Registers, including their types, contents and existing condition; furthermore, using these data from the registers, a brief analysis of the inventories of the Treasury from 1667 to 1774 and the Treasury income structure in some selected years (1725, 1753 and 1812) is given. However, since the author read just a small part of the Treasury's archives, it still lacks a fuller discussion on the revenues, expenditures and inventories of the Qing Silver Treasury.

3 It merged into the Institute of Social Sciences of Academia Sinica in 1934.

and the Institute of Arts at Peking University, in order to copy these Yellow Registers. The copies made at that time later became part of the Qing archive collections stored in the Institute of Economics, Chinese Academy of Social Sciences (CASS). These copies of the Yellow Registers are fully consistent with the originals in their content, but the data are recorded in Arabic numerals and presented in carefully designed tables. They are, thus, easier to use than the originals.

Ever since I joined the Institute of Economics as a researcher in 1988, I have been thinking about writing a book on the subject of the Qing Silver Treasury. However, as I was constantly preoccupied with other research projects and various assignments, until recently I was only able to make some informal use – every now and then – of a small amount of the data recorded in the registers. Fortunately my participation in the compilation of the national Qing history project gave me time to thoroughly study the copies of the Silver Treasury Yellow Registers stored in the Institute of Economics, resulting in the monograph before you. In it you will find not only the revenues and expenditures for each month but also the figures registered in the Treasury's annual four-column inventories. I have also included whatever supplementary materials I found in the original Silver Treasury Yellow Registers, which are kept in the First Historical Archives of China (FHAC), as well as material gathered from other archival sources. All these can be found in tabular form throughout the chapters and appendices of this book. I believe the publication of these valuable historical data will help advance the study of the fiscal history of the Qing dynasty.

CHAPTER 1

# The Central Government's Silver Treasury

## 1.1 Set-up and Evolution of the Three Stores

The Three Stores of the Ministry of Revenue located in the capital were national treasuries set up by and exclusively accessible to the central government[1]. The first national treasury of the Qing dynasty was set up at the back of the Ministry of Revenue immediately after the Manchu court entered Beijing and declared its rule of the whole empire in 1644. This treasury, due to its location, was called "the Back Store" (*Hou Ku* 后库) in its first few years but was renamed the Silver Treasury in 1656. In that same year the Store of Silk Fabrics and the Store of Dyes were set up outside the Donghua and the Xi'an Gates (respectively) of the Forbidden City. From then on, the system of the Qing's national treasuries *San Ku* ("the Three Stores") was established[2]. As their names indicated, the holdings in the Three Stores were different. The Silver Treasury mostly held gold, silver and copper coins, while the Store of Silk Fabrics held cloth, leather, cotton, thread, linen and all kinds of silk fabrics. The Store of Dyes stored copper, iron, lead, tin, cinnabar, yellow lead, fragrant rosewood, yellow tea, white wax, yellow wax, paper, tung oil, rosewood, red sandalwood and various other articles; this store was also responsible for making joss sticks and candles for the imperial court or use in state sacrificial ceremonies .

In terms of management, the Back Store was original placed directly under the Ministry of Revenue but this changed in 1650, when the Qing court decided that taxes and other provisions sent to the capital from the provinces had to be

1 In addition to the Three Stores of the Ministry of Revenue, there were other stores in the capital. Among these, the Six Stores (the stores of sliver, leathers, satin, clothing, tea and porcelains) under the Storage Office (*Guangchu Si* 广储司) of the Department of Internal Affairs (*Neiwu Fu* 内务府) were also famous. Belonging to and mainly serving the imperial family, these were not national stores, athough there were some overlaps between them and the Three Stores of the Ministry of Revenue during the Qing period, especially in the late Qing. The holdings in these six stores mainly produced by the Department of Internal Affairs and its affiliates or purchased in different regions of the country, as well as some tributes regularly submitted by the provinces.

2 According to the Yellow Registers, during the *Shunzhi* and the early *Kangxi* the three stores were also called *Jinyin Ku* (金银库, the Gold and Silver Treasury), *Duanpi-Pizhang Ku* (缎匹皮张库, the Store of Silk Fabrics and Leathers) and *Yanliao-Zhizhang Ku* (颜料纸张库, the Store of Dyes and Paper).

 | DOI 10.1163/9789004307339_003

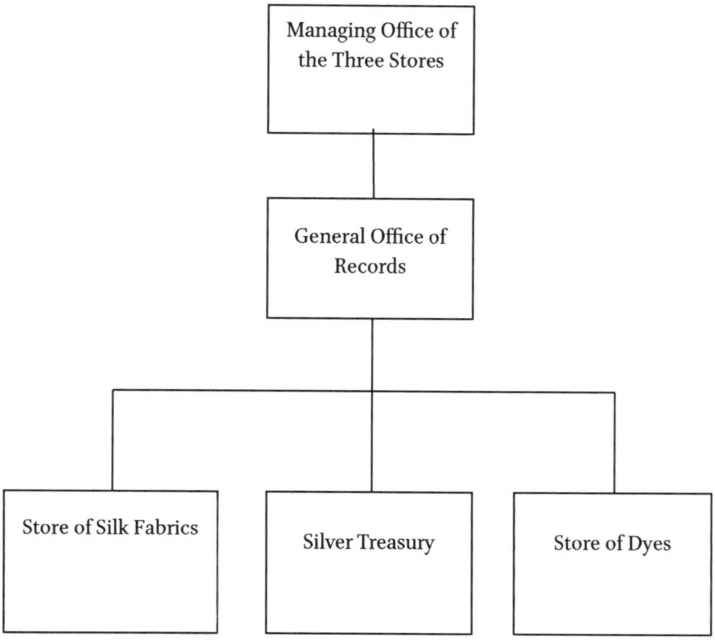


FIGURE 1.1 *The administrative structure of the Three Stores (1730–1902)*

managed by government ministries separately, instead of solely by the Ministry of Revenue. Nevertheless, in 1664 the management of the Three Stores reverted again to the Ministry of Revenue. Princes and ministers began to be appointed to manage the Three Stores from 1723 onwards, and the official seal with characters *Guanli Hubu Sanku Yamen* (管理户部三库衙门, Managing Office of the Three Stores of the Ministry of Revenue) was cast and conferred in 1730. Thus, the Three Stores had in time become a relatively independent department of the government. In 1902, when the Qing court abolished *Guanku Dachen* (The Minister of Management of the Three Stores), this independent status ended and the Three Stores were once more put under the Ministry of Revenue. In 1906, along with *Hu Bu* being renamed *Duzhi Bu* (度支部, the Ministry of Finance), the Store of Silk Fabrics and the Store of Dyes were placed under *Kucang Si* (库藏司, Department of Storage) of the new ministry, while the Silver Treasury, being renamed *Jinyin Ku* (金银库, the Gold and Silver Treasury), remained directly under the authority of the Ministry of Finance.

From the early 1720s to 1906, the Three Stores had been managed by high-ranking imperial officials called *Guanku Dachen* (管库大臣, Minister of Management of the Three Stores), who were selected from members of the Manchu nobility or from among the Manchu and Han ministers. All *Guanku Dachen* were appointed by the emperor personally and put in charge of "checking inventories and managing revenues and expenditures (of the Three stores)"[3]. There were generally four positions available for *Guanku Dachen*: two for ethnic Manchu and two for ethnic Han. Their tenure of office was not fixed until 1801, when it was set at one year. In 1809, this was changed to three years.

The main administrative department under the Managing Office of the Three Stores was called *Zong Dangfang* (总档房, General Office of Records) or *Dangfang* (档房, Office of Records). This office, composed of five persons – one *Zhushi* (主事, an official title of grade six in the nine civilian ranks. As the director, the *Zhushi* kept the seal of the office); two *Bitieshi* (笔帖式, an official title, no grade, handling documents affairs in the office); and two *Jingcheng* (经承, a kind of service official running errands in the office) – was responsible for the following affairs: (1) keeping the records of the Three Stores; (2) managing and supervising officials and servants of the Three Stores; and (3) handling documents regarding the inflow of taxes and other provisions sent to the capital by the provinces, such as checking the delivery documents carried by provincial officials, issuing receipts, and so on.

In addition of the *Dangfang* officials, the Three Stores also had their own officials:

- *Langzhong* (郎中), an official title of grade five in the nine civilian ranks. As the top official appointed to administer the store, the *Langzhong* held the store's seal and was overall in charge of its affairs. There were four such positions of *Langzhong* during the period of the Back Store (from mid-1640s to 1656). After the separation of the Three Stores, two *Lishiguan* (理事官, a Manchu official title, equivalent to *Langzhong* in position and level of rank)in charge of the unified management of the Three Stores were appointed by the Qing court. As from 1686, with each store beginning to have its own team of officials according to an order from the imperial court, *Langzhong* replaced *Lishiguan* once again and began to be called *Zhangyin Langzhong* (掌印郎中, meaning *Langzhong* as a seal-keeper). The total number of positions of *Zhangyin Langzhong* was three – each store had one.
- *Yuanwailang* (员外郎), an official title of grade six, the deputy of *Langzhong*. There were two *Yuanwailang* in the period of the Back Store, three after the separation of the Three Stores (each store had one), which increased to six in 1724 (each store had two).
- *Siku* (司库), an official title of grade seven. As a storekeeper, *Siku* was responsible for the safety of the money or goods stored and was required to ensure they were kept in good condition. There were six *Siku* during

3 *Qianlong Huidian*, Volume 8.

the period of the Back Store. After the separation of the Three Stores, the total quotas were unchanged but were appointed to each store (two for each) in 1686. As from 1724 the number of *Siku* in the Silver Treasury was cut to one.

- *Dashi* (大使), an official title. The position of *Dashi* together with a new office called *Dashiting* (大使厅, *Dashi's Office*)were set up in the Three Stores in 1724 to be in charge of incoming and outgoing official documents between the Three Stores and the provinces, as well as other government departments or offices. In the beginning there was one *Dashi* set up for each store, but this increased to two in 1738.
- *Bitieshi* (笔帖式), handled documentary affairs in the stores. There were thirteen *Bitieshi* in the late Qing: six in the Silver Treasury, three in the Store of Silk Fabrics and four in the Store of Dyes.
- *Kushi* (库使), no grade, in charge of keeping records and handling teller-related affairs in the store. In the late Qing, the Silver Treasury had four *Kushi*, the Store of Silk Fabrics had nine *Kushi* and the Store of Dyes had eleven *Kushi*.
- *Jingcheng* (经承). As service officials running errands, each of the three stores had two *Jingcheng* in the late Qing.

In addition to all these officials, there were a number of other staff and servants, such as *Tiexie* (贴写, copyist in the store), *Yangjiang* (验匠, craftsman in charge of checking the percentage of silver coming into the Silver Treasury), *Kubing* (库兵, soldiers sent to guard the stores) and so on. According to the *Hubuzeli* (户部则例, Regulations of the Ministry of Revenue), edited in 1874, altogether 24 such persons served the Silver Treasury in the late Qing period: ten *Tiexie* (five under the regular budget and five under special funding), twelve *Kubing* and two *yanjiang*.

As from 1744 the tenure of most of the official positions in the Three stores, i.e. those from *Langzhong* through to *Kushi*, became three years (before then, *Siku* and *Dashi* could hold their posts for five years). And according to regulations of the Qing dynasty, with the exception of *Guanku Dachen*, all officials serving the Three Stores had to be Manchus. At least two of the four *Guanku Dachen* had to be Manchus; Han ministers could be selected and appointed to any of the other two positions remaining unfilled .

## 1.2 Management of the Silver Treasury

The Silver Treasury of the Ministry of Revenue stored most fiscal receipts of the central government. They mainly came from taxes on agricultural land, salt gabelle, customs duties, and miscellaneous levies, which were sent to the capital from all over the country every year. Of these, according to the regulations of the Qing dynasty, taxes on agricultural land and the miscellaneous levies, both of which had been collected from *xian* (县, county), or *zhou* (州) and *ting* (厅) – the lowest administrative districts of the country, were submitted by provincial treasuries (*Buzhengshi Si* 布政使司) after they had deducted the amounts needed to cover their provincial budget and items related to inter-provincial assistance (*xiebo* 协拨). The salt gabelle and customs duties were sent on by the collecting authorities set up in provinces after deducting an amount for use by these authorities themselves.

Besides taxes mentioned above, the Silver Treasury had other revenues. For example, according to the *Hubu zeli* (户部则例, Regulations of the Ministry of Revenue), edited in 1874, in the late Qing period, in addition to regular provisions to the capital, at least 77 items of *nian'e jiekuan* (年额解款, annually forwarded funds) had to be sent to the Silver Treasury by provincial treasuries or salt administration authorities, 63 of which were fixed amounts and 14 unfixed. The revenues of the Silver Treasury also included forwarded funds called *suishi jiekuan* (随时解款, occasional funds), such as *zangfa yinliang* (赃罚银两, silver from confiscations and fines) submitted by provincial judges (*Anchashi Si* 按察使司) or handed in by relevant government departments in the capital; donations for purchasing official ranks or titles collected by the Donation Office (*Juanna Fang* 捐纳房); and copper coins produced by *Baoquan Ju* (宝泉局, the Mint Bureau under the Ministry of Revenue) and *Baoyuan Ju* (宝源局, the Mint Bureau under the Ministry of Works) each year.

The Silver Treasury was divided into two parts: "the inner treasury" (*nei ku* 内库), and "the outer treasury" (*wai ku* 外库). Located behind the Donghua Gate of the Forbidden City, the inner treasury was set up during the reign of Emperor *Kangxi* (1662–1722). It held a silver reserve of more than one million taels that could not be drawn on unless for emergencies, such as a siege of the capital by enemy troops. The outer treasury, which was situated at the back of the Ministry of Revenue and stored the central government's revenues for its daily use, was what we generally call "the Silver Treasury".

All silver sent into the Treasury was weighed using the standard Treasury scale *kuping* (库平). In 1732 the Qing government conferred upon each province "original weights of scale" (*zheng fama* 正砝码), together with copies (*fu fama* 副砝码), cast by the Ministry of Revenue. It ruled that any escorting officer sent by the provinces to submit silver to the capital had to carry a duplicate balance scale with him and use it to weigh the silver handed in once he had arrived and calibrated his scale against the original treasury scale. If there was

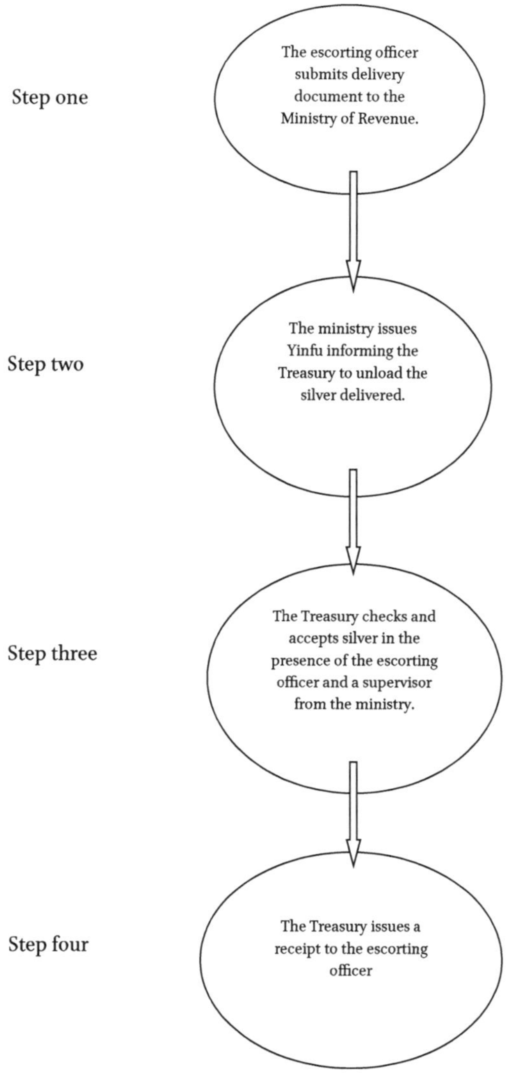


FIGURE 1.2
*Procedures for sending silver to the Silver Treasury*

too little silver, or the balance scale he carried was found to have been falsified, or the treasury official in charge of receiving silver had cheated in calibrating the two scales, the responsible person(s) – the escorting officer or the treasury official, or both – would be punished according to law. In 1734, the Qing government stipulated, furthermore, that if there was a shortage of silver submitted, the official of the province responsible for remitting the silver had to go to the Silver Treasury himself and check the weight of the silver again, together with the escorting officer and the treasury official in charge of receiving silver: if there was in fact no shortage, the treasury official was to be heavily punished;

if there was, the provincial official issuing the silver would have to supply the missing silver himself and both he and the escorting officer would be punished.

In 1734 the Qing government also stipulated that the *diding* (地丁) silver (the main part of agricultural land tax collected in all provinces) sent to the capital by the provinces had to be cast in silver ingots called *yuanbao* (元宝), weighing 50 *kuping* taels each, while it was permitted that *caoxiang* (漕项)[4], the additional tax on *caoliang* (漕粮)[5], together with the salt gabelle and customs duties, be sent in small pieces of silver (*sansui yinliang* 散碎银两")[6]. From 1738 onwards, all silver ingots delivered to the Treasury were to carry marks indicating where and by whom they were cast (after 1776, the year and month of casting also had to be added). Upon receiving small pieces of silver, according to regulations, a certain additional amount of silver (i.e. a handling fee) called *jiaping* (加平) had to be paid into the Silver Treasury. In 1761, the Qing government stipulated that the ratio of additional *jiaping* was to be 15/1000 for sending taxes on the salt gabelle and customs duties, and 5/1000 for sending *caoxiang*. After 1843, all silver paid into the Treasury was subject to *jiaping* at a ratio of 25/1000, in addition to the *diding* silver and the rent silver collected on eight-banner land in Zhili province.

There were strict procedures to be followed when sending silver to the Treasury. These included four main steps: (1) upon his arrival in the capital, the escorting officer went to the Ministry of Revenue to submit the delivery document issued by his province; (2) the relevant department of the Ministry issued a document with the seal of the Ministry (*yinfu* 印付) informing the Treasury that the delivery document had been checked and the silver escorted by the officer could be unloaded; (3) a Treasury official checked and accepted the silver in the presence of the escorting officer and a supervisor sent by the relevant department of the Ministry; and (4) the Treasury issued a receipt to the escorting officer. All these steps were accompanied by elaborately documented

4 As the extra collection on *caoliang*, *caoxiang* were levied in silver to cover various expenses and losses of *caoliang* occurring during its collection, transportation and storage.

5 *Caoliang* (tribute) was a special kind of land tax paid in grain (mainly rice) in ancient China. During the Qing dynasty it was collected mainly in eight provinces (Jiangsu, Anhui, Jiangxi, Zhejiang, Hubei, Hunan, Shandong, and Henan) and transported to the capital each year by the Grand Canal.

6 From 1738 onwards, according to a new stipulation, the salt gabelle collected in *lianghuai* (两淮) (referring to areas north and south of the Huai River, one of the main salt producing areas; under the Qing's system of salt monopoly, the sales territory of *lianghuai* salt covered parts of Jiangsu, Anhui, Henan, Jiangxi, Hubei and Hunan provinces) was also to be cast into silver ingots, after which it was sent to the capital.

procedures and had to comply with various rules and regulations that changed – from the simple to the complex – continuously during the Qing period. Although the Qing government had been checking for errors at the very outset and tried various devices to defend its lifeline – the revenue of the Silver Treasury – fraudulent practices still occurred from time to time, in spite of the red tape it put in place.

There were also numerous rules and regulations for paying out silver. Any government department or office in the capital requesting to withdraw money from the Treasury had to send an application in both the Manchu and Han languages to the Ministry of Revenue in advance, specifying the purpose of the withdrawl, the amount, and who (name and title) would be sent to withdraw the money. After receiving the application, the relevant department of the ministry would investigate and if the application was found to be in order an approval document was issued. The latter document served as credentials for withdrawing the money from the Treasury, and detailed the purpose of use and amount to be payed out, to whom (name and title) the money would be paid, and which person (name and title) would be sent by the Ministry to supervise the payment. The payment had to be done at the appointed time and in the presence of both the persons sent by the department or office withdrawing the money and the supervisor sent by the relevant department of the Ministry; if substantial amounts were to be paid out, the *Guanku Dachen* were also required to be present.

According to regulations, silver payed out from the Treasury had to be drawn from the old storage, while the new receipts in the year were to be stored in another place so as to facilitate inspection and counting (stipulated in 1706). Pay for Eight-Banner soldiers had to be drawn by their officers, who were required to go to the Treasury in person, after which they returned to camp to pay each soldier personally (stipulated in 1734). For non-regular payments, such as those for construction, after its arrival at the Ministry of Revenue the application document had to be re-verified with the *yamen* (i.e. office) that applied for the money (stipulated in 1734). For the payout of funds for engineering appropriations, the official directly responsible for the engineering was required to go in person to the Treasury and be accompanied by a supervisor from the Ministry of Revenue (stipulated in 1809).

Regulations also stipulated that *yuanbao* ingots were only to be used for paying the salaries of Manchu and Mongolian nobles and government officials in the capital, and for appropriations for military actions (from 1761 onwards, special appropriations for disaster relief ordered by the emperor were also permitted to use *yuanbao*), while other expenditures had to be paid in small pieces of silver unless they were in short supply. When paying small pieces of silver

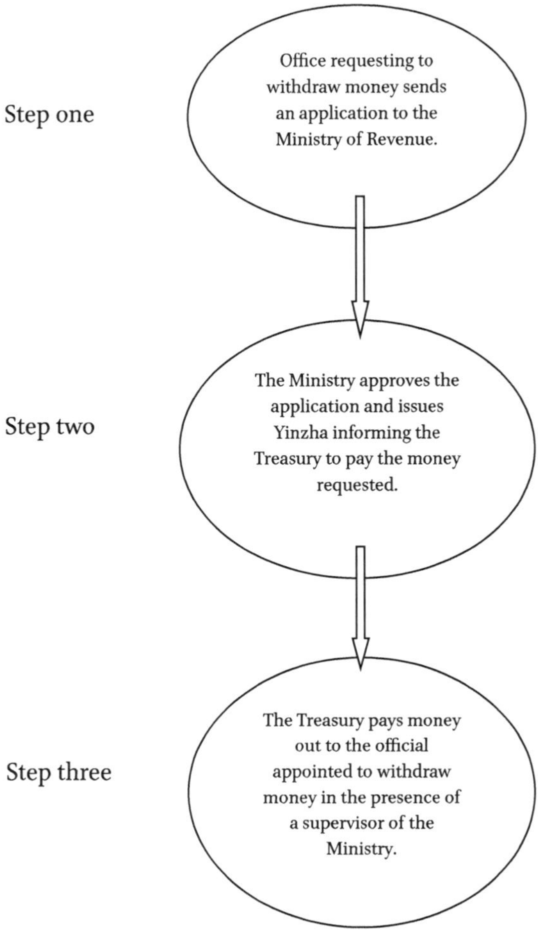


FIGURE 1.3
*Pay-out procedures of the Silver Treasury*

out, according to regulations, a certain portion of silver called *pingyu* (平余, balancing surplus)[7], generally being about 36/1000, had to be deducted from the approved amount of silver. Some payments were stipulated to ration a certain portion of *chengse yin* (成色银), which had a lower purity than the official standard percentage of “full silver” (*shizu wenyin* 十足纹银)[8].

7 All silver sent into the Treasury was weighed by the treasury-standard scale *kuping*. But for some payments, the Treasury would use the market-standard scale *shiping* (市平) to weigh the silver being payed out. Since the weight of *shiping* was lower than that of *kuping*, the Treasury would benefit from the difference in weight between the two scales; this was called *pingyu* (平余).

8 In the Qing dynasty, the official standard of purity of *kuping* silver was 93.5374%. The purity of silver that actually circulated on the market varied – it was often lower than 93.5374%.

Besides silver, copper coins (*zhiqian* 制钱") produced mainly by the Baoquan Mint Bureau (宝泉局) under the Ministry of Revenue, were the second most important currency stored and used in the Treasury[9]. From the *Yongzheng* period (1722–1735) onwards, the total amount of copper coins flowing in and out of the Treasury each year was at least several hundreds of thousands of strings (*chuan*, 串), with a maximum of sometimes more than one million strings[10]. The main use of copper coins was for the pay of Eight-Banner soldiers (according to regulations, soldiers had to be paid partly in copper coins). The same held for some other payments such as engineering appropriations.

Silver Treasury regulations concerning days of operation, staff management, entry- and exit-examination procedures, patrolling and guarding, and stock-taking are not dealt with here.

---

9 Some of the copper coins stored in the Silver Treasury came from the Baoyuan Mint Bureau under the Ministry of Works.

10 One *chuan* had 1000 copper coins and was equal to one tael of silver (according to the official rate of exchange).

CHAPTER 2

# Silver Treasury Registers and Their Copies

## 2.1 Yellow Registers of the Silver Treasury

Yellow Registers of the Silver Treasury were the annual financial reports submitted by the Treasury to the imperial throne. In order to understand the significance of these registers it is necessary to briefly consider two basic systems maintained during the Qing dynasty: one concerning fiscal administration, the other concerning official documentation.

The first of these is *zouxiao* (奏销), one of the most important fiscal administration systems in the Qing dynasty. According to the regulations established in the early Qing, all imperial revenues and expenditures originating or taken place inside and outside the capital had to be reported to both the emperor and the Ministry of Revenue[1] by the responsible officials or government departments. Upon receiving these reports the Ministry would start an audit process to review whether or not the revenues and expenditures were consistent with statutes or established cases: if they were, it would submit an audit report to the emperor for approval; if not, it would indicate the mistakes and order the reporter to make corrections. This process was called *zouxiao*. There were two kinds of *zouxiao*: the regular (routine) *zouxiao* and the special *zouxiao*. The regular *zouxiao* referred to current fiscal items such as the annual revenues of *diding, caoliang*, salt gabelle and customs duties, and yearly expenditures such as official salaries, soldiers' pay, government administrative expenses and so on. For each of these *zouxiao*, the item names and prescribed formats of reports, as well as a time limit (usually in the next fiscal year), had been set. Special *zouxiao* referred to the cases of irregular appropriations, such as those for military actions, special projects, disaster relief and the like. This kind of *zouxiao* was generally presented after the case no longer existed, although if a case lasted for years an annual report was also needed. The system of *zouxiao* enabled the emperor and the Ministry of Revenue to exercise effective supervision and have control over revenues and expenditures.

The other basic system is that of official documentation through a system of registers. In the Qing dynasty, whenever a report to the throne needed

1 If the reporting matters referred to military and project funds or fines and confiscated silver they also had to be reported to the Ministry of Defence, the Ministry of Works or the Ministry of Justice.

 | DOI 10.1163/9789004307339_004

(according to regulations) more details, such as the fiscal report for *zouxiao*, a register with all details of the matter would have to be attached to the memorial (the main statement) by the reporting official and, at the same time, the copy or copies of this register would be sent to the relevant government department(s) for verification. Since the registers presented to the throne were conventionally covered in yellow silk, and their copies sent to the relevant government departments were covered in blue paper or silk, the former were called "Yellow Registers" (huang ce 黄册), while the latter were called "Blue Registers" (qing ce 青册); also called inventory registers (清册). Once the issues concerned had been dealt with, the Yellow Registers would be transferred to the Certification Office of the Grand Secretariat (*neige dianjiting* 内阁典籍厅) and stored in the Archives of the Grand Secretariat (*neige daku* 内阁大库), while their copies would remain at the *yamen* to which they had been sent.

Surviving Yellow Registers of the Silver Treasury were the products of the above two systems: they were registers compiled for *zouxiao* and were the ones presented to the throne; their blue copies were sent to relevant government departments. According to their nature, they were also called *zouxiao ce* (奏销册, registers for *zouxiao*) or *zouxiao huangce* (奏销黄册, Yellow Registers for *zouxiao*).

According to the regulations of *zouxiao* recorded in *Daqing Huidian* (大清会典, Collected Statutes of the Qing Dynasty) and *Hubu Zeli* (户部则例, Regulations of the Ministry of Revenue), the Three Stores had to record their revenues and expenditures and submit a report to the throne at the end of each month. This report, called *yuezhe* (月折, monthly report), together with a detailed register attached, would be sent for verification to the *Jiangnan Dao* (江南道) of the Court of Censors (*Ducha Yuan* 都察院) within the first 10 days of the following month. In addition to the monthly report, at the end each year, the whole year's revenues and expenditures had to be aggregated from the monthly accounts and compiled into a register, thus preparing for *zouxiao* in the following year.

No specified time limit for *zouxiao* of the Three Stores can be found in the official statutes and regulations of the Qing dynasty. The surviving Yellow Registers of the Three Stores compiled after *Yongzheng* (1723–1735) did not give the date for submission either. But before the reign of *Yongzheng*, a date was always given on the first page. From these we know that the reporting time for the Three Stores was in the 3rd or 4th month of following year during the reign of *Shunzhi* (1644–1661) and in the 5th or 6th month or even later during the reign of *Kangxi* (1662–1722). Considering the submitting date recorded in the Yellow Registers of *Shunzhi* and *Kangxi*, and the practices of *zouxiao* for regular fiscal items, the date of presentation of the Yellow Registers of the Three Stores from *Yongzheng* onwards was most likely also in the following year.

Under *Shunzhi* and *Kangxi*, each of the Three Stores only compiled an annual four-column register called *Qianliang Shumu Ce* (钱粮数目册). In these registers, according to the prescribed formats of *sizhu ce* (四柱册) (also called *sizhu zouxiao ce* (四柱奏销册), the initial balance of the year, the total amounts of revenues and expenditures during that year, and the final balance at year-end were listed. From the reign of *Yongzheng* onwards, in addition to the four-column registers, the annually compiled *dajin ce* (大进册, register of aggregate revenues) and the *dachu ce* (大出册, register of aggregate expenditures) were also included. These newly included registers recorded in full detail all revenues/expenditures in the year, including the item's name, the amount and the date of entering or leaving the store, and also included which yamen sent/withdrew the item and the responsible department or office of the Ministry of Revenue. All items were listed monthly and this produced total amounts at the end of each month; a few registers also gave a total sum at year-end. The four-column register and the two newly added registers were supplementary to each other: one could know not only the overall condition of a certain store over a particular year but also obtain the details of revenues and expenditures during that year. From a simple four-column register through to the interconnected three registers, the evolution of the complilation of the Yellow Registers reflected the improvement of administration of the Three Stores.

Because of poor conditions for preservation, some of the Yellow Registers stored in the Archives of the Grand Secretariat became damaged or lost, even as early as in the early and middle Qing period[2]. Since the late Qing, these precious archives have suffered from even more serious losses. During the ill-fated period of the late Qing and the early Republic of China, many Yellow Registers of the Three Stores, together with many other archives of the Qing palace, were carted away from the palace where they had been stored, moved from one place to the next, sold and resold, falling into the hands of organizations and even individuals. Many were damaged or lost in the process[3].

---

2 For example, in 1775, when Emperor Qianlong ordered the Grand Councillors (*junji dachen* 军机大臣) to investigate and report on the annual inventories of the Silver Treasury from *Kangxi* to that year, he received a report in which he was told that since many of the registers of *Kangxi* had become "mildewed and rotten", the inventories during the reign could not be listed year by year (see the memorial to the throne by Grand Councillors in the 40th year of *Qianlong*).

3 See Xu Zhongshu (徐中舒), "Neige Dang'an zhi Youlai jiqi Zhengli" (内阁档案之由来及其整理) in *Ming Qing Shiliao* (明清史料), Volume 1, pp. 1–3; and "Zhongyang Yanjiuyuan Lishi

In the 1930s, the Documentation Office of the Palace Museum (now FHAC) rearranged and catalogued over 6,600 volumes of Chinese Yellow Registers that had remained in the palace, and published in 1936 *Neige Daku Xiancun Qingdai Hanwen Huangce Mulu* (内阁大库现存清代汉文黄册目录, Catalogue of Extant Chinese Yellow Registers of the Archives of Grand Secretariat in the Qing Dynasty). At nearly the same time, similar work was being done by the two major collectors of the scattered palace archives: the Department of Sinology of the Institute of Arts, Peking University; and the Institute of History and Philology, Academia Sinica. In 1947, these three institutes compiled and published *Qing Neige Jiucang Hanwen Huangce Lianhemulu* (清内阁旧藏汉文黄册联合目录, Union Catalogue of Chinese Yellow Registers stored in the Grand Secretariat of the Qing Dynasty), which, containing over 17,000 volumes of Chinese Yellow Registers, is by far the most complete catalogue of surviving Chinese Yellow Registers in existence. In 1952, after the foundation of the People's Republic of China, collections of the Grand Secretariat archives scattered throughout China, including the Yellow Registers, were all returned to the Archives of the Palace Museum (except those transported to Taiwan) and are now kept by FHAC[4].

---

Yuyan Yanjiusuo Suocang dang'an de Fenxi – zaishu neige daku dang'an zhi youlai jiqi zhengli" (中央研究院历史语言研究所所藏档案的分析－再述内阁大库档案之由来及其整理) in *Zhongguo Jindai Jingjishi Yanjiu Jikan* (中国近代经济史研究集刊), Volume 2–2 (May 1934), pp. 166–221. See also Li Pengnian (李鹏年), "Neige Daku – Qingdai Zuizhongyao de Dang'an Ku" (内阁大库－清代最重要的档案库), in *Gugong Bowuyuan Yuankan* (故宫博物院院刊), 3 (1981). Furthermore, in his essay "Tan Suowei Danei Dang'an" (谈所谓 '大内档案), based on his own experiences, Lu Xun (鲁迅) also disclosed relevant inside stories about how the Grand Secretariat archives were stolen or damaged during his service in the Ministry of Education of the Beiyang government (see Lu's *Eryi ji* (而已集).

4 Before the foundation of the People's Republic of China, the scattered Grand Secretariat archives were mainly collected by the Institute of History and Philology of the Academia Sinica, the Institute of Arts of the Peking University, the History Museum and the Fengtian Library in Shenyang. These archives were all taken over by the Archives of Palace Museum (originally the Documentation Office of the Palace Museum, now FHAC) in 1952, except for the 100 volumes transferred to Nanjing before the War of Resistance against Japan by the Institute of History and Philology and then transported to Taiwan before 1949 (the ones stored at the Meridian Gate and the Upright Gate of the Forbidden City by the Institute of History and Philology were also taken over by the Archives of Palace Museum in 1952) and a small number kept by the History Museum.

## 2.2 Copies of the Yellow Registers of the Silver Treasury

Copies of the Yellow Registers of the Silver Treasury are part of the more than 120,000 Qing archive copies now held by the Institute of Economics, CASS. They were copied from several institutes in Peiping during the seven years from winter 1930 to summer 1937, thanks to the efforts of Tang Xianglong and the support of Tao Menghe. Most copies of the Registers came from the Documentation Office of the Palace Museum, with a small number of them coming from the Department of Sinology of the Institute of Arts at Peking University. According to my investigations the collection of the Institute of History and Philology of the Academia Sinica was not copied. As far as the Silver Treasury is concerned the copied information is quite complete. It comprised almost all usable Yellow Registers still in existence at that time, including some extremely rare examples that can never be seen today. Table 2.1 gives an overview of volumes of surviving Yellow Registers of the Silver Treasury included in *Lianhemulu*, collected in FHAC and their copies kept in the Institute of Economics[5]:

First, as we can see from Table 2.1, the majority of Yellow Registers of the Silver Treasury in existence in the 1930s were collected by the Documentation Office of the Palace Museum and the Institute of Arts at Peking University, with only a small number being held in the Institute of History and Philology. The collection of the first two institutes (now the FHAC collection) amounts to more than 80 % of the volumes recorded in *Lianhemulu*. Second, almost all the Yellow Registers were copied, except for a notable difference in the number of volumes under the reign of *Guangxu* held in the collections of the Institute of Economics and FHAC. From my investigations, I suggest that there are two

5 The records did not include those volumes that had missed their compiling years. And the numbers of surviving volumes collected by the FHAC shown in Table 2.1 were based on the *Catalogue of Extant Chinese Yellow Registers of the Grand Secretariat Archives in the Qing Dynasty* and the *Catalogue of Yellow Registers* compiled by the Department of Sinology of the Institute of Arts of Peking University, which were merely the ones accessible now but not the entire collection of Yellow Registers held by FHAC. Its collection should also include those originally stored at the Meridian and Upright Gates of the Forbidden City by the Institute of History and Philology. However, these have never been touched since their arrival at FHAC, nor have they been catalogued. Therefore, the number of these volumes remains unknown. In fact, even the Yellow Registers originally stored in the Documentation Office and the Institute of Arts at Peking University have also not yet been thoroughly cleaned ever since they were accepted by the FHAC. So, sometimes you cannot always find a special register even it is indeed listed in a catalogue.

TABLE 2.1 *Volumes of surviving Silver Treasury Yellow Registers included in Lianhemulu, collected in FHAC, and their copies in the Institute of Economics (IE)*

| Period | Included in *Lianhemulu* | In FHAC collection | Copies with IE |
|---|---|---|---|
| *Shunzhi* | 2 | 0 | 1 |
| *Kangxi* | 2 | 0 | 1 |
| *Yongzheng* | 19 | 15 | 14 |
| *Qianlong* | 94 | 79 | 78 |
| *Jiaqing* | 52 | 46 | 43 |
| *Daoguang* | 65 | 56 | 56 |
| *Xianfeng* | 18 | 17 | 15 |
| *Tongzhi* | 10 | 8 | 8 |
| *Guangxu* | 26 | 19 | 7 |
| Total | 288 | 240 | 223 |

likely explanations for registers not being copied: either they were left out[6], or the originals were so badly deteriorated that they could not be copied. Yellow Registers copied in the 1930s were what remained after disasters. Some were mildewed and rotting, others were broken and some were destroyed. In the case of a defective register, if the missing part was only the last several pages, the loss would be limited to the data of the 12th month (if only the last page was lost, that would be no serious loss at all, since the monthly totals could still be obtained by adding up all the detailed amounts of the month); but if the missing part was the first page, the register would be of no use, because in that case we would never know when it was compiled. And if a significant part of the register had deteriorated or was glued or stuck together, the entire register would also become practically useless. In my opinion (I have checked all the accessible registers), the latter was the primary cause.

Table 2.1 also shows that none of the four remaining volumes of *Shunzhi* and *Kangxi* included in the *Lianhemulu* are in the collections of FHAC (at least they

6 When Tang Xianglong organized the copying of palace archives in the early 1930s, the rearrangement of Yellow Registers had not yet started, or at least had not been completed, both in the Documentation Office and the Institute of Arts at Peking University. In other words, the archives were still in a state of chaos then. So, it would be understandable if some registers were left uncopied. In addition, some registers might not have been collected until the copying had been completed, as some archives kept by the Documentation Office were gradually purchased from non-governmental sources.

are not in the catalogue). Nevertheless, two copies of them are to be found in the collections of the Institute of Economics – the *Yinku Qianliang Shumu Ce* (银库钱粮数目册, Register for Amounts of Money and Grain of the Silver Treasury) compiled in the 17th year of *Shunzhi* (1660) and the 44th year of *Kangxi* (1705). Unfortunately, both of them are incomplete. The *Shunzhi* register is practically unusable due to its severe data loss. The *Kangxi* register contains the revenues and expenditures for the year of 1705 but the initial and final balances of the year are missing. Incomplete as the two copies are, since they nevertheless contain precious early-Qing data of the Silver Treasury, they are still valuable.

The copies of the Silver Treasury Yellow Registers kept by the Institute of Economics are more complete from the reign of *Yongzheng* onwards. Although records of many years are incomplete, as a whole they still constitue a chain of revenue/expenditure data spanning a period of around 170 years, from the 1720s to the 1890s[7]. A systematic data chain for such a long period is rare in the fiscal history, as well as the entire economic history, of the Qing dynasty.

The copies have the same contents as their originals but the manner of recording the data is different. In the originals, the revenues/expenditures were recorded in chronological order by month, like a journal account, giving a monthly total at the end. The recording format of the original registers (*Dajin Ce* /*Dachu Ce*) was:

> The amounts of aggregate revenues/expenditures of the Silver Treasury from the 1st month to the 12th month of *xx* year are now listed as:
> The 1st month
> – With the *yinfu* (*yinzha*)[8] of *xx* department or office (of the Ministry of Revenue), *xx yamen* handed in/withdrew silver/coins *xx* (amounts of silver or copper coins) for *xx* item
> – With the *yinfu* (*yinzha*) of *xx* department or office (of the Ministry of Revenue), *xx yamen* handed in/withdrew silver/coins *xx* (amounts of silver or copper coins) for xx item
> …
> The total amount of revenues/expenditures of the month was silver *xx*
> Coins *xx*
> … (and so on until the 12th month)

7 The data in aggregate revenue registers continued until 1896, while data in aggregate expenditure registers and four-column registers continued until 1891.

8 *Infu* (印付) and *yinzha* (印札) were documents bearing seals of the Ministry of Revenue. The former was issued for informing the Silver Treasury to accept money coming in and the latter for paying money out.

However, in the copies, instead of by mere chronological order, the data were tabulated and classified first by the responsible departments or offices of the Ministry of Revenue, and then by months, as shown in Table 2.2.

TABLE 2.2 *Table format of Yellow Register copies*

| | **xx Year of xx reign** | **xx Department/Office (of the Ministry of Revenue)** | | |
|---|---|---|---|---|
| **Month** | **Revenues/Expenditures** | **Silver** | **Coins** | **Notes** |
| 1st month | xx *yamen* handed in/withdrawn *xx* item | (amount) | (amount) | – |
| | xx *yamen* handed in/withdrawn *xx* item | (amount) | (amount) | – |
| | … | … | … | – |
| … | … | … | … | – |
| 12th month | … | … | … | – |

There is a summary at the end of each volume of the copies, recording all monthly totals of the year. Obviously, the way the data has been recorded is clearer and more convenient for use in the copies than in the original registers.

Data in the four-column copies were arranged in the same way as in the originals, except that the figures in the four columns were changed from Chinese characters into Arabic numerals. The data recorded in these copies are quite reliable – all figures had been carefully checked by a corrector as well as the scribe: accurate entries were ticked with a pencil, while errors were corrected with red ink. I have compared some copies with the originals collected in the FHAC and also the figures in the aggregate revenue/expenditure registers with the four-column registers[9] and found few errors. Even if there is an error, it is mostly an accurate copy of the original rather than a slip of the pen. For some copies, a general check of the figures was done in addition to the careful copying work and as a result some errors in the originals were found.

9 The yearly total of revenues/expenditures obtained by adding up monthly totals in a register should be consistent with the figure of "new incomes/expenditures" in the four-column register of the same year. For the four-column registers, the "original balance" in a register should be consistent with the "final balance" in the previous year's register, and the "final balance" in it should be consistent with the "original balance" in the following year's register. For a four-column register itself, the difference obtained by deducting "expenditures" from the sum of the "original balance" and "new revenues" should be equal to the "final balance". These are the methods used to check the figures in the registers.

For example, in the copy of the aggregate revenue register of the 14th year of *Daoguang* there is a note after the total number of coins of the 11th month that reads: "The total number of coins of the 11th month does not match the sum of the detailed amounts. There are errors in the detailed amounts". Another note is to be found after the monthly totals in the copy of the aggregate revenue register of the 20th year of *Daoguang* that reads: "Totals of the 3rd and 12th months do not match the sums of the detailed amounts". These notes are manifest of the conscientiousness of the copyists and are of great help to researchers today.

Unlike their independent originals, the copies of Yellow Registers of the Silver Treasury collected in the Institute of Economics are bound into 35 thick volumes, which are arranged in three categories: "Registers of Aggregate Revenue", "Registers of Aggregate Expenditure" and "Four-column Registers"; within each category, the individual registers are arranged by reign and years. Table 2.3 summarizes the contents of these 35 volumes.

TABLE 2.3 *Contents of volumes of copies of the Silver Treasury's Yellow Registers collected in the Institute of Economics*

| Volume no. | Categories | Years |
|---|---|---|
| 1 | Aggregate revenue – *Yongzheng* | 2, 3, 5, 7, 9, 10, 11, 13 |
| 2 | Aggregate revenue – *Qianlong* | 1, 2, 5, 9 |
| 3 | Aggregate revenue – *Qianlong* | 11, 14, 16, 18 |
| 4 | Aggregate revenue – *Qianlong* | 19, 20, 25, 26 |
| 5 | Aggregate revenue – *Qianlong* | 28, 29, 30, 35, 37, 39 |
| 6 | Aggregate revenue – *Qianlong* | 41, 43, 46, 47, 48, 49 |
| 7 | Aggregate revenue – *Qianlong* | 50, 51, 55, 57, 58, 59, 60 |
| 8 | Aggregate revenue – *Jiaqing* | 1, 3, 6, 7, 9, 10, 12 |
| 9 | Aggregate revenue – *Jiaqing* | 13, 14, 17, 19, 20, 22, 24 |
| 10 | Aggregate revenue – *Daoguang* | 1, 2, 3, 4, 5, 7, 8, 9, 10, 12 |
| 11 | Aggregate revenue – *Daoguang* | 13, 14, 16, 19, 20, 21, 22, 23, 25, 26, 28, 29, 30 |
| 12 | Aggregate revenue – *Xianfeng, Tongzhi* and *Guangxu* | *Xianfeng*: 1, 2, 3, 5, 6, 9, 10<br>*Tongzhi*: 4, 5, 6<br>*Guangxu*: 18, 22 |
| 13 | Aggregate expenditure – *Yongzheng* | 3, 7, 8, 9, 11 |
| 14 | Aggregate expenditure – *Qianlong* | 1, 3, 5, 8 |
| 15 | Aggregate expenditure – *Qianlong* | 9, 14, 15, 17 |

TABLE 2.3 *Contents of volumes of copies of the Silver Treasury's Yellow Registers* (cont.)

| Volume no. | Categories | Years |
|---|---|---|
| 16 | Aggregate expenditure – *Qianlong* | 18, 22, 23, 25 |
| 17 | Aggregate expenditure – *Qianlong* | 26, 27, 29, 30 |
| 18 | Aggregate expenditure – *Qianlong* | 31, 32, 35, 36 |
| 19 | Aggregate expenditure – *Qianlong* | 37, 38, 40, 43 |
| 20 | Aggregate expenditure – *Qianlong* | 45, 46, 47, 49 |
| 21 | Aggregate expenditure – *Qianlong* | 50, 51, 53, 54 |
| 22 | Aggregate expenditure – *Qianlong* | 55, 56, 58, 59 |
| 23 | Aggregate expenditure – *Jiaqing* | 1, 2, 4, 5 |
| 24 | Aggregate expenditure – *Jiaqing* | 7, 8, 9, 10 |
| 25 | Aggregate expenditure – *Jiaqing* | 12, 14, 16, 17 |
| 26 | Aggregate expenditure – *Jiaqing* | 18, 19, 20, 21 |
| 27 | Aggregate expenditure – *Jiaqing* | 22, 23, 24, 25 |
| 28 | Aggregate expenditure – *Daoguang* | 1, 2, 3, 5, 6 |
| 29 | Aggregate expenditure – *Daoguang* | 7, 8, 9, 10, 11 |
| 30 | Aggregate expenditure – *Daoguang* | 12, 13, 14, 17, 18 |
| 31 | Aggregate expenditure – *Daoguang* | 19, 20, 21, 22 |
| 32 | Aggregate expenditure – *Daoguang* | 23, 24, 25, 27, 29, 30 |
| 33 | Aggregate expenditure – *Xianfeng* | 2, 3, 8, 9 |
| 34 | Aggregate expenditure – *Tongzhi* | 2, 4, 5, 6, 8 |
| 35 | – Aggregate expenditure: *Guangxu*<br>– Four columns: *Shunzhi* – *Guangxu*<br>– Appendix: *fanyin sizhu* (饭银四柱) and *yinqian riqing* (银钱日清) | – Expenditure, *Guangxu*: 5, 9, 17<br>– Four columns, *Shunzhi*: 17; *Kangxi*: 44; *yongzheng*: 1; *Qianlong*: 13, 18, 20, 22, 28, 38, 40, 41, 42, 45, 60; *Jiaqing*: 1,3, 7, 10, 12, 16, 20, 21, 22, 23; *Daoguang*: 1, 2, 7, 8, 10, 13, 14, 23; *Xianfeng*: 4, 6, 9, 11; *Guangxu*: 9, 17 |

## 2.3 Use in this Book of Copies of Yellow Registers

In this book I present two types of records concerning the silver and copper coins stored in the Silver Treasury: (1) annual aggregate revenues, expenditures and their surpluses/deficits; (2) annual inventories of the Silver Treasury. Both kinds are based mainly on those copies held by the Institute of Economics, CASS, and supplemented with data found in the archives of FHAC.

### 2.3.1 *Annual Aggregate Revenues, Expenditures and Their Surpluses/ Deficits*

These records were compiled from data recorded in the Yellow Registers of aggregate revenues/expenditures, together with the use of the four-column registers. The principal tables of this type of records are those concerning aggregate revenues/ expenditures categorized according to imperial reigns. Monthly figures in tables have been copied from the original registers; the annual totals are the sums of monthly figures. In addition to these tables, years with complete data of revenues and expenditures have been arranged in independent tables to show the yearly surpluses/deficits under the reigns of each emperor[10].

The surviving Yellow Registers of the Silver Treasury did not come through the centuries completely unscathed, i.e. they are fragmentary rather than abundant or complete – only a few annual registers contain complete data for all three volumes of revenues, expenditures and yearly four-column records. In order to make the data more complete and put present resources to better use, in this part of the records, data on "new revenues" and "expenditures" in the four-column registers have been used to supplement the missing data in the registers of aggregate revenues/expenditures (the former has been used to supplement missing revenue data and the latter has been used to supplement missing expenditure data). Figures from the four-column registers are all marked with an asterix (*) in the tables and explained in the notes.

The four-column registers have also been used when some of the monthly totals in a Yellow Register of aggregate revenues/expenditures have been lost (in most cases, the lost or incomplete data is that of the 12th month because a few of the last pages are missing) and, as a result, an accurate yearly total cannot be obtained. In that case, the figure of "new revenue"/"expenditure" recorded in the same year's four-column register (if it still exists) has been added in the corresponding column of the aggregate revenue/expenditure tables along with the sum of monthly total and marked "*". If the monthly

10 For *Yongzheng* and *Qianlong*, there are two surplus/deficit tables: one is based solely on the tables of aggregate revenues and expenditures of the period; the other is supplemented with those years of revenue/expenditure data that can be calculated from the inventory figures occurring on a list submitted to the emperor in 1775. The inventory figures on this list are complete from *Yongzheng* onwards, by which, together with the revenue/expenditure data already known, the missing data for some years can be calculated according to the following formula: a year's revenue = the year's expenditure + the year's inventory – last year's inventory; a year's expenditure = the year's revenue – the year's inventory + last year's inventory.

records are complete but their sum does not match the yearly total recorded in the four-column register, the figure found in the latter is also listed.

Some original registers not included in the Institute of Economics copies have also been used in this book in order to complete the Silver Treasury's historical records. These originals, in the possession of the FHAC, are: the aggregate revenue register of the 3rd year of *Qianlong*, the aggregate expenditure register of the 13th year of *Jiaqing*, and the aggregate revenue, expenditure and four-column registers of the 23rd, 24th and 25th years of *Guangxu*. Original FHAC registers not used in this book (eight in total) had deteriorated too much for them to be used. In conclusion, I have made full use of all accessible resources of the Yellow Registers of the Silver Treasury.

### 2.3.2 *Annual Inventories of the Silver Treasury*

These records have been compiled mainly based on extant four-column registers, using their "initial balance" and "final balance" figures. Two kinds of tables have been included: tables designed according to the original copies, listing all the four-column figures in them, and tables of annual inventories of the Silver Treasury, categorized by imperial reign.

Since the extant four-column registers are more incomplete than the registers of aggregate revenues and expenditures – all usable four-column registers date from *Yongzheng* onwards – I have supplement these records using data from a list provided to the throne dated the 40th year of *Qianlong*. This list, attached to a memorial submitted by *Junji Dachen* (军机大臣, Grand Minister of the Strategy Board) in 1775, was a detailed report on annual inventories of the Silver Treasury from the 6th year of *Kangxi* to the 39th year of *Qianlong* (1667–1774). Of the combined 78 years' inventory data on this list, 26 years fell under the reign of *Kangxi* – an excellent remedy for the lack of four-column registers of the *Kangxi* period; the other 52 years' data were a complete record from the 1st year of *Yongzheng* to the 39th year of *Qianlong* that can be used to supplement the missing data and check the existing data in the four-column registers for that period. This document was published in full in the 4th volume of *Lishi Dang'an* (历史档案, Historical Archives) in 1984. Were it not for Mr Lü Jian's discovery of this precious document, I would never have been able to cite this publication here.

In this book, directly copied silver/copper coin figures in the tables (monthly total figures in the aggregate revenue/expenditure tables and figures in the four-column tables) are all specified to three decimals, i.e. the smallest value is li (厘, 1/1000 of a tael) for silver and *wen* (文) for copper coins (according to Qing official rate of exchange, 1000 wen equalled one tael of silver). And for the calculated figures (yearly totals in the aggregate revenue/expenditure tables, figures in the surplus/deficit tables and the annual inventory tables), the numbers of silver and copper coins are expressed in taels and *chuan* (串), respectively; one chuan is equivalent to 1000 wen of copper coins)

CHAPTER 3

# Silver Treasury Revenues during the Qing Dynasty

## 3.1 Provisions to the Capital and Silver Treasury Revenues

Apart from some income obtained directly from within the capital, most revenues of the Silver Treasury came from *Jing Xiang* (京饷, provisions to the capital by provinces). From the early Qing up until the *Daoguang* era (1821–1850), land tax, salt gabelle, customs duties and miscellaneous levies were the four main sources of *Jing Xiang* sent to the Silver Treasury each year. From the *Xianfeng-Tongzhi* period (1851–1874), *likin* (厘金) and maritime customs duties (*yangshui* 洋税), two new pillars of taxation in the late Qing, were included in the submission of *Jing Xiang*.

Based on a highly centralized structure, the financial management of the Qing dynasty treated the entire country as one single unit under the complete control of the central government. Under such a structure "the Ministry is in charge of expenditures, while the provincial governors are responsible for revenues"[1], i.e. all taxes collected by provinces as part of national revenue had to be managed and distributed by the authorized department of the central government (the Ministry of Revenue) and not by the provinces – they had no right to decide how to spend what they collected. Allocating *Jing Xiang* arising from provincial taxation was a product of this structure, which lasted throughout the entire period of the Qing dynasty. However, due to a loosening of the central government's grip over the provinces in the late Qing, both the operational mode and the degree of realization of this centralized fiscal administrative structure saw considerable change. This evolution manifested itself in many aspects, but here I will only deal with changes in the system of allocating *Jing Xiang*.

In the early Qing, under the absolute authority of the central government, all taxes collected by provinces were controlled by the Ministry of Revenue. The Ministry took total control of the distribution of these revenues. According to regulations, both salt gabelle and customs duties collected in the provinces had to be sent directly to the capital and stored in the Silver Treasury – except for a certain portion that was kept for use by the collection authorities

1 Quoted from a memorial to the throne dated the 16th of the 6th month of the 8th year of *Shunzhi* (August 1, 1651) by Wei Xiangshu 魏象枢, *Xingke Jishizhong* 刑科给事中 of the "Six Sections 六科", see CSL: *Shizu Shilu*, Volume 57.

 | DOI 10.1163/9789004307339_005

themselves. As was the case for *diding* (the most important part of the agricultural land tax) and the miscellaneous levies, once these had been collected from *xian* 县/*zhou* 州/*ting* 厅 (i.e. the lowest level administrative districts), they first had to be sent to the provincial capitals, where they were stored in the Provincial Treasury (*Fanku* 藩库), also known as *Buzhengshisi Ku* (布政使司库). Without a directive from the capital, these *qianliang* (钱粮)[2] could not be put to any use unless in cases of emergency[3]. Three times a year, according to regulations, the provinces had to send fiscal reports called *donggu* (冬估, winter estimate), *chunbo* (春拨, spring allocation) and *qiubo* (秋拨, autumn allocation) on the inventories of their *Fanku* to the Ministry of Revenue in winter, spring and autumn, respectively. The system of these three reports, set up in 1725 under the reign of *Yongzheng* emperor, formed the basis for allocating *Jing Xiang* by the Ministry of Revenue.

The winter report was presented before the end of the fiscal year (generally in the 10th month). In this report, each province had to submit a budget estimate, with detailed registers attached, of the following year's payments of officers' salaries and soldiers' pay of the garrison troops; the provincial recurrent expenditures such as salaries of officials, cost of maintenance workers and servants, administrative expenses at all levels, funds for post stations, and so on, were paid according to regulations and needed no estimate in this report. Following the winter report, in the 2nd and 8th months of the following year the provincial governors had to submit spring and autumn reports requesting allocations (*qingbo* 请拨), once more accompanied by detailed accounts of the actual amounts of silver stored in *Fanku*.

After receiving these three reports the Ministry would start its bi-annual allocation process on the basis of all the arrangements. First, it would approve expenditures for the garrison troops estimated by provinces in their winter reports, as well as their recurrent provincial payments; these expenditures would be deducted from the amounts of silver stated in the inventories of each *Fanku*. Then, it would make arrangements for inter-provincial assistance, called *xiebo* (协拨) or *xiexiang* (协饷), by transferring funds from those provinces with financial surpluses to those that had deficits. After deducting all these items, the Ministry would allocate *Jing Xiang* to each province. In

2 The literal meaning of the word *qianliang* (钱粮) is "money and grain", but in many cases it refers only to silver and copper coins, as it does here.

3 In the early *Qing*, urgently needed provincial payments could be taken from *Fanku* inventories without prior approval from the court, although this had to be immediately reported to the Ministry of Revenue. From 1698 onwards, recurrent provincial expenditures were allowed to be paid without prior approval but had to be reported at the time of payment.

principle the remaining surplus would be earmarked as *Jing Xiang* to be sent to the capital[4].

There were strict rules for delivering this *Jing Xiang*. According to regulations stipulated in 1726, after receiving the directive document issued by the Ministry of Revenue for delivering *Jing Xiang*, provinces had to start their shipment in full amount without delay. The time limits stipulated for delivery of *Jing Xiang* varied according to the distance of a province from the capital: for Zhili, Shandong, Shanxi and Henan provinces it was within 60 days upon receiving the directive document; for Jiangsu, Anhui, Jiangxi, Zhejiang, Hubei and Hunan provinces it was within 80 days; and for Fujian, Guangdong and Guangxi provinces it was within 100 days.

This system remained unchanged until the *Daoguang* (1821–1850) era. However, the rebellion of the Taiping Heavenly Kingdom (1851–1864) brought about a profound shift in economic and political power between the central and provincial governments. During that rebellion and the re-establishment of imperial order that followed, it became increasingly difficult to maintain the fiscal management systems previously in place, including that of *Jing Xiang*. The highly centralized fiscal administration of the early Qing was based on the premise that the central government could exert absolute authority over the provinces. Only under this premise could taxes collected by provinces but managed by the central government, and could the Ministry of Revenue extract any surpluses, such as *Jing Xiang*, from provincial revenues. After the war, with the rise of a group of warlords, the Qing central government lost its complete control over the provinces. The dominant position of these actual holders of provincial power was strengthened and consolidated in the ensuing post-war reconstruction. They contributed greatly to the restoration of the imperial order, and through doing so they acquired control over all affairs – including foreign affairs – in their own "territories". They came to hold almost complete control over the collection and use of *likin*, one of the main tax revenues exploited by the warlords during the war to put down the Taiping Rebellion, and which formed a stable pillar of provincial finances during the late Qing period. Against such a background, along with the power shift from a highly centralized system to a pattern of "strong provincial governments and a weak central government" in the late Qing, the centralized fiscal management

4 In 1727, all provinces were ordered to keep a certain amount of fiscal reserves in *Fanku* for emergencies; this was called *siku fengchu* (司库封储, keeping reserves in *Fanku*). From 1730 onwards, similar funds were also established in stores of prefectures. Hence, when the Ministry of Revenue allocated *Jing Xiang*, the amount of provincial silver reserves kept at all levels had to be deducted from the provincial fiscal surpluses in order to ensure they would be refilled.

originally established in the early Qing was severely undermined, resulting in a "devolution of fiscal power", i.e. the creation and expansion of provincial fiscal autonomy. Nominally, a complete structure of fiscal systems reflecting central government control over the provinces remained, but the actual scope and practice differed greatly as it adapted to the reality of the increasing local autonomy.

Early in the 1850s, as the rebellion spread rapidly over a greater part of the country, the crisis of Qing's centralized fiscal management became apparent. Under fire, tax revenues in the war zones decreased markedly, while at the same time military supplies became the first priority for all provinces, and they devoured, directly or indirectly, much of the provincial revenues. More and more provinces became unable to comply with the allocation directives of the Ministry of Revenue – whether it concerned *Jing Xiang* or *xiexiang* – because of their own fiscal woes. Under such an unprecedented fiscal crisis, the Ministry of Revenue ceased to be the centre of control of national financial resources. It had to allow the provinces to finance themselves by any means. And in 1856 it was also forced to accept a new method for the allocation of *Jing Xiang*: instead of requisitioning all provincial surpluses, from that year on the Ministry began to allocate in advance a fixed quota of *Jing Xiang* to each province in the winter, asking them to send the funds to the capital in batches the next year. Initially the national total of *Jing Xiang* was 4 million taels per year, subsequently increasing to 5 million taels in 1860 and 7 million taels in 1861. In 1867, another 1 million taels, called *Xubo Jingxiang* (续拨京饷, additional *Jing Xiang*) was added; the original 7 million taels were referred as *Yuanbo Jingxiang* (原拨京饷, original *Jing Xiang*). From then on till the end of the Qing dynasty, it became standard practice for the Ministry of Revenue to allocate 8 million taels of *Yuanbo Jingxiang* and *Xubo Jingxiang* each year to the provinces and the customs income.

Originally, altering the way of allocating *Jing Xiang* was a temporary measure taken because of the war. However, once the war ended, faced with the reality of much greater provincial autonomy, the Ministry of Revenue had no choice but to maintain the new measure, although nominally the whole set of previous fiscal management systems, including *donggu*, *chunbo* and *qiubo*, were still in place.

Besides *Jing Xiang*, since the *Tongzhi* era (1862–1874), the Ministry of Revenue also allocated other capital funds in fixed quotas. In the late Qing, expenditures of the central government, just like those of the provinces, increased vastly, extending far beyond past levels. Often, when additional expenditures were needed the Ministry would raise a special fund and allocate additional quotas to the provinces and the customs. Special funds routinely required by the capital during the late Qing period were:

1. *Guben Jingxiang* (固本京饷, literally meaning "*Jingxiang* for consolidating the basis"). This was originally called *Guben Bingxiang* (固本兵饷, solidiers' pay for consolidating the basis); a total of 0.66 million taels each year, allocated from 1863 onwards, was sent to the *Fanku* of Zhili province, to pay soldiers of the four *zhen* (镇) divisions of the "new army" (*xinjun* 新军) and the four battalions of *Shenji Ying* (神机营, one of the praetorian guard units set up in 1861). In the 8th month of 1866, the fund was renamed *Guben Jingxiang* (固本京饷) and sent to the Silver Treasury of the Ministry of Revenue to be used for establishing six corps of cavalry and infantry.
2. *Dongbei Bianfang Jingfei* (东北边防经费, fund for the defence of the northeast border). Allocated from 1880 onwards, and totalling 2 million taels each year, these were used for northeastern border defence (when China was negotiating with Russia on the problem of Ili).
3. *Dimin Jingxiang* (抵闽京饷) and *Jiafang Fengxiang* (加放俸饷). In 1874, the Qing Government borrowed 2 million taels from HSBC to defend Taiwan against an invasion from Japan. Since the principal and interest of the loan was to be repaid from the annual *Jing Xiang* of *Fujian* customs, the shortfall of an additional 0.2 million taels was then levied by the Ministry of Revenue from other provinces and customs. This additional allocation was thus called *Dimin Jingxiang*. In early 1886 (the 12th month of the 11th year of *Guangxu*), in order to fully restore the payment of official salaries in the capital – because of the war these had been paid with a discount since the *Xiangfeng* period – the Ministry of Revenue changed the name of the fund to *Jiafang Fengxiang* (fund for restoring official salaries, one of the special funds submitted to the capital by provinces in the late Qing) and used it for this purpose. The total amount of *Jiafang Fengxiang* allocated was 1.2 million taels per year. Besides the 0.2 million taels of *Dimin Jingxiang,* the remaining one million taels came from an external capital fund called *xizheng yangkuan* (西征洋款), which was originally allocated by the Ministry to provinces and customs for the repayment of the principal and interest of foreign loans borrowed by Zuo Zongtang during his campaigns in Shaanxi and Gansu provinces. At this point, *xizheng yangkuan* was renamed *Jiafang Fengxiang*, becoming one of the special funds annually sent to the capital. In 1902, the entire 1.2 million taels of *Jiafang Fengx-*

*iang* was used to help pay the Boxer Rebellion Indemnity and ceased to be submitted to the capital.

4. *Jingguan Jintie* (京官津贴, allowances of capital officials) and *Jiafu Fengxiang* (加复俸饷, fund for restoring official salaries). From 1883 onwards, the Ministry of Revenue allocated 0.26 million taels of funds from the provincial *yangyao likin* (洋药厘金, *likin* levied on imported opium) for the payment of allowances to capital officials lower than the 4th grade (there were nine civilian grades). In 1886, after fully restoring the salaries of officials in the capital, this fund was renamed *Jiafu Fengxiang*. In 1902 it, too, was used to help pay the Boxer Rebellion Indemnity.
5. *Beihuang Jingfei* (备荒经费, fund for relief of natural disasters) This was allocated from 1883 onwards for famine relief and totalled 0.12 million taels per year.
6. *Qiying Jiaxiang* (旗营加饷). This was allocated from 1885 onwards to the provinces and *Caoyun Zongdu* (漕运总督, Governor of Tax Grain Transport), for increasing the pay of Eight-Banner soldiers in the capital; it totalled 1.33 million taels per year.
7. *Choubei Xiangxu* (筹备饷需, fund for soldiers' pay). In 1885, the Qing court redirected 2 million taels of "saved military funds in the westward march" to pay soldiers defending the region around the capital (*Jinji Fangxiang* 近畿防饷). In 1886 this fund was renamed *Choubian Junxiang* (筹边军饷), and was to be used for the southeastern coastal defence. In 1892 the fund was once again renamed *Choubei Xiangxu* and sent each year to the Silver Treasury of the Ministry of Revenue.
8. *Haifang Jingfei* (海防经费, fund for coastal defences). From 1875 onwards, the Qing Government allocated 4 million taels annually to provinces and the customs income for defence of the southeast coast. After 1877, this fund was divided into two and 2 million taels each sent to the *Nanyang Dachen* (南洋大臣, Southern Commissioner of Trade) and *Beiyang Dachen* (北洋大臣, Northern Commissioner of Trade). After the establishment of *Haijun Yamen* (海军衙门, the Navy *yamen*) in 1885, the fund began to be used for Naval military spending. After the *Haijun Yamen* was dissolved in 1895, the fund was sent to the capital.
9. *Tielu Jingfei* (铁路经费, Railway fund). This fund of 2 million taels per year was set up in 1889 for the construction of the Lu-Han (Lugouqiao-Hankou) Railway. An amount of 1.2 million taels were paid by the Ministry and 0.8 million taels were levied from provinces. As from 1891 the fund was used for the construction of the Guandong Railway.

Of Silver Treasury revenues in the late Qing, in addition to special funds named after specific expenditures, some were named after their sources, such as *sicheng yangshui yin* (四成洋税银, 40% of import duties), *yangyao likin* (洋药厘金, *likin* on imported opium), *tuyao shuili* (土药税厘, tax and *likin* on domestic opium), *Xin Haifang Juanxiang Yin* (新海防捐项银, newly contributed silver for coastal defence), and so on. Of these, *sicheng yangshui yin* came from customs duties. After the Second Opium War (also called the Arrow War by the British, 1856–1860), according to the *Conventions of Peking*, the Qing Government had to pay Britain and France 8 million silver taels each as indemnities from the "40% of import duties" collected in treaty ports. This special fund, after the indemnities had been paid off in 1866, was redirected to the Ministry every year and it became one of the stable revenue flows at the disposal of the central government.

*Yangyao likin* and *tuyao shuili* were taxes collected from the opium trade. In the *Xianfeng* era coastal provinces in the southeast had begun to levy *likin* on opium in order to raise funds with which to put down the Taiping Rebellion. After the Second Opium War, along with the legalization of opium trade, customs services in treaty ports began to levy duties on imported opium, while *likin* collecting offices in the provinces levied an additional *likin* on opium transported inland. In 1885, China and Britain signed the *Additional Articles to the Chefoo Convention*, which specified that both customs duties and *likin* on foreign opium had to be collected by the customs service at its point of import at a rate of 30 taels per 100-catty case for customs duties and "no more than 80 taels for *likin*". Thereafter, "*likin* on imported opium" was submitted as a special fund to the Ministry of Revenue each year. After the introduction of taxes on foreign opium, taxes and *likin* on domestic opium were levied all over the country. From 1890 onwards, taxes and *likin* on domestic opium were combined and collected by special offices set up in provinces and submitted annually as a special fund to the Ministry of Revenue.

Newly contributed silver for coastal defence was collected as from 1889, when the Navy *yamen* was in urgent need of funds for coastal defence. The Ministry of Revenue considered inventing another title to collect money for use, since the Contribution for Yellow River Works in Zhengzhou (*Zhenggong Juanshu* 郑工捐输) had expired by that time. Since there had been an instance named "Contribution for coastal defence" during the Sino-French War several years earlier, in order to distinguish the new case from the old one this new case was called *Xin Haifang Shili* (新海防事例, new case for coastal defence).

The special funds mentioned here were usually recorded as separate accounting items in the Yellow Registers of the Silver Treasury of *Guangxu*, with revenues and expenditures being listed separately.

The change from extracting all the surpluses in provincial tax revenues to allocating fixed levies not only came about because of the strengthening of provincial independence during the late Qing, it also reflected the nature of provincial revenues and expenditures at that time. In the early Qing, all taxes collected in the provinces and provincial expenditures were fixed by the central government and recorded in official statutes without changes unless approved by the emperor himself. Under the principle of "cut the coat according to the cloth", both provincial revenues and expenditures in the early Qing were rather stable with a current-account surplus. Such a fiscal system enabled easy control of provincial finances by the central government. However, in the late Qing, ever since the provinces had been allowed to finance themselves during the war against the Taiping Rebellion, a great deal of new items appeared in provincial revenues and expenditures. Brought about by the expansion of provincial fiscal autonomy, these new items were not recorded in the official files and their exact details could not always be ascertained by the central government unless provincial administrators reported them faithfully. In the face of this reality, and since it lacked the power to monitor the actual state of provincial finances, the central government had to make the best of things by taking the practical measure of levying capital funds in fixed quotas. The new way of levying capital funds meant that the central government had given recognition to the vested fiscal interests of the provinces, i.e. it would no longer be able to intervene in the provinces' actual revenues and expenditures as long as they submitted their regular tax quotas to the capital.

Nevertheless, there were also problems in the new equilibrium because provinces might not have enough funds or be willing to submit the prescribed amounts. In the late Qing, the submission of *Jing Xiang* and other special capital funds became a process of bargaining between the Central Government and the provinces. On the one hand, the central government, the Ministry of Revenue would emphasize the importance of the levies and the difficulties of the Ministry, demanding that the provinces place national interests above their own and submit all the funds as soon as possible and "by all means". On the other hand, the provinces might ignore these demands or prevaricated by making all kinds of excuses, such as pleading financial difficulties, shortage of revenues, mounting expenditures, and so on. As a result, the provinces might delay payments or only submit part of the amount due despite being urged again and again to pay up. In its turn, the Ministry of Revenue, once it had some funds in hand, might take no action against the provinces for late payment or shortfalls between the required and the submitted amounts. This bargaining process would repeat itself year after year.

The default of capital funds was most serious from the 1850s up to the early 1860s. *Jing Xiang* was seldomly submitted in full without delay in this period. In the 11th month of the 2nd year of *Tongzhi* (1863), an imperial edict read: "over the years, *Jing Xiang* has been allocated in advance from provincial *diding*, salt gabelle, customs duties and miscellaneous levies for the expenditures of the next year. Since the 11th year of *Xianfeng*, the allocated quota has been 7 million taels annually. However, except for Shanxi province, all other provinces have either failed to meet the deadline or have made no submission even after the deadline (from the 8th month till now) very few of the provinces have submitted this year's *Jing Xiang*, even after having been urged in official documents from the Ministry of Revenue again and again"[5]. After the Taiping Rebellion was put down and the march to the northwest came to an end, in mid-1870s the situation improved. However, following the First Sino-Japanese War (1894–1895) and especially after the *Gengzi* Incident (Boxer Rebellion, 1900), the Qing government lost control over almost all customs duties and most of the salt gabelle, because of a wave of huge war indemnities and foreign debts, while its expenditures continued to increase. Forced by extreme circumstances, the central government began to impose heavy provincial levies without regard for their actual revenues. Consequently, provincial defaults and shortages – and even resistance to the central levies – became more and more acute, which eventually led to an unprecedented financial crisis in both the central government and provinces. The crisis eventually resulted in experimental financial clean up and reform as from the late *Guangxu*, when the fall of the Qing dynasty was not far away.

## 3.2 Silver Treasury Revenues from *Kangxi* to *Daoguang*: 1662–1850

There are complete revenue figures for the Silver Treasury for 90 of the 189 years from *Kangxi* to *Daoguang* (1662–1850). Except for the *Kangxi* era, for which there is data for only one single year, there are revenue figures available for at least two-thirds of the succeeding reigns (see Table 3.1). On the whole, therefore, the data available for this period are sufficient for my research.

---

5 CSL: *Muzong Shilu*, Volume 85.

TABLE 3.1 *Number of years of revenue figures from* Kangxi *to* Daoguang *and their proportions relative to the total years of each reign*

| Reign | Years | Number of years with revenue figures and their proportions relative to years of reign | |
|---|---|---|---|
| | | Number of years | % |
| *Kangxi* (1662–1722) | 61 | 1 | 1.6 |
| *Yongzheng* (1723–1735) | 13 | 10 | 76.9 |
| *Qianlong* (1736–1795) | 60 | 39 | 65.0 |
| *Jiaqing* (1796–1820) | 25 | 17 | 68.0 |
| *Daoguang* (1821–1850) | 30 | 23 | 76.7 |
| Total | 189 | 90 | 47.6 |

*Source*: The numbers of years for each reign are in accord with the data available in Tables A.6, A.10, A.11 and A.14, including those for which missing revenue figures can be calculated using data already known.

The number of these years at different revenue levels under each reign is shown in Table 3.2. The distribution of the total number of these years at classified levels is shown in Figure 3.1. The revenue variations from *Yongzheng* to *Daoguang* are shown in Figures 3.2 and 3.3.

TABLE 3.2 *Number of years with revenue figures at different levels, from* Kangxi *to* Daoguan

| Revenue level (million taels) | Kangxi (1662–1722) | | Yongzheng (1723–1735) | | Qianlong (1736–1795) | | Jiaqing (1796–1820) | | Daoguang (1821–1850) | | Total | |
|---|---|---|---|---|---|---|---|---|---|---|---|---|
| | No. of years | % | No. of years | % | No. of years | % | No. of years | % | No. of years | % | No. of years | % |
| Below 6 | – | – | – | – | – | – | 1 | 5.9 | – | – | 1 | 1.1 |
| 6–8 | – | – | – | – | 1 | 2.6 | 2 | 11.8 | 7 | 30.4 | 10 | 11.1 |
| 8–10 | 1 | 100 | 2 | 20.0 | 7 | 17.9 | 5 | 29.4 | 9 | 39.1 | 24 | 26.7 |
| 10–12 | – | – | 2 | 20.0 | 12 | 30.8 | 2 | 11.8 | 4 | 17.4 | 20 | 22.2 |
| 12–14 | – | – | – | – | 5 | 12.8 | 5 | 29.4 | – | – | 10 | 11.1 |
| 14–16 | – | – | 1 | 10.0 | 8 | 20.5 | 1 | 5.9 | 2 | 8.7 | 12 | 13.3 |
| 16–18 | – | – | 4 | 40.0 | 4 | 10.3 | 1 | 5.9 | – | – | 9 | 10.0 |
| 18–20 | – | – | 1 | 10.0 | 2 | 5.1 | – | – | – | – | 3 | 3.3 |
| Above 20 | – | – | – | – | – | – | – | – | 1 | 4.4 | 1 | 1.1 |
| Total | 1 | 100 | 10 | 100 | 39 | 100 | 17 | 100 | 23 | 100 | 90 | 100 |

*Source*: based on Tables A.6, A.10, A.11 and A.14.

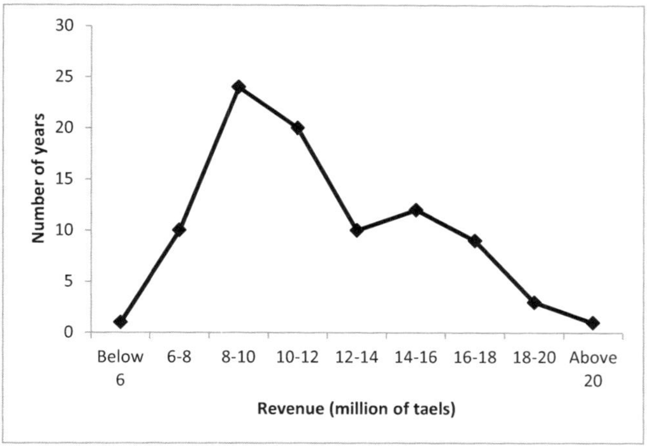


FIGURE 3.1
*Distribution of number of years at different revenue levels, 1662–1850*

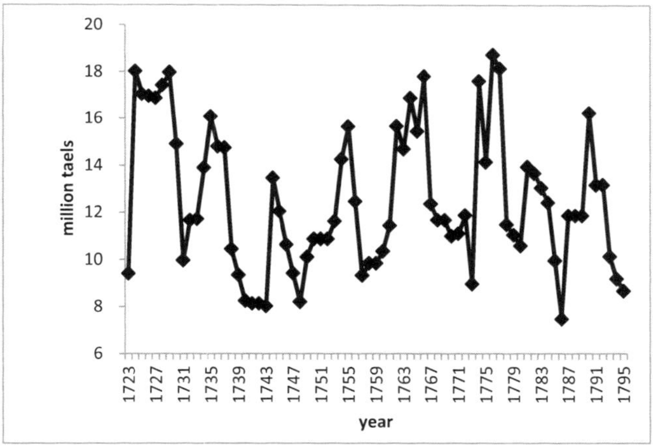


FIGURE 3.2
*Variations in revenue from* Yongzheng *to* Qianlong, *1723–1795*

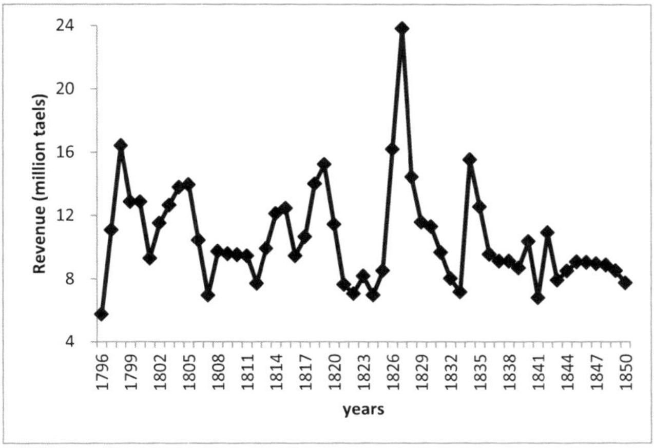


FIGURE 3.3
*Variations in revenue from* Jiaqing *to* Daoguang, *1796–1850*

As shown in Table 3.2, among the total of 90 years of revenue figures during the period, there is only one year with an amount below 6 million taels and one year with an amount above 20 million taels. The 5.73 million taels of revenue in 1796 is only a little more than half the average revenue (11.05 million taels) under the reign of *Jiaqing* (1796–1820). And the 23.8 million taels of revenue in 1827 is more than double the average revenue (9.9 million taels) found under the reign of *Daoguang* (1821–1850).

The very low revenue in 1796 might have been caused by the outbreak of two large-scale rebellions, one in 1795 and one in 1796. During the last few years under the reign of *Qianlong*, the Qing dynasty was hit by a series of natural calamities and man-made misfortunes. In 1795, an uprising of the Miao people, led by Shi Liudeng (石柳邓), broke out in the border areas of Guizhou and Hunan provinces, soon spreading to many other regions in Guizhou, Hunan and Sichuan provinces; it took a dozen years to quell the uprising. In 1796, the White Lotus Rebellion broke out in Hubei province. This uprising spread across Hubei, Sichuan, Henan, Shaanxi and Gansu provinces and lasted for nine years. Although the two rebellions did not take place in key regions of the country and posed no threat to the throne, due to their vast geographic scope, their effect on national tax revenues should not be underestimated. Moreover, since troops had to be sent to stamp out these rebellions, huge amounts of military funds were needed, which pushed up the expenditures of provinces that were directly or indirectly involved; these suffered as a consequence of the provisions that had to be sent to the capital.

The relation between social unrest and falling Silver Treasury revenues is reflected in fluctuations in the revenues and expenditures of the Silver Treasury and its inventory levels after 1793 (see Table 3.3).

TABLE 3.3 *Fluctuations in revenues/expenditures and inventories (in million taels) of the Silver Treasury, 1793–1796*

| Year | Revenue | Expenditure | Surplus/Deficit | Inventory |
|---|---|---|---|---|
| 1793 | 10.11 | 9.72 | + 0.39 | – |
| 1794 | 9.18 | 12.67 | – 3.49 | 71.47 |
| 1795 | 8.67 | 10.75 | – 2.08 | 69.39 |
| 1796 | 5.73 | 18.54 | – 12.81 | 56.58 |

*Source*: see Tables A.9, A.13, B.43 and B.44.

Table 3.3 shows revenues of the Silver Treasury dropped after 1793, while its expenditures simultaneously rose. After all expenses were paid, the Silver Treasury ran huge deficits in each of the three years following 1793; in 1796 in particular, the deficit exceeded revenues/expenditures of ordinary years. Precisely because of the huge deficits, the Treasury's year-end inventory declined from 71.47 million taels to 56.58 million taels – a 21% fall within 2 years. There will be further discussion on changes in revenues/expenditures and inventories of the Silver Treasury during the *Qianlong* and *Jiaqing* eras in the following chapters. Here I would only like to point out that the changes in Silver Treasury figures after 1894 proved beyond question that the low level of revenue in 1796 was clearly linked to military actions that had been ongoing in many provinces over the years.

The high level of revenue for 1827 was rather abnormal: at 23.8 million taels it was roughly twice that of the Silver Treasury's annual revenues in ordinary years. In realation to the stability of provincial revenues and expenditures at that time, it was almost impossible for provinces to double the usual amount of provisions they sent to the capital, unless new financial sources were explored. But the only new source instituted in 1827 was a special contribution called *Zhuozeng Changli* (酌增常例, Increasing Contributions to Routine Case). This special levy, according to historical records, was set up in 1826 after a flood washed out the dams and blocked the channel of the Grand Canal. Since the project of dredging and rebuilding the canal was very costly, and additional military funds were needed to put down the Jahangir Rebellion in the northwest, which had been going on for years, the Qing court decided to introduce this special levy and began to accept contributions from the 1st month of the 7th year of *Daoguang*.[6] The total amount of silver collected remained unknown, but in its first two terms (3 months per term) over 7.5 million taels were received. If one supposes receipts for this item for the whole year reached 10 million taels or more, then that would account for the high level of Silver Treasury revenue in the year, although there may be other, as yet unkown, explanations.

The revenues of the Silver Treasury in 1796 and 1827 were special cases that are not representative of the general level of revenues in the early Qing. As Table 3.2 and Figure 3.1 show (see also Figures 3.2 and 3.3), among the 90 years of revenue data available for the period *Kangxi* to *Daoguang*, 46 of those years show revenue levels of between 8 and 12 million taels. The average of revenues in all these years was 11.71 million taels, which probably represents the general revenue level of the Silver Treasury up to the late Qing. Average revenues under

6 *Zhuozeng Changli · Yuanzou* (酌增常例· 原奏), the 7th year of *Daoguang* (1827).

each reign in this period was: 14.36 million taels for *Yongzheng*, 12.42 million taels for *Qianlong*, 11.05 million taels for *Jiaqing* and 9.9 million taels for *Daoguang*. As for the average during the *Kangxi* era, since there was only data for one year available it is hard to obtain an average figure. Nevertheless, considering the general situation of taxation and economic development under this reign, the 9.1 million taels of revenue collected in 1705 might be close to the average level for the period, or at least close to the average for the mid- and late *Kangxi*.

What was the proportion of Silver Treasury revenues in relation the total financial income of the country during the early Qing period? The following passages set out by reign the findings of my investigations into this question.

***Kangxi***. In the early days of his reign, the main task of the emperor was to eventually reunify the country and solidify the rule of the new Manchu court. Signified by the putting down of the rebellion of the Three Feudatories in South China in 1681 and the surrender of the Zheng family in Taiwan in 1683, this goal was finally achieved. From the mid-1680s onwards, in the *Kangxi*, *Yongzheng* and *Qianlong* eras, the Qing dynasty flourished. However, during the mid- and late *Kangxi* periods, as the social economy had not fully recovered from the chaos resulting from long wars preceding these periods, and the taxation systems were still imperfect and incomplete, as well as being influenced by the Kangxi emperor's policy of showing leniency to his people, the annual amount of taxes levied at the time was still less than that under the Ming dynasty. Taxes levied annually in provinces during the mid- and late *Kangxi* can be roughly estimated: (1) about 29 million taels from land and poll taxes – including 25 million taels from land tax on common land, more than 3 million taels from poll tax, and several hundreds of thousands of silver taels from both military lands and their population; (2) more than 3 million taels of salt gabelle; (3) more than 1 million taels from customs duties; and (4) several hundreds of thousands of silver taels from miscellaneous levies. Furthermore, *juanna* (捐纳, purchasing offices by contributions) was also an important source of revenue. Ever since Kangxi's early years the Qing government had begun to sell offices and titles on a large scale in order to raise money for the quelling of the rebellion of the Three Feudatories. There were at least 29 types of contributions under various names during Kangxi's reign. The average income from contributions at that time, according to my estimate, should have been at least 1–2 million taels per year. In total, the national aggregate revenue during the mid- and late *Kangxi* may have been around 35 million taels per year, excluding taxes levied in kind. If the average revenue of the Silver Treasury was a little more than 9 million taels at that time, it would account for about 26 % of the national total.

***Yongzheng.*** In the early *Yongzheng* era, on average the Qing government collected annually 26.36 million taels from land tax on common land, 0.43 million taels from land tax on military lands, more than 3 million taels from poll tax, 4.43 million taels of salt gabelle, and 1.35 million taels from customs duties. Besides this, it also collected at least several hundreds of thousands of taels via miscellaneous levies and no less than 2 million taels of recurrent contributions every year. In total the annual national aggregate revenue in the early *Yongzheng* era was about 38 million taels. Of this total, the 14.36 million taels of average revenue of the Silver Treasury in Yongzheng accounted for 37.8 % of the national total. However, because the figure for national revenue used here comes from the early *Yongzheng* era this amount might be lower than the average taken over the entire reign. The actual proportion should be slightly lower than the above result, but in any case it should be at least one-third (~ 33%).

***Qianlong.*** According to *Qingshi Gao* (清史稿, Draft History of the Qing Dynasty), besides the *waixiao* (外销) items (funds at the disposal of provinces that did not have to be reported to the Ministry of Revenue), the total national revenue in 1766 was 48.54 million taels, composed of 29.91 million taels from land and poll taxes, more than 3 million taels of *haoxian* silver (耗羡银, a land-tax surcharge levied under the name of meltage fees), 5.74 million taels of salt gabelle, 5.4 million taels from customs duties, 1.49 million taels from miscellaneous levies, and 3 million taels from recurrent contributions[7]. Since this list of revenues is incomplete – for example, according to the *Qingchao Wenxian Tongkao* (清朝文献通考, Encyclopaedia of Official Documents of the Qing Dynasty), in addition to the revenues just listed, another 0.78 million taels of *tunfu yin* (屯赋银, land tax on military lands) was also levied in provinces in 1766 – in this situation the annual national aggregate revenue in the mid-*Qianlong* period should have been at least 50 million taels (excluding revenues levied in kind). Of this total, the 12.54 million taels of average revenue of the Silver Treasury in *Qianlong* accounted for 25.1 % of national aggregate revenue.

***Jiaqing.*** Detailed revenue figures can be obtained by integrating various records from this period: 30.23 million taels from land tax (1820), 6.37 million taels of salt gabelle (1812), 4.81 million taels from customs duties (1812), about 4 million taels of "*haoxian* silver", about one million taels from miscellaneous levies, and about 3 million taels from recurrent contributions. In total, the national aggregate revenue was about 50 million taels, i.e. roughly the same as that during the *Qianlong* era. Nevertheless, the figure for land tax listed above is the *ezheng shu* (额征数, regular quota) and not the actual amount levied,

7 See *Qingshi gao*, Volume 125, p. 3703.

which was usually higher (since there had always been exemptions and suspensions). Here, I take 47–48 million taels as the estimate of the average annual national revenue in the *Jiaqing* era. The 11.05 million taels of average revenue of the Silver Treasury at that time therefore accounts for 23.3 % of the national total (based on a national total of 47.5 million taels).

***Daoguang.*** According to a memorial to the throne by the Ministry of Revenue in 1850, "during the last decade or more … the actual annual revenue was only 40 million taels or so", about 4–5 million taels less than the regular quota[8]. As this was the figure from the late *Daoguang*, when Qing revenues had declined, and the "quota of annual revenue" mentioned in this memorial might only refer to major entries such as land and poll taxes, salt gabelle, customs duties and miscellaneous levies, but would not have included "*haoxian* silver", recurrent contributions and the like[9], here I estimate general annual revenue in the *Daoguang* to be 45 million taels. The 9.9 million taels of average revenue of the Silver Treasury at that time accounts for 22 % of the national total. All these conclusions are shown in Table 3.4.

TABLE 3.4 *Proportions of the average revenue of the Silver Treasury relative to national totals under each reign from* Kangxi *to* Daoguang

| Reign | National aggregate revenue (million taels) | Average revenue of the Silver Treasury (million taels) | Proportion (%) |
|---|---|---|---|
| *Kangxi* | 35.00 | 9.10 | 26.0 |
| *Yongzheng* | 38.00 | 14.36 | 37.8 |
| *Qianlong* | 50.00 | 12.54 | 25.1 |
| *Jiaqing* | 47.50 | 11.05 | 23.3 |
| *Daoguang* | 45.00 | 9.90 | 22.0 |

*Source*: Average revenues of the Silver Treasury: see Tables A.1, A.6, A.10, A.11 and A.14.

8 See *Huobi Shi Ziliao*, 1–1, p. 170. Also see *Wang Qingyun*'s Zhisheng Suiru Zongshu Biao (直省岁入总数表, Table of Provincial Annual Total Revenues) and Zhisheng Churu Suiyu Biao (直省出入岁余表, Table of Provincial Annual Balance of Payments), in *Shiqu Yuji*, Volume 3, and the *Daoguang Shiba Nian Zhi Ershiba Nian Suiru Suichu Ce* (道光十八年至二十八年岁入岁出册).

9 *Wang Qingyun*'s Zhisheng Suiru Zongshu Biao (直省岁入总数表), in *Shiqu Yuji*, Volume 3.

As shown in Table 3.4, in the early Qing it was under the reign of *Yongzheng* that the proportion of average revenues of the Silver Treasury in national total revenue was the highest. The proportions decreased from reign to reign thereafter. The figure for the *Kangxi* era was also much lower than that in the *Yongzheng* era, but a little higher than that in the *Qianlong*, *Jiaqing* and *Daoguang* eras. The high proportion of the Silver Treasury revenue in *Yongzheng* was related to two factors: the relatively low level of national aggregate revenue and the high level of average revenue of the Silver Treasury. During *Yongzheng*'s reign, although national aggregate revenue had increased in comparason to that under *Kangxi*'s reign, after a series of tax reforms, such as improving land tax collection procedures, *tandingrudi* (摊丁入地, merging the poll tax into land tax), *haoxian guigong* (耗羡归公, transferring meltage fees into the public state), increasing salt gabelle and customs duties, and so on, it still could not compare with the best of Qing's national aggregate revenues, such as those achieved during the *Qianlong* era. As I have already estimated, the national aggregate revenue during *Yongzheng* might have been only 38 million taels, or so, and it would never have exceeded 40 million taels, even in cases of over-estimation. In other words, it was at least 10 million taels less than that in the *Qianlong* era. On the other hand, central government expenditures increased more than national revenues did. For example, from 1728 onwards the Qing court doubled the salaries of officials in the capital. Later on, after the "anti-corruption allowance" (*yanglian yin* 养廉银) had become common in the provinces, this additional allowance was also added to the payment of capital officials. Furthermore, during the short 13 years of his reign, the Yongzheng emperor launched a series of significant but costly measures in political, military and economic fields, such as implementing *gaitu guiliu* (改土归流, introducing regular government in tribal areas) in the southwestern provinces, undertaking military action in the northwest, constructing irrigation works and creating paddy fields in Jifu (畿辅, capital territory), rebuilding seawalls in Jiangsu and Zhejiang provinces, etc. Although most of the costs of these major measures had to be borne by provinces, rather than being paid by the Ministry of Revenue, the central government still had to increase its spending, which in turn demanded larger payments by the provinces to the capital.

The fiscal expansion of the central government was also closely related to the personal administrative style of the emperor. He was a conscientious and meticulous person who was impatient, tough and strict in handling affairs. During his reign, the economy recovered its prosperity and the country grew stronger. Faced with the difficulties of a messy administration, wide-spread corruption and shortages of funds inherited from late *Kangxi* era, Yongzheng had to act vigorously to combat corruption and carry out thorough financial reform aimed at tightening central control and improving the central government's fiscal administration. Deficits were thoroughly investigated and had to be settled within a set time. A comprehensive raft of fiscal management systems, including *donggu*, *chunbo*, *qiubo*, *jingxiang*, *xiexiang* and *zouxiao*, was established, strictly followed and carefully monitored. The vigorous and resolute process of rectification and improvement that had been set in motion brought about a tremendous change. From the perspective of central finances, the average revenue of the Silver Treasury climbed to the highest point of the early Qing and the inventories of the Treasury greatly increased. Thanks to all of these factors, Silver Treasury revenues occupied a great share of national total revenues under the reign of Yongzheng.

Silver Treasury revenues in the *Kangxi* era as a portion of national total revenues was also higher than that of other reigns except for that in *Yongzheng*, for the national aggregate revenue was very low. Nevertheless, the fact that the central government could still operate with such limited revenues (the smallest of all five reigns) shows that the court must have been quite thrifty with its expenditures. The Kangxi emperor's approach of advocating frugality and opposing extravagance in the administration of the country was well known, indeed he made comments to this effect several times and his attitude can be found in official records.

The proportion of the Silver Treasury revenues in national aggregate revenues in *Qianlong* was significantly lower than those in *Yongzheng*, due to increases in national aggregate revenues and a decrease in provisions made by the provinces to the capital. During the *Qianlong* era, extravagance started to prevail and profligate government spending would have been unimaginable under previous reigns, e.g. the emperor's inspection tours and birthday celebrations, military actions taken both inside and outside the country (called *shiquanwugong* (十全武功, ten military exploits), large-scale river works and disaster-relief project. Nevertheless, the extent of recurrent central-government expenditures did not increase in line with the growth of national aggregate revenue. In fact, under the traditional fiscal administrative system the government had little room to increase its spending, for "all expenditures had to be based on rules and regulations". Even during *Yongzheng* period, the intent to increase provisions to the capital by provinces was not so much meant to cover the daily expenses of the central government, but rather to strengthen central control and refill the national treasury. The rapid growth of Silver Treasury inventories from about 30 million taels to more than 60 million taels during the first seven years of Yongzheng's reign was clearly the result of this. After his accession to the throne, the Qianlong emperor imitated in many ways his grandfather rather than his father – emphasizing leniency over the amassing of wealth was one manifestation of this. Thus, instead of increasing Silver Treasury revenues, the Qing court reduced them, along with an increase of expenditures by the central government. With increasing national aggregate revenues and a decrease in Silver Treasury revenues, the latter's share in the national totals dropped.

The decline of the Silver Treasury's share in total national revenues in *Jiaqing* and *Daoguang* was caused by financial difficulties. During these two reigns the Qing dynasty had to deal with a series of long-standing, deep-seated social contradictions that became increasingly apparent and intense. Natural calamities and man-made misfortunes followed one upon the other. Tax collection became increasingly difficult, while unexpected expenses continued to present themselves. As a result, the value of inventories of government treasuries at all levels plummeted year after year. Throughout both reigns, national aggregate revenues fell continually and in the final dozen years of *Daoguang* almost fell to levels seen in *Yongzheng*. In this light, the decline in the Silver Treasury's share could only mean that the central government found itself in unprecedented financial straits. The memorial of the Ministry of Revenue in 1850 (mentioned above) reported: "revenues are ever-decreasing, while (the provincial) expenditures are ever-increasing ... thus less and less funds are left for submitting to our Ministry ... (Until now) although more than 10 million taels have been transferred from the royal stores as financial aid, 10 million taels have been saved from expenditures on garrison troops outside the capital, and over 17 million taels of arrears have been collected, ... there still remains a huge financial gap"[10]. The description here paints a vivid picture of the dire financial straits faced in the late *Daoguang*.

## 3.3 Silver Treasury Revenues during *Xianfeng* and *Tongzhi*: 1851–1874

By far the most difficult challenge in researching the financial history of *Xianfeng* – *Tongzhi* eras is the dearth of relevant materials and data. The long period of war experienced under these reigns seriously affected the sophisticated system of fiscal reporting and record keeping. For a period of more than 10 years, the provinces rarely submitted any reports to the central government. A great many of the original archives were also either destroyed or simply went missing. As a result, it is almost impossible to draw a picture of national finances at that time. Fortunately, most of the Silver Treasury data of the *Xianfeng* and *Tongzhi* reigns have been preserved, especially the *Xianfeng* data.

10 *Huobishi Ziliao*, 1–1, p. 171.

We may, therefore, still be able to get a general idea of the fiscal situation of the central government. The aggregate revenue figures of the Silver Treasury under these two reigns are shown in Tables 3.5 and 3.6.

TABLE 3.5 *Aggregate revenue of the Silver Treasury during* Xianfeng

| Year | Silver (million taels) | Coins (ten million wen) | | | |
|---|---|---|---|---|---|
| | | Copper coins | *Jingpiao** | *Baochao*** | Total coins |
| 1851 | 7.64 | 125 | – | – | 125 |
| 1852 | 8.36 | 143[a] | – | – | 143[a] |
| 1853 | 4.44 | 120 | – | – | 120 |
| 1854 | 5.00 | 305 | 785 | – | 1090 |
| 1855 | 3.07 | 190 | 779 | 409 | 1378 |
| 1856 | 2.67 | 81 | 788 | 728[b] | 1597 |
| 1859 | 4.46 | 97 | 1913 | 213 | 2223 |
| 1860 | 5.43 | 37 | 432 | 332 | 801[c] |
| 1861 | 6.68 | 30 | 41 | 16 | 87 |
| Average | 5.31 | 125 | 790[d] | 340[e] | 840 |

*Source*: based on Tables A.17 and A.18.

* *Jingpiao* (京票), also called Jing qianpiao (京钱票), means "Beijing Notes", paper money issued during *Xianfeng*.

** *Baochao* (宝钞, Precious Paper Notes), issued during *Xianfeng*.

*Notes*: [a] Peng Zeyi (彭泽益) recorded this year's aggregate revenue figure as 0.84 million strings in his Hubu Yinku shouzhi ji yingkui qingkuang biao (户部银库收支及盈亏情况表, table of revenues, expenditures and surpluses/deficits of the Silver Treasury of the Ministry of Revenue) attached to Xianfeng chao Yinku shouzhi pouxi (咸丰朝银库收支剖析, an Analysis on Revenues and Expenditures of the Silver Treasury during the Reign of Xianfeng); see also his *Shijiu shiji houbanqi de zhongguo caizheng yu jingji* (十九世纪后半期的中国财政与经济, Finance and Economy of China in the second half of the 19th Century), People's Publishing House, 1983, p. 74. The figure Peng Zeyi recorded here is different from the sum of monthly totals calculated according to the original register.

[b] The four-column register recorded this year's income in Precious Paper Currency as 4,405,082 strings, while if calculated using the monthly totals recorded in the aggregate revenue register of that year the yearly sum ought to be 7,282,490 strings. Furthermore, the figure of this year's total coins listed in Peng Zeyi's table (see above) is also different from what I list here. Peng Zeyi's figure was calculated from four-column register data.

[c] Some of the monthly totals in this year's aggregate revenue register do not match the sums of the detailed amounts. The figure used here is the sum of monthly totals. The amount of total coins listed in Peng Zeyi's table is 7.94 million strings.

[d] Average of the figures from 1854 to 1861 (6 years).

[e] Average of the figures from1855 to 1861 (5 years).

TABLE 3.6 *Aggregate revenue of the Silver Treasury during* Tongzhi

| Year | Silver (million taels) | Coins (ten million wen) |
|---|---|---|
| 1865 | 8.50 | 19 |
| 1866 | 8.58 | 14 |
| 1867 | 12.35 | 15 |
| Average | 9.81 | 16 |

*Source*: based on Table A.24.

As shown in Table 3.5, until 1853, revenues of the Silver Treasury consisted of silver pieces (of various weights) and copper coins, the two major metal currencies it stored. But from 1854 onwards, *Jing Piao* (京票) and *Baochao* (宝钞) were added, both of which were paper monies denominated in copper cash. Issuing paper money was a measure adopted by the Qing government in response to the unprecedented financial crisis brought on by war (i.e. the taiping Rebellion). After the outbreak of war in early 1851, although the Ministry of Revenue could still get by with limited provincial provisions (as well as its Treasury reserves) for the first couple of years, by the third year of *Xianfeng* it could no longer manage, as the war had expanded to the lower Yangtze region – one of China's wealthiest areas – marked by the fall of Nanjing in 1853. According to a memorial submitted to the throne by the Ministry of Revenue in the 6th month of the year, the silver reserves of the Treasury were nearly depleted and were "not enough even for the soldiers' pay of the 7th month"[11]. These financial straits left the Ministry of Revenue no choice but to cast *Daqian* (大钱, large coins, or token coins) and issue *Guanpiao* (官票, Official Notes) and *Baochao* (宝钞, Precious Paper Notes), which it began in 1853.

The *Daqian*, issued in two forms – copper and iron coins – were token coins of large denominations expressed in *wen* (文) or *qian* (钱, cash). During the period 1853–1855 the Ministry of Revenue issued successively six copper tokens (tong daqian 铜大钱), including coins with face values of 5, 10, 50, 100, 500, and 1000 wen[12]. But except for the *dang shi qian* (当十钱, 10-cash), all of these were discontinued within one or two years. *Dang shi qian*, circulated mainly in the capital, continued to be cast until being replaced by *tong yuan* (铜元, copper

11 *Huobi shi ziliao* 1–1, pp. 175–177.

12 *Huobi shi ziliao* 1–1, pp. 203–208.

yuan) in *Guangxu*. Besides copper tokens, a considerable number of iron tokens (*tie daqian* 铁大钱) were also issued in *Xianfeng*, but only for a short time.

*Guanpiao* and *Baochao* were officially called *Hubu Guanpiao* (户部官票, Official Notes of the Ministry of Revenue) and *Daqing Baochao* (大清宝钞, Precious Paper Notes of the Great Qing), respectively. The former, issued in the 2nd month of the 3rd year of *Xianfeng*, was expressed in taels of silver – thus also being called *yinpiao* (银票, silver notes) – of five denominations: 1, 3, 5, 10 and 50 taels. The latter, issued as from the 9th month of the same year, was expressed in *wen* (as copper coins) – thus also being called *qianpiao* (钱票, cash notes) – of eight denominations: 500, 1000, 1500, 2000, 5000, 10,000, 50000 and 100,000 wen. According to the official rate of exchange, a tael of *Guanpiao* was equal to 2000 official copper coins, and 2000 wen of *Baochao* were equal to one tael of silver.

At the same time as the issuing of *Guanpiao* and *Baochao*, in the 3rd and 4th years of *Xianfeng*, a number of official banks (*guan yinqianhao* 官银钱号) were set up in Beijing[13]. These were authorized to issue *Jingpiao* (京票, also called *Jing qianpiao* (京钱票)) for the Silver Treasury to pay Eight-Banner soldiers' wages (thus the notes were also called *xiangpiao* (饷票, meaning "notes for soldiers' pay"). According to regulations, these official banks were also in charge of cashing *Guanpiao* and *Baochao* on behalf of the government, for the purpose of maintaining the credit of these paper notes and promoting their circulation in the market. But in fact, since there were not enough silver or copper coins to back the paper money up, these official banks could not exchange *Guanpiao* and *Baochao* for cash, nor could they guarantee the credit of *Jingpiao* they issued. These official paper notes rapidly depreciated in value not long after their issue. By the end of 1856 the market price for a one tael silver note had fallen to about 30% of its face value, falling further to 3% in 1861. The market price for a 1000 wen of *Baochao* was about 40–50% of its face value between summer and autumn of 1856, and it fell to 5% in the autumn of 1857. During

---

13 Those set up in the 3rd year of *Xianfeng* were: *Qian Yu* (乾豫), *Qian Heng* (乾恒), *Qian Feng* (乾丰) and *Qian* (*Yi* 乾益), which were attached to the Ministry of Revenue and collectively called *Si Qian Guanhao* (四乾官号, four official banks with *Qian* in their names). In the 4th year of *Xianfeng*, the Ministry set up another five banks called *Yu Sheng* (宇升), *Yu Heng* (宇恒), *Yu Qian* (宇谦), *Yu Tai* (宇泰) and *Yu Feng* (宇丰), which were collectively called *Wu Yu Guanhao* (五宇官号, five official banks with *Yu* in their names). At that time, the *Si Qian Guanhao* together with another five banks attached to the Department of Internal Affairs (*Tian Yuan* (天元), *Tian Heng* (天亨), Tian *Li* (天利), *Tian Zhen* (天贞) and *Xi Tian Yuan* (西天元)) were also collectively called *Qian-Tian Jiu Hao* ( 乾天九号, nine official banks with *Qian* or *Tian* in their names).

early *Tongzhi*, as the war (Taiping Rebellion) ended, soon both *Guanpian* and *Baochao* disappeared from circulation – most became waste paper, although a small part was withdrawn by the government.

The new "currencies" – *Daqian, Guanpiao* and *Baochao* – helped the Ministry of Revenue to get through the hard times following the breakout of war in *Xianfeng*. But these "currencies" have also created some confusion for today's economic researchers. These new "currencies" and real silver and copper coins were not always recorded separately, so it is not always possible to distinguish between paper and cash transactions. On paper, the Silver Treasury still had an income of several million taels during *Xianfeng* (see Table 3.5), but in reality, as Professor Peng Zeyi, who has probed deeply into the Silver Treasury data of the time, pointed out that the amount of silver revenue in the Treasury in *Xianfeng* "was merely a figure on paper, a total sum of all entries expressed by taels of silver, including actual silver and the silver notes"[14]. The figures of copper coins recorded in *Xianfeng* registers were also a mixture. From the 4th year of *Xianfeng* (1854), the revenue registers did not record real copper coins as they did before, but a mixture of various currencies expressed by the cash unit wen, including copper coins and *Daqian*, as well as the paper notes *Jingpiao* and *Baochao*. Though according to official regulations all these currencies were exactly the same if they had the same face value, in fact they were different. The new currencies were guaranteed by the government but not backed up by metal. As products of an inflationary policy of the Qing government, which wished to replenish its depleted treasury reserves, they lost their credibility from the moment they were produced. As a result, *Daqian* stopped being cast soon after its issue; *Baochao* and *Guanpiao* rapidly depreciated in value within one or two years and became eventually waste paper. In short, Silver Treasury data after 1853 greatly overstate the actual value of currencies received by the Silver Treasury. This needs to be clarified before beginning to analyse the Silver Treasury data of the time.

According to Table 3.5, the average silver revenue of the Silver Treasury during *Xianfeng* amounted to 53.6 % of the *Daoguang* average (9.9 million taels); in 1856 the percentage was only 27%. The figure for revenue in coins, on the other hand, increased many-fold after *Daqian* and *Baochao* were issued in 1853. This trend continued until 1861, when the Qing government stopped issuing *Baochao* and *Guanpiao* and nearly all new currencies, with the exception of the 10-cash, had been withdrawn from circulation. On average, the annual revenue in copper coins in *Xianfeng* was 7.1 times as large as that in *Daoguang*.

---

14 Peng Zeyi, *Shijiu Shiji Houbanqi de Zhongguo Caizheng yu Jingji*, p. 76.

Because of all these changes, the proportions of silver and copper coins in the total revenue of the Silver Treasury during *Xianfeng* differed markedly from those in *Daoguang*, as Table 3.7 shows.

TABLE 3.7 *Proportions of silver and copper coins relative to total revenue of the Silver Trea*

| Year | Total revenue of silver and copper coins (million taels) | Silver | | Copper coins | |
|---|---|---|---|---|---|
| | | Revenue (million taels) | % | Revenue equivalent to silver (million taels) | % |
| Average of *Daoguang* | 11.08 | 9.90 | 89.4 | 1.18 | 10.6 |
| Average of *Xianfeng* | 9.73 | 5.31 | 54.6 | 4.42 | 45.4 |
| 1851 | 8.89 | 7.64 | 85.9 | 1.25 | 14.1 |
| 1852 | 9.79 | 8.36 | 85.4 | 1.43 | 14.6 |
| 1853 | 5.64 | 4.44 | 78.7 | 1.20 | 21.3 |
| 1854 | 10.45 | 5.00 | 47.8 | 5.45 | 52.2 |
| 1855 | 9.96 | 3.07 | 30.8 | 6.89 | 69.2 |
| 1856 | 10.66 | 2.67 | 25.0 | 7.99 | 75.0 |
| 1859 | 15.58 | 4.46 | 28.6 | 11.12 | 71.4 |
| 1860 | 9.44 | 5.43 | 57.5 | 4.01 | 42.5 |
| 1861 | 7.12 | 6.68 | 93.8 | 0.44 | 6.2 |

*Source*: based on Table 3.5. Strings (1 string = 1000 wen) have been converted into taels at the rate of 1:1 for years up to and including 1853 and at 2:1 from 1854 to 1861.

As shown in Table 3.7, in the first two years the proportions of silver in the total revenues of the Silver Treasury during *Xianfeng* remained roughly the same as those in *Daoguang*, but these began to drop rapidly from 1853 onwards and fell to a low of 25 % in 1856. Compared to that in *Daoguang*, during 1854–1859 the proportions of silver and copper coins in total revenue became reversed. On average, the percentage of silver revenue was 54.6 %, while that of copper coins was 45.4 % – a situation that was unique in the history of the Qing dynasty. Under the circumstances of reduced provincial submissions, it was monetary policies, such as issuing *Daqian*, *Guanpiao* and *Baochao*, that supported the revenues of the Silver Treasury and ensured the payment of basic expenses of the capital. Without such policies, the central government could never have managed.

The severity of the financial crisis was also reflected in the structure of silver revenues in the Treasury. On paper, during *Xianfeng*, although silver revenues had decreased in comparison with those in *Daoguang*, it still maintained a level of several million taels each year. But in fact, except for the first two years, the amount of actual silver revenue during *Xianfeng* was dwarfed by the paper silver. According to an inventory attached to a memorial by Zao Bao, *Zuo Shilang* (左侍郎, assistant minister) of the Ministry of Revenue, dated on the 13th of the 3rd month of the 4th year of *Tongzhi* (1865), on average, the actual receipts in silver of the Silver Treasury during 1853–1861 were only a little more than 0.2 million taels annually, thus only accounting for a few percent of the total silver revenue in the period (see Table 3.8). Such low revenues in silver further explains the weakness of the Silver Treasury at that time. Obviously, without the replenishment by large amounts of paper currencies the Silver Treasury could never have overcome this crisis.

TABLE 3.8 *Actual silver revenues of the Silver Treasury and their proportions relative to total silver revenues during* Xianfeng

| Year | Total silver revenue (million taels) | Revenue actually in silver (million taels) | Proportion of actual silver revenue (%) |
|---|---|---|---|
| 1853 | 4.44 | 0.48 | 10.8 |
| 1854 | 5.00 | 0.22 | 4.4 |
| 1855 | 3.07 | 0.14 | 4.6 |
| 1856 | 2.67 | 0.15 | 5.6 |
| 1857 | – | 0.20 | – |
| 1858 | – | 0.18 | – |
| 1859 | 4.46 | 0.19 | 4.3 |
| 1860 | 5.43 | 0.15 | 2.8 |
| 1861 | 6.68 | 0.15 | 2.2 |

*Source*: Actual silver figures come from an inventory attached to the memorial by Zao Bao on the 13th of the 3rd month of the 4th year of *Tongzhi* (1865).

The situation of Silver Treasury revenue in *Tongzhi* is unclear, because the data in existence only covers three years. However, from the figures listed in Table 3.6 we can roughly judge that by the time the Taiping Rebellion was put down in early 1864 the most difficult time had passed. The figure of 9.8 million taels of average revenue of the Silver Treasury during 1865–1867 was close to the *Daoguang* average, and exceeding that of any year in *Xianfeng*. But it should also be noted that such a situation did not appear until after the recapture of Nanjing in 1864, an event that had practically ended the war. In the few years prior to that, the revenue situation of the Silver Treasury was not at all promising. Based on Zao Bao's inventory, the actual silver revenues of the Silver Treasury during the period 1862–1864 were only 0.194, 0.118 and 0.174 million taels, respectively, so we conclude that the financial difficulty in the early *Tongzhi* was as serious as in *Xianfeng*.

## 3.4 Silver Treasury Revenues during *Guangxu*: 1875–1908

Although revenue data of the Silver Treasury during *Guangxu* (1875–1908) are also incomplete – there are only figures for seven years – the general situation during the early and middle parts of the era can still be established, as is shown in Table 3.9.

TABLE 3.9 *Silver Treasury revenues during* Guangxu

| Year | Silver (million taels) | Copper coins (million strings) |
|---|---|---|
| 1883 | 15.64 | 0.23 |
| 1891 | 19.27 | 1.39 |
| 1892 | 20.86 | 1.58 |
| 1896 | 22.78 | 0.44 |
| 1897 | 23.28[a] | 0.34 |
| 1898 | 28.80[b] | 0.43 |
| 1899 | 24.45[c] | 0.37[c] |
| Average | 21.80 | 0.71 |

*Source*: based on Table A.25.

[a] This figure is from the four-column register. The figure in the aggregate revenue register is 22.99 million taels; [b] This figure is from the four-column register . The figure in the aggregate revenue register is 27.57 million taels; [c] These figures are from the four-column register. In the aggregate revenue register, the figures are 23.47 million taels of silver and 0.59 million strings of copper coins.

Table 3.8 shows that the annual silver revenue in early *Guangxu* had been at a rather high level, similar to that in the early Qing. Thereafter, it continued to increase and after the First Sino-Japanese War was even double the average of early Qing.

The increase in Silver Treasury revenue was related to the expansion of fiscal revenue in the late Qing period. In the early Qing, revenues mainly came from land tax, salt gabelle, customs duties and miscellaneous levies. Other revenues, such as provisional contributions for special funds (*zanxing shili* 暂行事例) and contributions by businessmen (*Baoxiao* 报效) were all temporary money-raising measures. Although the imperial court considered them to be very important, they were, nevertheless, not recurrent revenues (except for their routine contribution).

During *Xianfeng*, however, major changes in fiscal revenues took place.The first was the introduction of the levy of *likin*. As a new tax, *likin* was firstly levied in Jiangsu in 1853 and spread rapidly to all provinces during *Xianfeng*, with the exception of Yunnan (Yunnan began to levy *likin* in 1874, the 13th year of *Tongzhi*). *Likin* was introduced to raise funds for putting down the Taiping Rebellion. In the period from late *Tongzhi* through to the first decade of *Guangxu*, *likin* became the second largest tax source after land tax[15].

Another change resulted from the the Second Opium War, which broke out between China and Great Britain and France during *Xianfeng*. After its defeat, China had to increase the number of treaty ports, further lower its import/export tariffs and permiting foreign goods to enter inland without being charged internal transit duties (50% of import/export tariffs). Through the implementation of these preferential trade conditions, China's foreign trade greatly expanded and maritime customs duties at treaty ports became an important source of tax revenue from 1860s onwards. After 1887, when both import tax and inland *likin* on foreign opium were combined and collected uniformly by the maritime customs, the annual amount of revenues from the maritime customs exceeded that of *likin* and thus became the second largest tax source[16].

---

15 According to Luo Yudong, the reported amount of *likin* collected in the provinces from 1869 to 1894 was 14–15 million taels each year; see Luo's *Zhongguo Likin Shi*, Volume 2, p. 469. But this is not the actual amount of *likin* collected, which, according to some estimates made at that time, may be two or three times more than the reported amount.

16 See Tang Xianglong: Quanguo Haiguan Linian Gexiang Shuishou Tongji Zongbiao (全国海关历年各项税收统计总表, Statistical Summary of Annual Revenues of National Maritime Customs), in *Zhongguo Jindai Haiguan Shuishou he Fenpei Tongji* (中国近代海关税收和分配统计), pp. 63–68. The amount of maritime customs duties from 1887 to the end of the 19th century was about 22–23 million taels annually; before this, in 1860s, it

Chinese government also began to borrow from abroad, the sums of which were small in the beginning but grew uncontrollably some time thereafter. Although the data are incomplete, by the eve of the First Sino-Japanese War in 1894 the cumulative amount of foreign debt had reached 67 million treasury taels, climbing as high as 500 million taels just before the Boxer Rebellion in 1900[17]. Internal debt also began to occur in the late *Guangxu*. Both foreign and internal debt played an important role in government finances in late Qing period, especially in *Guangxu*.

All the new sources of revenue just described greatly expanded the fiscal income of the Qing dynasty. In 1884, the Ministry of Revenue modified its accounting rules on the basis of a comprehensive survey of the actual revenues and expenditures of the government at that time. According to these new accounting rules, all revenues were divided into three categories, namely "routine revenues" (*changli zhengshou* 常例征收), "new levies" (*xinzeng zhengshou* 新增征收) and "current year's receipts" (*bennian shoukuan* 本年收款). Of these, "routine revenues" were composed of traditional revenues such as land and poll taxes (*diding* 地丁), *haoxian* (耗羡, land tax surcharge levied under the name "meltage fees"), miscellaneous levies, rents from land (revenue from leasing state-owned land), salt gabelle, and *changshui* (常税), also called *changguan shui* (常关税), which referred to the collection of the Chinese regional customs. The "new levies" included *likin*, *xinguanshui* (新关税), also called *yangshui* (洋税), which referred to revenues from maritime customs collected at treaty ports, and *anliang jintie* (按粮津贴), a surcharge on land tax levied in Sichuan province since the *Xianfeng* era. The "current year's receipts" referred to contributions (*juanshu* 捐输), arrears collected in the current year (*xuwan* 续完), and so on. Based on these new accounting items, the figures of national aggregate revenue from 1885 to 1894 are shown in Table 3.10; detailed revenue figures for 1891 are shown in Table 3–11.

was no more than 10 million taels, in 1870s it was 11–13 million taels and from 1880 to 1886 it was 14–15 million taels.

17 See *Zhongguo Qingdai Waizhai Shi Ziliao* (中国清代外债史资料), (1853–1911) pp. 136–140, 247 and 315.

TABLE 3.10 *National aggregate revenues, 1885–1894*

| Year | Annual revenue (million taels) | Year | Annual revenue (million taels) |
|---|---|---|---|
| 1885 | 77.09 | 1890 | 86.81 |
| 1886 | 81.09 | 1891 | 89.68 |
| 1887 | 84.22 | 1892 | 84.36 |
| 1888 | 87.79 | 1893 | 83.11 |
| 1889 | 80.76 | 1894 | 81.03 |
| Average: 83.59 | | | |

*Source*: Liu Yueyun: Ruxiang Zongbiao (入项总表, The Summary Table of Revenues), in *Guangxu Kuaiji Biao* (光绪会计表, Accounting Tables of Guangxu), Jiaoyu Shijie She (教育世界社). Educational World Press, 1901, Volume 1, pp. 1–5.

TABLE 3.11 *Revenues and their proportions relative to the national total, 1891*

| Item | Amount (million taels) | Proportion to total (%) |
|---|---|---|
| **Routine revenues** | **43.32** | **48.31** |
| Land and poll tax (*diding* 地丁) | 23.67 | 26.39 |
| Grain tax levied in silver (*liangzhe* 粮折) | 4.26 | 4.75 |
| Meltage fees (*haoxian* 耗羡) | 3.00 | 3.35 |
| Salt gabelle | 7.17 | 8.00 |
| Chinese regional customs | 2.56 | 2.85 |
| Miscellaneous levies | 1.81 | 2.02 |
| Land rent and others | 0.84 | 0.94 |
| **New levies** | **34.53** | **38.50** |
| *Likin* | 16.33 | 18.21 |
| Maritime customs | 18.21 | 20.30 |
| **Current year's receipts** | **11.83** | **13.19** |
| Official salary deductions (*jiekou* 节扣) | 2.00 | 2.23 |
| Collected arrears (xuwan 续完) | 7.23 | 8.06 |
| Contributions | 2.60 | 2.90 |
| Total | 89.68 | 100 |

*Source*: see sources of Table 3.10.

As Tables 3.10 and 3.11 show, the national aggregate revenue in early *Guangxu* was almost double that in *Daoguang,* thanks to the addition of "new levies". But the revenue items recorded by Liu Yueyun are still incomplete. For example, his total figures did not include foreign loans. This omission is not just a statistical oversight but is rooted in a classification error in the new accounting items made by the Ministry of Revenue. The Ministry mistakenly put foreign funds (*yangkuan* 洋款), together with their repayment and interest (*huanjie xikuan* 还借息款), under "new expenditures", which according to its nature, ought to be put under the "new levies" as a revenue item. Liu not only continued this error, but further combined the two items, collectively called *yangkuan* (洋款) in his statistics on expenditures. According to the *Zhongguo Qingdai Waizhai Shi Ziliao* (Historical Materials on Foreign Debts of the Qing Dynasty, 1853–1911), the Qing government during 1885–1893 borrowed through foreign loans 20 times, the amount totalling 67 million treasury taels: 8 times in 1885, amounting to 12.09 million taels; twice in 1886, amounting to 1 million taels; once in 1887, amounting to 0.98 million taels; six times in 1888, amounting to 6.23 million taels; twice in 1890, amounting to 0.22 million taels; and once in 1893, amounting to 0.15 million taels.

Furthermore, the revenue figures for maritime customs listed in Liu's table are incorrect. Compared with maritime customs data, his figures are quite small; especially those for 1888–1893 "are about five million taels lower each year"[18].

Taking all these factors into consideration, I have modified Liu's national aggregate revenues for the period 1885 - 1894 as shown in Table 3.12.

Concerning the revenues before the First Sino-Japanese War, George Jamieson, the British consul in Shanghai (November 1897–May 1899), also made an estimate on the basis of provincial reports during the early 1890s. According to his estimate, Qing annual revenue in 1893 was about 88.98 million taels, including 25.09 million taels from land tax, 6.56 million taels from tribute rice levied in silver (*caomi zhejia* (漕米折价), 13.66 million taels from salt gabelle and *likin* on salt (*yanli* (盐厘), 12.95 million taels from *likin* on general merchandise, 21.99 million taels of revenues from maritime customs, 1 million taels of revenues from Chinese regional customs, 2.23 million taels of tax and *likin* on domestic opium, and 5.5 million taels from miscellaneous levies[19]. Jamieson's estimate is roughly the same as Liu's corrected data: they appear to corroborate each other.

---

18 See *Qingchao Xu Wenxian Tongkao* (清朝续文献通考), p. 8228.

19 Jamieson: *Zhongguo Duzhi Kao* 中国度支考, p. 20.

TABLE 3.12 *Corrected national aggregate revenues, 1885–1894*[a]

| Year | Annual revenue (million taels) | Year | Annual revenue (million taels) |
|---|---|---|---|
| 1885 | 89.83 | 1890 | 92.30 |
| 1886 | 82.99 | 1891 | 94.54 |
| 1887 | 85.96 | 1892 | 89.55 |
| 1888 | 99.36 | 1893 | 88.53 |
| 1889 | 85.92 | 1894 | 93.15 |
| Average: 90.21 | | | |

[a] My corrections are based on data from two sources: (1)Tang Xianglong: Quanguo Haiguan Linian Gexiang Shuishou Tongji Zongbiao (全国海关历年各项税收统计总表, Statistical Summary of Annual National Revenues of the Maritime Customs), in *Zhongguo Jindai Haiguan Shuishou he Fenpei Tongji* (中国近代海关税收和分配统计, Statistics of Revenues and their Distribution of Chinese Modern Maritime Customs), Zhonghua Book Company, Beijing: 1992, pp. 63–68; (2) *Zhongguo Qingdai Waizhai Shi Ziliao (1853–1911)* (中国清代外债史资料, Historical Documents of Foreign Debts in the Qing Dynasty (1853–1911), China Financial Publishing House, 1991. Figures have been calculated according to the following formula: Liu's total revenue figure (see Table 3.10) + foreign loans − Liu's revenue figure for Maritime Customs + Tang's revenue figure for Maritime Customs.

In the 1890s, within the space of a few years China became involved in two wars: the First Sino-Japanese War (1894–1895); and the Boxer Rebellion and the beleaguering of Beijing in 1900 that followed. These wars resulted in large indemnity payments being demanded from the Qing government and, as a result, a new round of taxes and the expansion of levies.

There are no official statistics on national revenue in the period from the First Sino-Japanese War until 1908, when the Qing government decided to clean up provincial finances in order to establish and implement its first western-style budget. Nonetheless, several estimations have been made by individuals. Robert Hart, Inspector-General of the Chinese Maritime Customs Service, estimated China's aggregate revenue before the Boxer Rebellion to be:

1. Land tax = 26.5 million taels
2. Tribute rice levied in silver = 3.1 million taels
3. Salt gabelle and *likin* levied on salt = 13.5 million taels
4. Chinese regional customs duties = 2.7 million taels
5. *Likin* = 16 million taels
6. Maritime customs duties and opium taxes = 23.8 million taels

7. Miscellaneous provincial and other levies = 2.6 million taels
Total = 88.2 million taels[20]

Hart's estimate did not include some items, such as taxes and *likin* levied on domestic opium by the provinces, Contributions (a new contribution for coastal defence starting from 1889 (*xin haifang shili* 新海防事例), a contribution for preparing the defence of southern regions of the Yangtze River (*Jiangnan Chouban Fangwu Li* 江南筹办防务例) starting from 1894), and the price markup on salt (*yanjin jiajia* 盐斤加价) instituted in most provinces after 1894. However, Hart's estimate did not match expenditures, which he also estimated. According to this estimate, total expenditure of the Qing dynasty on the eve of the Boxer Rebellion was about 101.12 million taels, i.e. 13 million taels higher than the national revenue. Where did this deficit come from, and how did the Qing government close the gap? Well, if one checks expenditures in detaile one would find that domestic expenses (of both the central government and provinces) were even a little lower than those before war, rather than being higher. The deficit came from the 24 million taels of expenditure made on repayments of and interest on foreign debts – 21–22 million taels higher than the average before war. This newly increased expenditure was related to a series of foreign loans acquired during and after the Boxer Rebellion, especially three large loans – a Franco-Russian loan in 1895 and two Anglo-German loans, one in 1896 and the other in 1898 – that were used to pay war reparations to Japan. Since the repayment of these loans has been listed as an expenditure item, it is reasonable that the loans themselves should have been included in revenue items. In fact, after the First Sino-Japanese war, due to large additional reparations, the Qing government had to further reduce its daily expenses and at the same time seek all kinds of new sources of revenue, including levying heavier taxes and foreign loans. In his work *China: Past and Present* Edward. H. Parker has estimated that both revenue and expenditure of the Qing dynasty reached an average of 101.57 million taels per year during the period 1894–1900[21]. To me, his estimate is appears credible.

As far as national aggregate revenue of the Qing dynasty after the 1900 Incident goes, some foreign observers have estimated it was still slightly more than 100 million taels in the early 1900s[22]. But according to the reports by prov-

20 See *Zhongguo Hanguan yu Yihetuan Yundong* (中国海关与义和团运动), pp. 64–65.

21 See Liu Jinzao, *Qingchao Xu Wenxian Tongkao* (清朝续文献通考), p. 8248.

22 根岸佶 estimated Qing's national revenue in 1903 to be about 104.9 million taels, see *Qingchao Xu Wenxian Tongkao*, p. 8249. H.B. Morse's estimate for 1905 was 102.9 million

inces after the cleaning up of their finances already mentioned, the total sum of annual revenue by 1908 and 1909 was at least 230–260 million taels[23], more than twice as large as what people had estimated just a few years earlier. How to explain the huge jump? The difference in times the figures are linked to is obviously not a reason, for it is impossible that national revenue should double within the space of a few years. The only reasonable explanation for this is that after the thorough cleanup of provincial finances, a lot of revenues not included in the past were at last acknowledged and officially incorporated into national aggregate revenue statistics by the Qing government. Cleaning up provincial finances was part of a plan to thoroughly reform the Qing's traditional fiscal management on the basis of dividing the state and local tax/expenditure systems, the ultimate goal of this reform being to establish and implement western budget accounts in both central government and the provinces, coordinating with the constitutional reform taking place from the late *Guangxu* onwards. The cleanup operations began in early 1909 (the end of the 34th year of *Guangxu*) and lasted nearly two years, focusing on investigating all revenues and expenditures from 1908. Financial investigators were sent to each province by Beijing to lead the cleanup operation and compile the provinces financial specifications. After such an operation unprecedented in Qing history, although not all financial details of the time were clarified at least most revenues could be specified, both those instituted after the Boxer Rebellion and those from way before.

In the practice of financial management of the Qing dynasty, there had always been a grey area called *waixiao* (外销). According to regulations, all financial activities of provinces had to be reported to the throne and the Ministry of Revenue and would be subject to supervision. But this only referred to revenues and expenditures stipulated in rules and regulations. For those not stipulated, which had always existed in provincial fiscal activities, there was no need to report. So, the financial records of the Qing government obtained through *zouxiao* each year were not complete records of all fiscal activities of the dynasty, but only those stipulated under its rules and regulations. *Waixiao* revenues generally came from extra levies attached to normal taxes, being used to supplement local administration fees not covered by rules and regulations – a considerable part of which might fall into the pockets of officials at all levels.

---

taels, see his *The Trade and Administration of the Chinese Empire*, p. 115.

23 According to the reports by provinces, the total revenue figure was about 235 million taels for 1908 and 263 million taels for 1909; see *Qingchao Xu Wenxian Tongkao*, pp. 8233–8234.

In this respect, there was no difference between the early and late Qing periods. However, in the early Qing, under its highly centralized management and control, the provinces had little financial autonomy, and the scope and content of government activities were after all imited, i.e. the scale of *waixiao* revenues and expenditures could not be very large. I estimate that the percentage of these revenues and expenditures might be no more than 20–30% of the revenues reported by provinces each year[24]. Things were, however, different in the late Qing. Along with the reduction of central control, the financial autonomy of provinces expanded unprecedentedly. The scope and content of the activities of the provincial governments were also different from those in the past. During this period, many emerging government affairs, such as the management and levying of *likin*, foreign affairs, establishing new industrial enterprises, founding and training new armies, etc., were usually carried out by the provinces themselves, instead of being financed by the central government. Traditional administrative affairs also underwent a marked change, with more government agencies and administrative personnel being involved. The financial resources to maintain these provincial governmental activities came either from sharing new taxes, such as *likin* and domestic opium taxes – which had never been controlled by the central government – or from collecting all kinds of additional miscellaneous levies attached to normal taxes. Considering this situation had lasted for decades, when these *waixiao* revenues and expenditures were cleaned up at last, it was inevitable that the scale of national finances would suddenly expand.

I have introduced the issue of *waixiao* to give a better idea of the proportion of the Silver Treasury's revenue in the national total and to illustrate the changes occurring in fiscal relations between the central government and the provinces in the late Qing. As I have already mentioned, in early *Guangxu* (before the First Sino-Japanese War), national aggregate revenue was about 90 million taels per year (see Table 3.12). However this figure does not include *waixiao* items. If these are added, I estimate that the actual scale of revenues before 1894 might be no less than 146 million taels, as Table 3.13 shows.

24 See Shi Zhihong and Xu Yi: *Wanqing Caizheng* (晚清财政) ：1851~1894, p. 250.

TABLE 3.13 *Estimate of actual national aggregate revenue before 1894*

| Item | Amount (million taels) |
|---|---|
| Land tax[a] | 35.00 |
| Salt gabelle[b] & tea tax | 30.00 |
| Chinese regional customs | 5.50 |
| Maritime customs | 23.00 |
| *Likin* | 30.00 |
| Miscellaneous levies | 10.00 |
| Miscellaneous receipts[c] | 10.00 |
| Contributions | 2.66 |
| Total | 146.16 |

*Source*: see Shi Zhihong and Xu Yi: *Wanqing Caizheng* (晚清财政：1851~1894), pp. 253–264; p. 279 (Table 4.17); [a] Includes land and poll tax (*diding* 地丁), grain tax levied in silver (*liangzhe* 粮折) and meltage fees (*haoxian* 耗羡); [b] Includes *likin* on salt (*yanli* 盐厘) 。); [c] Referred to non-tax incomes.

As for the scale of national aggregate revenues around 1900, the estimated amount of about 100 million taels also does not include *waixiao* revenues[25]. I estimate that the actual revenue of that time could be increased to about 200 million taels if *waixiao* revenues are added. With the 230–260 million taels of national aggregate revenue after 1908 in mind, my estimate might not be too high.

There are six years of revenue figures that can be used to calculate the proportion of Silver Treasury revenues in the national totals: two before 1894, and four between 1896 and 1899 (see Table 3.9). The average figure of revenues for the two years before 1894 is 20.07 million taels; that for the four years after 1894 is 24.2 million taels. With these two averages, one can calculate the proportion of Silver Treasury revenues in the national totals before 1894 and around 1900, as Table 3.14 shows.

25 My detailed comments on these estimates can be seen in *Wanqing Caizheng*, pp. 283–290.

TABLE 3.14 *Estimate of the proportion of Silver Treasury revenue relative to the national total before 1894 and around 1900*

| Year | Silver Treasury revenue (million taels) | National aggregate revenue and the proportion of Silver Treasury revenue in it | | | |
|---|---|---|---|---|---|
| | | National total: number of *zouxiao* (million taels) | Proportion of Silver Treasury revenue in the total of *zouxiao* (%) | Estimated national total revenue (million taels) | Proportion of Silver Treasury revenue in the estimated total (%) |
| Before 1894 | 20.07 | 90.21[a] | 22.2 | 146.16 | 13.7 |
| Around 1900 | 24.20 | 103.92[b] | 23.3 | 200.00 | 12.1 |

[a] This figure is the average of revenues during the period1885–1894 (see Table 3.12).
[b] This figure is the average of revenues estimated by 根岸佶 (for 1903) and H.B. Morse (for 1905).

If one limits oneself to official statistics obtained by *zouxiao* or to foreign observers' estimates based on official reports, the proportion of Silver Treasury revenues in the national aggregate revenues did not change much before and after 1894: it was basically the same as that in the early Qing, i.e. it had been growing at roughly the same rate as national aggregate revenue. However, this situation does not square with the historical fact of the continuous weakening of the central control over the provinces, along with the expansion of provincial financial autonomy during the late Qing period. My estimates might not be accurate, but I believe they are more comprehensive than the official reports or contemporaries' observations. Based on these estimates, the proportions of Silver Treasury revenue in national aggregate revenue were lower by about one half: 13.7% before 1894 and 12.1% around 1900. This result shows that during the late Qing period, central finances played a less important role in national finances, especially toward the end of the period. Thus, China's crumbling unity and shift to greater provincial power was reflected in the weakening position of central government finances[26].

26 Some acute observers of the late Qing noted the devolution of powers from the central government to the provinces. In 1867, Zhao Liewen (赵烈文), one of Zeng Guofan's (曾国藩) advisors, once when discussing with Zeng the consequences of the excessive power

high-rank officers' obtained from training armies and raising funds by themselves since the war against the Taiping Rebellion, commented that "after a long period of unity, signs of seperation are appearing"; see Zhao's *Nengjingju Riji* (能静居日记, Zhao Liewen's Diary, the 29th day of the 6th month of the 6 th year of *Tongzhi*). In 1871, Wang Kaiyun (王闓运), a famous scholar in the late Qing and the author of *Xiangjun* Zhi (湘军志, History of the Hunan Army), after comparing the situation of the country in 1860s with that during the period of "Five Dynasties and Ten Kingdoms" (907–960 A.D.) said he was afraid that the historical scene of "rich officers and violent soldiers with sparkling spears ready for use" "might reappear today" in *Xiangqilou Riji* (湘绮楼日记, Wang Kaiyun's Diary, the 16th day of the1st month of the 9th year of *Tongzhi*. By the end of the Qing dynasty, Liang Qichao(梁启超), when commenting on the difficulties of financial reform, pointed out further that the 18 provinces of China at that time were just like "18 countries" . He wrote: "Whenever the cleanup is mentioned, all the provincial governors will push up their sleeves and fight against it, fearing that the central government may take their purses away"; and even among the provinces, "the boundaries of each are also marked as an impassable gulf". Some western scholars have used the word "regionalism" in their studies to define the political structure in the late Qing, and thought that as the central authority became weakened through the rebellions that had taken place since the 19th century, local military and political powers had begun to grow in some core areas. As a result, nominally these areas still remained parts of a united country, but their "regionalism" had already allowed them virtually to perform some of the functions of a state, which was "an important phenomenon in the history of modern China" (Stanley Spector, *Li Hung-chang and the Huai Army, A study in nineteenth century Chinese regionalism*, Seattle, 1964, pp. 21–43). This analysis is very critical and hits the mark. Although the situation of separated provinces did not actually appear until the fall of the Qing dynasty, the problem had been brewing and gradually taking form back in the late Qing period.

CHAPTER 4

# Silver Treasury Expenditures and Payment Surpluses/Deficits during the Qing Dynasty

## 4.1 From *Kangxi* to *Daoguang*

The items and amounts of recurrent expenditures of the Silver Treasury in 1765, based on the *Qingchao Wenxian Tongkao,* are shown in Table 4.1. In order to facilitate the discussion below, I have divided these items into five categories (indicated by Roman numerals) by their nature of use; the amounts and percentages are shown in Table 4.2 and Figure 4.1, i.e. I is salaries of soldiers, II is salaries of officials, III is representation and work allowances for officials, IV are (disaster) relief funds, and V are living subsidies.

TABLE 4.1 *Recurrent expenditures of the Silver Treasury, 1765*

| Item | Amount | |
|---|---|---|
| | **Silver (taels)** | **Copper coins (strings)** |
| Salaries of princes and officials [II] | 938,700[a] | – |
| Soldiers' pay [I] | 5,033,045[a] (non–leap year) | 1,000,000+ |
| Salaries and pay for officers and soldiers (respectively) stationed at Mukden, the Jehol royal hunting ground, Eastern Royal Tombs and the Tai Tomb[I] | 1,300,000–1,600,000 | – |
| Salaries of feudatories and Mongol princes [II] | 128,300 | – |
| Meal allowance of the Grand Secretariat and other offices [III] | 18,300 | – |
| Anti–corruption allowance of the Ministry of Personnel and the Ministry of Rites [II] | 15,000 | – |
| Meal allowance and office expenses for Beijing officials [III] | – | 110,000 |
| Travelling expenses of tax collectors in Bagou and Tazigou [III] | 1,062 | – |

 | DOI 10.1163/9789004307339_006

| Item | Amount | |
|---|---|---|
| | Silver (taels) | Copper coins (strings) |
| Funds (beiyong yin 备用银) for the Department of Internal Affairs, the Ministry of Works, the Court of Sacrificial Worship, the Banqueting Court and the Court of Colonial Affairs [III] | 560,000 | – |
| Funds (beiyong qian 备用钱) for the Department of Internal Affairs [V] | – | 5,000 |
| Money and grains for Huitong Guan (会同馆, guesthouse for tributary envoys) and other departments of the Ministry of Defense [III] | 4,180 | – |
| Silver of the Court Trial (chaoshen 朝审) of the Ministry of Justice [III] | 60 | – |
| Bursaries (gaohuoyin 膏火银, lamp expenses) of the Imperial Academy (Guozi Jian 国子监) [III] | 60 | – |
| Almanac expenses (shixianshu yin 时宪书银) of the Bureau of Astronomy (Qintian Jian 钦天监) [III] | 498 (non–leap year)<br>516 (leap year) | – |
| Material costs of the Mint Bureaus of Baoquan and Baoyuan [III] | 107,671 (non–leap year)<br>113,518 (leap year) | – |
| Salaries of servants in offices in the capital [III] | 83,330 | – |
| Living subsidies (mizheyin 米折银) for camelmen of the Department of Internal Affairs [V] | 3,041 | – |
| Relief funds for refugee office of the Five Districts of the capital (wucheng qiliusuo 五城栖流所) [IV] | 200 | – |
| Grain rations for the orphans and poor (gupin kouliang qian 孤贫口粮钱)[IV] | – | 2,930 |
| Pasturing expenses of the Department of Internal Affairs and other yamen [V] | 83,560 | – |
| Rewards for tributaries from feudatories, Mongolia and Korea [III] | 10,000 | – |
| Total | About 8,300,000–8,600,000 | 1,117,930+ |

*Source*: *Guoyong* (II国用二, Public Outlays: II), in *Qingchao Wenxian Tongkao* (清朝文献通考, Encyclopaedia of Official Documents of the Qing Dynasty), Volume 49, p. 5227.

[a] Original note by the author: "These are payments in quotas. The actual amount of the sum of salaries of princes, officials and soldiers was more than 4 million taels per year."

TABLE 4.2 *Amounts and proportions of classified expenditures of the Silver Treasury, 1765*

| Item | Silver | | Copper coins | | Total of silver and copper coins[b] | |
|---|---|---|---|---|---|---|
| | Amount (1000 taels) | Proportion of the total (%) | Amount (1000 strings) | % of the total | Amount (1000 taels) | Proportion of the total (%) |
| Soldiers' pay (I) | 6483[a] | 76.8 | 1000 | 89.4 | 7483 | 78.3 |
| Salaries of officials (II) | 1082 | 12.8 | – | – | 1082 | 11.3 |
| Administrative costs (III) | 785 | 9.3 | 110 | 9.8 | 895 | 9.4 |
| Disaster relief and welfare funds (IV) | 0.2 | – | 3 | 0.3 | 3.2 | – |
| Funds used for the Royal Family (V) | 87 | 1.0 | 5 | 0.4 | 92 | 1.0 |
| Total | 8437.2 | 100 | 1118 | 100 | 9555.2 | 100 |

*Source*: based on Table 4.1.
[a] The amount for the salaries and pay of officers and soldiers (respectively) stationed at Mukden, and the Jehol royal hunting grounds, the Eastern Royal Tombs and the Tai Tomb have been counted as 1.45 million taels in this table; [b] Copper coins have been counted according to the official exchange rate of one string (1000 wen) = 1 tael of silver.

Items and their regular amounts listed in Table 4.1 represent the general situation of recurrent expenditures of the Silver Treasury in the mid-Qing. During the early and mid-Qing periods, regular government expenses were fixed in items and quotas, which, recorded in *Daqing Huidian* and *Hubu Zeli*, would remain in force for a long period of time, until the next time a new modification of the rules and regulations was ordered by one of the emperors. The actual amount of payments on these items might be different each year, but such changes would be small unless there was an imperial edict to increase or decrease a special payment for some reason. For example, during times of serious financial difficulty, salaries and additional allowances of government officials might be cut by a certain percentage, which would last for several

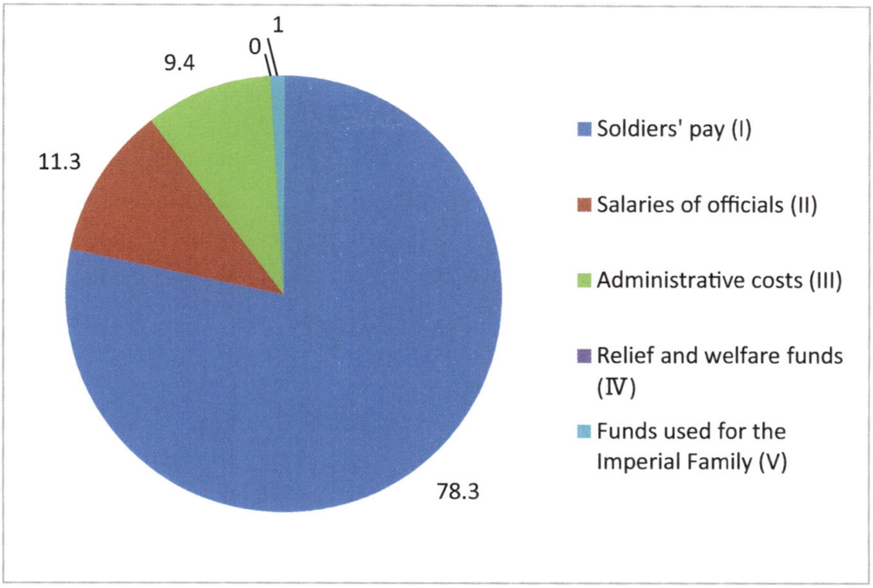


FIGURE 4.1 *Percentages of classified expenditures of the Silver Treasury, 1765*

years or even longer, until they were restored by a new imperial edict. Generally speaking, fixing regular government expenses in items and quotas, and keeping them stable, was a basic feature of financial administration in the early and mid- Qing.

Among the five categories of items, soldiers' pay and salaries of government officials took first and second place, respectively. In total these amounted to about 8.6 million taels per year, thus accounting for 90% of the aggregate expenditures of the Silver Treasury. But these were the quotas. The actual payments on these two categories in the capital (i.e. not including the salaries and pay of officers and soldiers (respectively) stationed at Mukden, the Jehol royal hunting grounds, the Eastern Royal Tombs, the Tai Tomb, and the salaries of feudatories and Mongol princes; also not including those paid in copper coins) were slightly more than 4 millions taels, or about two-thirds of their specified quotas. The two items of "meal allowance of the Grand Secretariat and other offices" and "meal allowance and office expenses for Beijing officials", classified under the category of administrative costs, were actually subsidies for the cost of living of government officials, i.e. these were paid in addition to their salaries. In total these amounted to about 130,000 taels, most of which was paid out in copper coins (see Table 4.1).

The expenses used for disaster and poor relief, as well as welfare payments for widowers, widows, orphans and other people without a provider, also accounted for a certain percentage of the annual expenditures of the Qing government. Disaster relief , especially, could cost thousands upon thousands of silver taels during times of flooding or drought., These belonged, however, in special expenses, which were usually supported by provisional contributions or special appropriations of the Silver Treasury ordered by emperors. As a recurrent item of expenditure, the relief and welfare funds only applied to government allocations to state welfare agencies, such as that for "refugee office of the Five Districts of the capital" (*wucheng qiliusuo* (五城栖流所) listed in Table 4.1, and did not amount to very much.

The "civil list" used for the imperial family was also part of the annual expenditures of the Silver Treasury. In the Qing dynasty, especially in its early and middle periods, supported by independent financial resources, the expenses of the imperial family ("the inner court") did not rely much on appropriations from the Silver Treasury. The related items listed in Table 4.1 only refer to payments made to the Department of Internal Affairs, which was also an organ of the central government. Besides, during mid-*Qianlong*, there were 120,000 taels of "purchasing expenses" (*caiban yin* 采办银) and 140 thousand taels of "weaving expenses" (*zhizao yin* 织造银) included in the annual financial report each year, some of which were for public uses and some for the inner court. These two items of silver were not paid for by the Silver Treasury but by related provinces.

In addition to recurrent expenditures, there were also unexpected provisional expenditures. Because of their unpredictability, these payments generally did not have stipulated supporting revenues and fixed quotas. They were taken mainly from the reserves of the Silver Treasury or covered by various temporary money-raisng measures, such as, for example, setting up provisional contributions for special funds and accepting contributions by businessmen. In the early Qing, provisional expenditures were mainly related to war expenses, disaster relief and extra costs related to major projects. Among these, war expenses occupied first place, extra costs incurred by the Yellow River works and the seawall engineering of Jiangsu and Zhejiang provinces ranked second, and disaster relief ranked third. According to incomplete statistics compiled by Zhou Yumin, military expenses resulting from major wars amounted to 376.13 million taels from 1736 to 1850, while in the period 1662–1850 the extra costs of major projects (Yellow River works, seawall engineering and others) and disaster relief were about 91.33 million taels and 54.38

million taels, respectively[1]. In total, these provisional expenditures paid in the early Qing amounted to over 500 million taels, i.e. equivalent to more than ten times annual national aggregate revenues at that time.

In order to cope with provisional expenditures, the Qing government had always to adopt various unconventional methods to raise money in addition to its normal annual revenues. Of these, the introduction of provisional contributions for special funds was the most commonly used method, although reducing recurrent expenses and using the reserves of the Silver Treasury were also measures often taken when extra payments were urgently needed. The drastic fluctuations in Silver Treasury inventories during the early Qing were usually caused by payments of provisional expenditures.

Except for the *Kangxi* era, for which data for only one year is available, the data of expenditures for all following reigns in the early Qing are relatively complete. The number of years for which expenditure figures are available is 10 for *Yongzheng*, 43 for *Qianlong*, 22 for *Jiaqing*, and 25 for *Daoguang*. For the sake of simplicity, I have divided the four reigns after the *Kangxi* era into two periods, (1) the *Yongzheng-Qianlong* period (1723–1795) and (2) the *Jiaqing-Daoguang* period (1796–1850), to analyse their changes in expenditures and balances of payments. Fluctuations in expenditures of the Silver Treasury during the two periods are shown in Figure 4.2 and Figure 4.3 respectively.

### (1) Yongzheng-Qianlong *Period (1723–1795)*

According to Figure 4.2, for most years in the *Yongzheng-Qianlong* period annual Silver Treasury expenditures fluctuated about the level of just above 10 million taels, the range being roughly ± 1.5 million taels. However, the curve in Figure 4.2 is not smooth: there are peaks in the middle, two of which, one during 1729–1737 and the other during 1771–1776, are most conspicuous. In the first few years of *Yongzheng*, expenditure figures fluctuate within the range of 9–10 million taels, but starting from 1729 the curve rises sharply to reached a peak of more than 24 million taels in 1731; thereafter it declines year by year, returning to a normal level of about 10 million taels in 1737. The second peak climbes from 9.45 million taels in 1771 to reach 12.07 million taels in 1772 and 19.03 million taels in 1773; after falling to 13.36 million taels in 1774 it once again climbs to peak at 23.08 million taels in 1775, only to fall back once more to 9 million taels in 1776.

These violent fluctuations in the expenditure figures of the Silver Treasury in these two periods are related to major wars. During the first period,

1 Zhou Yumin, *Wanqing Caizheng yu Shehui Bianqian*, pp. 41–45.

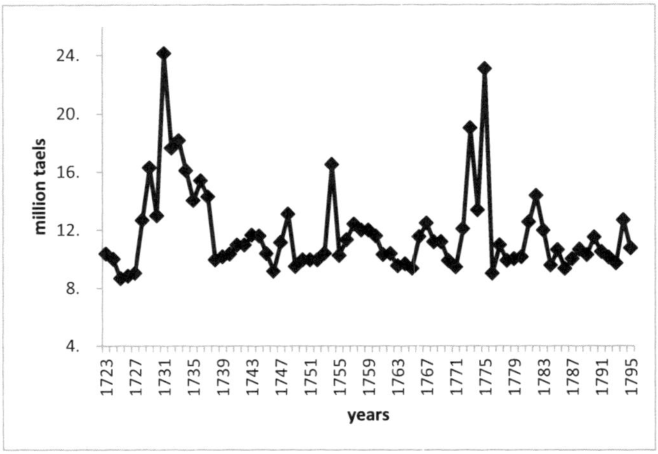


FIGURE 4.2 *Fluctuations in expenditure during the* Yongzheng-Qianlong *period, 1723–1795*

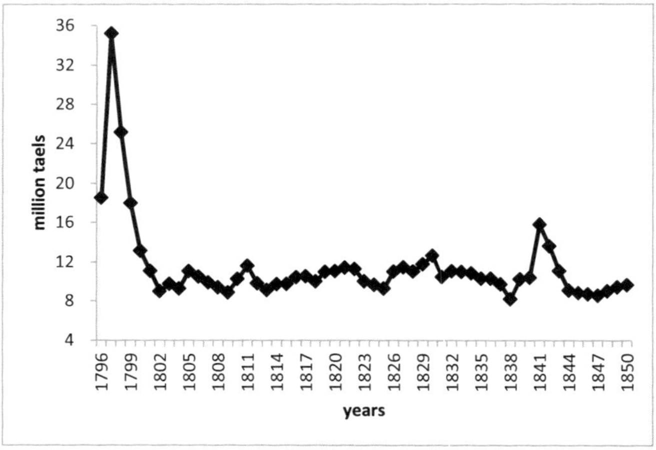


FIGURE 4.3 *Fluctuations in expenditure during the* Jiaqing-Daoguang *period, 1796–1850*

1723–1795, the Yongzheng emperor waged war against the Zunghar on the imperial northwest border; this was an important military action following the pacification of the Qinghai region in early *Yongzheng*. The war began in 1729 and did not cease until a peace agreement was reached six years later, in 1735. Since no provisional contributions were set up for special funds during the war, the huge costs of waging war had to come from the Silver Treasury and to some extent from provincial contributions. Table 4.3 shows the fluctuations in revenues/expenditures and inventories of the Silver Treasury during the war against the Zunghar.

TABLE 4.3 *Fluctuations in revenues/expenditures and inventories of the Silver Treasury during the war against the Zunghar (in million taels)*

| Year | Revenue | Expenditure | Surplus/Deficit | Year-end inventory |
|---|---|---|---|---|
| 1729 | 17.96 | 16.29 | +1.67 | 60.25 |
| 1730 | 14.89 | 12.96 | +1.93 | 62.18 |
| 1731 | 9.96 | 24.11 | −14.15 | 50.38 (48.03) |
| 1732 | 11.66 | 17.65 | −5.69 | 44.39 (42.34) |
| 1733 | 11.71 | 18.17 | −6.46 | 37.93 (35.88) |
| 1734 | – | – | −5.43 | 32.50 (30.45) |
| 1735 | 16.06 | 14.03 | +2.03 | 34.53 (32.48) |

*Source*: based on the Table A.6 and Table B.1. There are some slight differences between the changes in year-end inventory figures reported by the Grand Ministers of the Strategy Board (*Junji Dachen* 军机大臣) in 1775 (see Table B.1) and that of the surplus/deficit figures calculated according to the annual revenue/expenditure figures listed in this table. For the convenience of the reader, I have placed my revised figures in parentheses alongside the originals.

The changes in revenues/expenditures and inventory figures of the Silver Treasury shown in Table 4.3 reflect the course of the war. First, the changes in expenditure agree well with the levels of intensity of the war during the period: in 1729, when tens of thousands of soldiers (two Qing armies) led by Furdan (傅尔丹) and Yue Zhongqi (岳钟琪) set out for the northwest border, the expenditure figure of the Silver Treasury jumped from the 9–10 million taels of previous years to 16.29 million taels; and its falling back to about 13 million tales in 1730 was obviously connected with the fact that the Yongzheng emperor had begun peace negotiations and scaled back the campaign in that year. Expenses peaked at 24.11 million taels in 1731, when Yue Zhongqi was allowed to attack Urumqi and Furdan thrust deeply into Mongolia. However, after suffering several defeats at the hands of the Zunghars, the emperor once more scaled back operations and renewed peace negotiations. Connected to this, expenditure figures decreased in the following years. When at last a peace agreement was reached, in 1735, expenditures fell further and returned to normal levels two years later.

Second, the figures shown in Table 4.3 also reflect how the war had affected surpluses/deficits, as well as inventories, of the Silver Treasury. In the first two years, the costs of the war were paid by provincial allocations, not by the Silver Treasury of the Ministry of Revenue. Because of this, the financial situation of the Treasury did not deteriorate with the sudden increase of expenditure and continued to enjoy surpluses similar to those of the first half of *Yongzheng*. The inventories of the Treasury also continued to increase[2]. However, from 1731 onwards the revenues of the Silver Treasury fell, while expenditures continued to increase due to the hostilities, which resulted in huge deficits and a sharp drop in the Treasury's inventories. It was not until the war ended in 1735 that decreasing expenditures and recovering revenues brought the Silver Treasury back to a postion of surpluses. Over the period of the war the inventory of the Silver Treasury halved from 62.18 million taels to a little more than 30 million taels – a striking contrast with that in the first half of Yongzheng's reign, when the inventories of the Silver Treasury increased from 23.71 million taels in 1723 to more than 60 million taels. The surpluses of the Silver Treasury accumulated during the early *Yongzheng* were consumed during the war.

As for the sudden rise of expenditures of the Silver Treasury during 1771–1776, it was obviously related to the second *Daxiao Jinchuan* Campaign (大小金川之役) in Sichuan province. This military compaign, the longest and the most expensive war of the Qianlong emperor's "ten military exploits" (*shiquan-wugong* 十全武功), lasted for almost six years and cost 60–70 million taels of silver[3]. Fluctuations in revenues/expenditures and inventories of the Silver Treasury during that war are shown in Table 4.4.

TABLE 4.4 *Fluctuations in revenues/expenditures and inventories of the Silver Treasury during the Second Jinchuan Campaign (in million taels)*

| Year | Revenue | Expenditure | Surplus/Deficit | Year-end inventory |
|---|---|---|---|---|
| 1771 | 11.09 | 9.45 | +1.64 | 78.94 |
| 1772 | 11.87 | 12.07 | -0.20 | 78.74 |
| 1773 | 8.97 | 19.03 | -10.06 | 68.68 |
| 1774 | 17.59 | 12.36 | +5.23 | 73.91 |
| 1775 | 14.13 | 23.08 | -8.95 | 64.96 |
| 1776 | 18.71 | 9.01 | +9.70 | 74.66 |

*Source*: based on Table A.10.

2 See Table A.6.

3 According to Zhao Yi (赵翼): *Yanpu Zaji* (檐曝杂记), the Second Jinchuan Campaign cost 63.7 million taels.According to Qingshi Gao, however, the total sum of expenses of the campaign was more than 70 million taels.

As Table 4.4 shows, three of the most important four years of the campaign (1772–1775) suffered from payment deficits, the total sum of which reached 19.21 million taels. Among these, the deficits in 1773 and 1775 were 10.06 and 8.95 million taels, respectively, which resulted in unprecedented decreases in Silver Treasury inventories during the *Qianlong* era. However, as the table also shows, in its heyday the Qing court could easily cope with provisional expenditures and did not suffer as a result of the tens of million taels paid out to meet military expenses. Of the six years of war, besides the three years just mentioned, the other three had financial surpluses. In total, after six years of war that cost 60 million taels in military funding, the inventories of the Silver Treasury had decreased by only 4 million taels, i.e. by only 5.4% of inventory totals before war began.

The military funds for the Second Jinchuan Campaign came mostly from temporary money-raising measures rather than from the inventories of the Silver Treasury. For example, the contribution named *chuan yun junliang shili* (川运军粮事例, contribution for the transportation of army provisions in Sichuan province) was set up for this very purpose in 1774. Though the amount of revenue from this contribution remains unknown, the up to 17.59 million taels of aggregate revenue of the Silver Treasury in the first year that it was set up should be related to it. During the six years of the Campaign, average revenues of the Silver Treasury reached 13.73 million taels per year, about 3–4 million taels more than that in normal years and about 5 million taels more than needed to meet annual recurrent expenditures. The total sum of these six years of increased revenues that could be used for provisional expenditures was about 20–30 million taels. This extra money, together with provisional contributions, special military allocations over provinces (*junxu xiexiang* 军需协饷, a kind of inter-provincial assistance ordered by the Ministry of Revenue) and a small part of the inventories of the Silver Treasury, would have been the major sources of the 60 million taels of military funds raised to pursue the war.

There are also some smaller hillocks to be seen on the expenditure curve of *Qianlong* in Figure 4.2, such as the 13.09 million taels in 1748, 16.51 million taels in 1754, 12.39 million taels in 1757, 12.46 million taels in 1767, 14.36 million taels in 1782 and 12.67 million taels in 1794; the Silver Treasury also ran payment deficits in all these years. Most of these hillocks were related to military actions. The heaviest battles of the First Jinchuan Campaign (1747–1749) took place in the year 1748, while the two Zunghar campaigns under the reign of Qianlong started in 1754 and ended in 1757. And the heaviest battles of the Burma Campaign took place in 1767. Qianlong was a ruler who continually craved greatness and success and thus waged, either actively or passively, one war after another, be it inside and outside his empire.

Although the country was rich and powerful at that time, having vast financial resources to support provisional expenditures, traces of other activities during Qianlong could still be found among the records of the Silver Treasury. The over-expenditure of the Silver Treasury in 1782 was related to several important river works and seawall projects going on in Henan, Shandong, Hubei and Zhejiang provinces, which in total cost about 20 million taels[4]. As for the high levels of expenditure and payments deficits of the Silver Treasury in 1794, these were obviously related to the spread of social unrest and numerous disasters that occurred in the last few years of *Qianlong*. The revenue of the Silver Treasury was only 9.18 million taels in that year, which resulted in a deficit of 3.49 million taels. In 1795, the last year of the reign of *Qianlong*, revenue dropped further to 8.67 million taels, resulting in a deficit of 2.08 million taels, although expenditure was a mere 10.75 million taels. These figures reflect that the initial prosperity and easy financial circumstances had come to an end under the reign of Qianlong.

Nevertheless, the expenditure level of the Silver Treasury during *Qianlong* was generally not very high, the average of which, calculated from the 43 years of data surviving, was only 11.6 million taels per year; if the years of extremely high expenditure I have just described are excluded, the average figure of normal years would be only 10.24 million taels per year. With the over 12 million taels of average revenue per year, the Silver Treasury would have had an average annual surplus of more than 2 million taels during *Qianlong*. These financial surpluses, together with all kinds of money-raising measures for special funds, helped the Qing court to cope with the numerous provisional expenditures. The inventory of the Silver Treasury had always been 60–80 million taels ever since 1765, which was roughly equivalent to the two years' of national aggregate revenue at that time. As far as financial circumstances were concerned, *Qianlong* was the best among the reigns of the early Qing.

### (2) Jiaqing-Daoguang *Period (1796–1850)*

As Figure 4.3 shows, in marked contrast with the *Yongzheng-Qianlong*, the annual expenditure curve of the Silver Treasury during this period was quite smooth, fluctuating slightly around 10 million taels, except for two special periods, one from 1796 to 1800 and the other from 1841 to 1842. Calculated from all 22 years of data available, average annual expenditure during *Jiaqing* (1796–1820) was 12.7 million taels; if, however, the period of high expenditure during

4 See *Qingshi Gao* Volume 125; Wang Qingyun 王庆云, *Shiqu Yuji*, Volume 3; Zhang Xiaotang 张晓堂, "*Qianlong* Nianjian Qing Zhengfu Pingheng Caizheng Zhi Yanjiu 乾隆年间清政府平衡财政之研究".

its first five years (1796–1800) is excluded, it would be only 11.5 million taels per year. During the *Daoguang* era (1821–1850), calculated from all the 25 years of data available, average annual expenditure was 10.63 million taels, and 9.88 million taels if the period of high expenditure, from 1841 to 1842, is excluded.

The expenditure curve for the first few years of *Jiaqing* towers above the rest: starting from 18.54 million taels in 1796, it peaked at 35.17 million taels in 1797, but declined year by year thereafter. By the year 1802 annual expenditure had dropped to 8.97 million taels and in subsequent years fluctuated, within a very narrow range, around 10 million taels per year throughout the rest of the era of *Jiaqing*.

The period from 1796 to the early 1800s was notable for the campaign put down the White Lotus Rebellion (1796–1804), which, spreading across Hubei, Sichuan, Henan, Shaanxi and Gansu provinces and lasting nine years, was – with the exception of campaigns to crush the Revolt of the Three Feudatories in the early *Kangxi* and the Taiping Rebellion in *Xianfeng-Tongzhi* – the most expensive war to be fought during the whole Qing dynasty. To raise military funds with which to fight the war and cope with its aftermath, a provisional contribution called *Chuan-Chu Shili* (川楚事例, the Contribution for the Sichuan and Hubei Incidents) was set up in 1798. By the time the contribution was stopped, in early autumn 1801, a total sum of more than 30 million taels of revenue had been raised[5]. However, compared with the huge costs of over 100 million taels spent on the campaign[6], the contribution was far from enough. It was thus inevitable that the Qing court would look for other methods to raise the necessary funds, including using the inventories of the Silver Treasury. Of these, using the huge inventories of the Treasury left by the Qianlong Emperor was almost the only choice for the new successor, for at that time, as I have already pointed out, it was unlikely that the Qing court could collect enough money in any other way. Therefore, in the first three years prior to settting up the "Contribution for Sichuan and Hubei Incident, inventories of the Silver Treasury dropped sharply at a hitherto unprecedented speed from about 70 million taels in 1795 to a little more than 19 million taels in 1798. Even after the contribution had been set up, inventories continued to fall. By 1801, the 6th year after the rebellion had broken out, there were only 16.93 million taels left in the Silver Treasury. In total, the inventories of the Silver Treasury dropped by 52.46 million taels from 1796 to 1801. Such a dramatic decrease in Treasury inventories had been seldom seen in the early Qing. The decline consumed

5 Wei Yuan, *Shengwu Ji, Fulu* (圣武记・附录), Volume 11.

6 The record of Shihuo Zhi (食货志) in *Qingshi Gao* is 200 million taels.

almost all the financial surpluses accumulated in *Qianlong* and greatly undermined the finances of the Qing dynasty for years to come.

Another major but slighter rise in expenditures occurred during the Opium War of 1840–1842. Table 4.5 shows the revenues/expenditures and surpluses/deficits of the Silver Treasury during the period.

TABLE 4.5 *Revenues/expenditures and the surpluses/deficits of the Silver Treasury during the Opium War (in million taels)*

| Year | Revenue | Expenditure | Surplus/Deficit |
|---|---|---|---|
| 1840 | 10.35 | 10.31 | +0.04 |
| 1841 | 6.80 | 15.73 | −8.93 |
| 1842 | 10.91 | 13.52 | −2.61 |
| 1843 | 7.92 | 10.99 | −3.07 |

*Source*: based on Table A.16.

Table 4.5 shows that from 1840 to 1843 the Silver Treasury had payment deficits in all years except for 1840, 14.61 million taels in total. According to the four-column register, the inventory of the Silver Treasury was 9.93 million taels by the end of the year 1843. Based on this data, I estimate the inventory figure to be about 24.5 million taels in 1840. Ever since the White Lotus Rebellion ended in early 1800s, Treasury inventories had always been at a level of about 20–30 million taels – until the Opium War. So, during the war more than one-half of the Treasury's inventory – an unprecedented low level since mid-*Kangxi* – was consumed within the short span of two or three years. What was left was barely enough to meet the normal expenditures of a single year, showing how the war had greatly undermined the finances of the Qing government.

According to Zhou Yumin, taking military expenditures, the indemnity and losses of money and property all together, the cost of the Opium War amounted to more than 45 million taels[7]. This amount would have had no significance in *Qianlong*, but in late *Daoguang* it could indeed hit the beleaguered Qing's financial balance heavily, making it much weaker and unable to withstand even the slightest accident, as was demonstrated after the outbreak of the Taiping Rebellion a few years later.

Except for the two special periods mentioned above, the expenditures of the Silver Treasury were rather stable during the *Jiaqing-Daoguang* period.

7 Zhou Yumin: *Wanqing Caizheng yu Shehui Bianqian*, pp. 77–81.

However, revenues at that time fluctuated violently (see Figure 3.3), with low-revenue years being constantly present; in some years revenues were a mere 8–9 million taels, or even less. Such a situation resulted in frequent deficits at the time. Table 4.6 shows the number of years of surpluses/deficits during the period (the two special periods are not included):

TABLE 4.6 *Number of years of surpluses/deficits of the Silver Treasury during* Jiaqing *and* Daoguang

| **Reign** | **Total number of years** | **Number of deficit years** | | **Number of surplus years** | | **Average revenue (million taels)** | **Average expenditure (million taels)** | **Average surplus/deficit (million taels)** |
|---|---|---|---|---|---|---|---|---|
| | | **Number** | **% of total** | **Number** | **% of total** | | | |
| *Jiaqing* | 13 | 4 | 30.8 | 9 | 69.2 | 11.16 | 11.46 | −0.30 |
| *Daoguang* | 15 | 11 | 73.3 | 4 | 26.7 | 10.48 | 10.58 | −0.10 |

*Source*: based on Tables A.13 and A.16.

Table 4.6 shows the fiscal situation of the Silver Treasury, which during both *Jiaqing* and *Daoguang* was hardly able to break-even, even in normal years; the difference between the two was that it was slightly better off in *Jiaqing* than in *Daoguang*. In the *Jiaqing* period, the proportion of surplus years was higher than that of deficit ones, whereas in *Daoguang* the position was reversed. Though deficits during the *Daoguang* period were generally small, they eventually consumed the limited reserves, demonstrating that the central finances of the Qing dynasty were becoming weaker and weaker.

The fragile balance of payments in *Jiaqing* and *Daoguang* depended not merely on regular taxes, which were at most just enough to cover basic recurrent expenditures. The central government also had to use all kinds of temporary money-raising measures to cope with the various provisional expenses it had to meet. Of these, the most important measure was "provisional contributions" (*zanxing shili* 暂行事例). According to incomplete data, during 1798–1814 a total of nine provisional contributions were imposed under various names. Such contributions were also frequently imposed during *Daoguang*. In addition, the semi-compulsory apportioned "business contributions" (*shangjuan* 商捐) were used more frequently than before, especially in *Daoguang*. The amount of silver collected from each contribution varied from hundreds of thousands to millions of taels.

All these contributions were temporarily set up for special purposes and would be ended when the prescribed time limit had expired – only in exceptional circumstances could the time limit be extended. In addition to these, the recurrent contribution (*changli juanshu* 常例捐输 or *changjuan* 常捐for short) was also an important item of revenue during the *Jiaqing-Daoguang* period, yielding about 2 million taels per year at that time.

Contributions played an important role in the revenues of the Silver Treasury during*Jiaqing-Daoguang*, which included not only the silver received by the "donation office" (*juanna fang* 捐纳房) under the Ministry of Revenue, but also what was collected in the provinces. According to Tang Xianglong, on average 52% of the provincial revenues from selling the position of*Jiansheng* ( 监生, student of the Imperial College) were forwarded to the Silver Treasury during the reign of Daoguang[8]. And according to Luo Yudong, in 1802, a year having the highest revenue from contributions in both*Jiaqing* and *Daoguang*, the amount of contributions received by the Silver Treasury was as much as 9.52 million taels, accounting for 82% of its total revenues in that year[9]. The important position of contributions in the revenues of the Silver Treasury in *Daoguang* is shown in Table 4.7[10].

TABLE 4.7 *Total revenues of the Silver Treasury and the share of contributions during the period 1840–1849*

| Year | Total revenue of the Silver Treasury (million taels) | Amount of contributions in total revenue (million taels) | Proportion of contributions relative to total revenue (%) |
|---|---|---|---|
| 1840 | 10.35 | 2.49 | 24.1 |
| 1841 | 6.80 | 2.07 | 30.4 |
| 1842 | 10.91 | 8.95 | 82.0 |
| 1843 | 7.92 | 3.82 | 48.2 |
| 1845 | 9.07 | 1.49 | 16.4 |
| 1846 | 9.04 | 1.74 | 19.2 |
| 1849 | 8.51 | 1.07 | 12.6 |
| *Average* | *8.94* | *3.09* | *34.6* |

*Source*: The annual figures of Contribution revenues are based on page 7 of Luo's *Zhongguo lijin Shi*.

8 Tang Xianglong, "Daoguang Chao Juanjian zhi Tongji" (道光朝捐监之统计).

9 Luo Yudong, *Zhongguo Likin Shi*, 1, pp. 6–7.

10 The annual figures of Contribution revenues are based on page 7 of Luo's *Zhongguo Likin Shi*.

Table 4.7 shows that in late *Daoguang* the proportions of contributions in the total revenue of the Silver Treasury varied from over 10% to as much as 80%, averaging more than one-third. Such high proportions not only reflect the important position of provisional fund-raising measures in the central finances of that time, they also indicate that the traditional fiscal system of the early Qing was coming to its end.

## 4.2 The *Xianfeng – Tongzhi* Period

During the reigns of Xianfeng and Tongzhi, many changes took place in the Qing's traditional fiscal system, starting with an unprecedented financial crisis in early *Xianfeng*.

The crisis was triggered by the Taiping Rebellion, which had broken out at the beginning of the year 1851 but did not become widespread until two years later. During the first two years of the war that ensued, few changes were to be seen in the central finances of the Qing dynasty. At that time, the court deployed forces to pursue and encircle the rebel armies and the Ministry of Revenue dispatched military funds from the provinces to the front line, in doing so playing its role as the control centre of national financial resources, just as it had before. However, when the war spread to the middle and lower reaches of the Yangtze River and the rebels captured Jiangning (now Nanjing) in early 1853, the Qing Government could no longer bear the ever-increasing military expenses: the vast and very productive lands of the Yangtze were extremely important sources of taxation for the government. And the reserves of treasuries in both the capital and the provinces were becoming depleted after two years' excessive consumption. Thus, an unprecedented financial crisis arose, causing the Ministry of Revenue to described its financial situation in the 6th month of the year as follows:

> It has been three years since the war broke out in Guangxi province. The total sum of military funds allocated by our Ministry and paid from provincial retention money has reached 29.63 million taels. … Offices set up to supply army provisions (*liangtai* 粮台, to be set up for moving troops during wars) have already increased to six or seven. And the reports asking for funds from troops everywhere come in such large numbers that all our working time has been occupied every day. … Military funds are in urgent need, while the apportioned revenues are still up in the air. The land tax can no longer be counted on from the provinces in war zones; even in those that have always been called "perfect areas", since Jiangsu has applied for postponing its imposition, Shandong

> has requested to keep the collections for its own use, and in Shanxi, Shaanxi and Zhejiang everyone is preparing for war, such that the revenue of land tax collected there will not be able to meet the quota in full this year. Yangzhou was captured by the rebels already quite some time ago, Hankou has not yet recovered, and the administration of salt in Huainan is still a complete mess, and therefore most of the salt gabelle cannot be collected. Wuhu, Jiujiang, Jiangning and Fengyang have been harassed one after another; merchants are afraid of passing through Kuizhou and the Suzhou customs; even the Chongwen Men customs have also requested that they only have to submit the amount it has levied – because of all these factors, most of the revenue from customs duties has run out. All the above revenues allocated by our ministry for various payments each year cannot meet the need for military funds today. As a result, we have had to turn to introducing contributions; and when contributions have not worked well, we begged for the help of the imperial treasury. Recently, revenue from contributions decreased greatly and we dare not to think about approaching the imperial treasury any further. Dozens of other remedies have also been put into practice, including those suggested by us in the light of our limited experience and by other officials in the capital, such as withholding the payment of anti-corruption allowances, exploiting silver mines, withdrawing capital officially deposited in pawnshops, collecting storefront rents, and so on. Some of these are worth only a try, while others will not get instant results. The limited revenues can never meet insatiable demands. ... By the end of the 12th day of this month, there are only 227,000 taels left in the Silver Treasury for the recurrent payments, which is not enough even for the soldiers' pay of the 7th month ..."[11]

At its wit's end, the Ministry of Revenue at last gave up its role as the control centre of national financial resources from 1853 onwards, forced by the circumstances to allow the provinces and the military leaders to finance themselves by any means. In the capital, besides cutting down all unnecessary expenses, the ministry introduced a series of unconventional financial and monetary measures, such as the casting of metal tokens, issuing paper currencies, etc., in order to protect itself under the circumstances that provisions from the provinces would no longer be forwarded. Though its severity varied from one period to the next, this unprecedented crisis did not pass until the Taiping Rebellion was suppressed, in the early 1860s.

---

11 *Zhongguo Jindai Huobi Shi Ziliao*, 1–1, pp. 175–177.

There are nine years of expenditure data available or for which the data can be calculated based on known figures for the *Xianfeng* era. These data are shown in Tables 4.8, 4.9 and 4.10.

TABLE 4.8 *Aggregate expenditures of the Silver Treasury during* Xianfeng

| Year | Silver (million taels) | Coins (billion wen) | | | |
|---|---|---|---|---|---|
| | | Coins | *Jingpiao* | *Baochao* | Total |
| 1852 | 10.27 | 0.84 | – | – | 0.84 |
| 1853 | 8.47 | 1.37 | – | – | 1.37 |
| 1854 | 5.03 | 3.04 | 7.83 | – | 10.87 |
| 1855 | (3.23) | – | – | – | (13.69) |
| 1856 | 2.70 | 0.52 | 7.95 | 4.41 | 12.88 |
| 1858 | 3.06 | 0.63 | 11.36 | 1.51 | 13.50 |
| 1859 | 3.81 | 0.70 | 13.98 | 2.12 | 16.80 |
| 1860 | (7.28) | – | – | – | (11.11) |
| 1861 | 6.33 | 0.17 | 0.17 | 0.16 | 0.50 |
| *Average* | *5.58* | *1.04*[a] | *8.26*[b] | *2.05*[c] | *9.06* |

*Source*: see Tables A.19 and A.20. Figures in parentheses have been calculated according to the following formula: a year's expenditure = the year's revenue − the year's inventory + last year's inventory.
[a] The figures is the average of 7 years; [b] The figures is the average of 5 years; [c] The figures is the average of 4 years.

TABLE 4.9 *Proportions of silver and coins in the total expenditure of the Silver Treasury during* Xianfeng

| Year | Total expenditure of silver and coins (million taels) | Silver | | Coins | |
|---|---|---|---|---|---|
| | | Amount (million taels) | Proportion relative to total (%) | Amount equivalent to silver (million taels) | Proportion relative to total (%) |
| 1852 | 11.11 | 10.27 | 92.4 | 0.84 | 7.6 |
| 1853 | 9.84 | 8.47 | 86.1 | 1.37 | 13.9 |
| 1854 | 10.47 | 5.03 | 48.0 | 5.44 | 52.0 |
| 1855 | (10.08) | (3.23) | 32.0 | (6.85) | 68.0 |
| 1856 | 9.14 | 2.70 | 29.5 | 6.44 | 70.5 |

TABLE 4.9 *Proportions of silver and coins in the total expenditure of the Silver Treasury* (cont.)

| Year | Total expenditure of silver and coins (million taels) | Silver | | Coins | |
|---|---|---|---|---|---|
| | | Amount (million taels) | Proportion relative to total (%) | Amount equivalent to silver (million taels) | Proportion relative to total (%) |
| 1858 | 9.81 | 3.06 | 31.2 | 6.75 | 68.8 |
| 1859 | 12.21 | 3.81 | 31.2 | 8.40 | 68.8 |
| 1860 | (12.84) | (7.28) | 56.7 | (5.56) | 43.3 |
| 1861 | 6.58 | 6.33 | 96.2 | 0.25 | 3.8 |
| *Average* | *10.23* | *5.58* | *54.5* | *4.66* | *45.5* |

*Source*: Based on Table 4.8. Coins have been converted into taels at the rate of 1000 wen = 1 tael for 1852 and 1853, and 2000 wen = 1 tael from 1854 to 1861.

TABLE 4.10 *Actual silver expenditures of the Silver Treasury and their proportions relative to total expenditures (in million taels)*

| Year | Total expenditure of silver and coins | Total expenditure of silver | Actual silver expenditure | | |
|---|---|---|---|---|---|
| | | | Amount | Proportion relative to total expenditures of silver and coins (%) | Proportion relative to total expenditure of silver (%) |
| 1853 | 9.84 | 8.47 | 0.40 | 4.1 | 4.7 |
| 1854 | 10.47 | 5.03 | 0.21 | 2.0 | 4.2 |
| 1855 | (10.08) | (3.23) | 0.15 | 1.5 | 4.6 |
| 1856 | 9.14 | 2.70 | 0.17 | 1.9 | 6.3 |
| 1858 | 9.81 | 3.06 | 0.23 | 2.3 | 7.5 |
| 1859 | 12.21 | 3.81 | 0.16 | 1.3 | 4.2 |
| 1860 | (12.84) | (7.28) | 0.15 | 1.2 | 2.1 |
| 1861 | 6.58 | 6.33 | 0.15 | 2.3 | 2.4 |

*Source*: the amounts of actual silver expenditures listed in this table have been taken from the inventory attached to the memorial by Zao Bao, dated the 13th day of the 3rd month of the 4th year of *Tongzhi* (1865).

Just like revenue figures, expenditure figures of both "silver" and "coins" of the Silver Treasury were not all paid in actual silver or copper coins during *Xianfeng*. The "silver" figures are a mixture of actual silver and all kinds of paper currencies expressed in taels, and the figures for "coins" are a mixture of real copper coins, various metal tokens and paper notes expressed in the unit of copper coins (*wen* 文). Under the severe inflation being experienced at that time, neither the metal tokens nor the paper notes could be used at their nominal value in the market, i.e. their actual value was substantially less.

As shown in Table 4.9, even when using the face value of these alternative currencies, and, as well, adding the amount of coins to the total, aggregate expenditures of the Silver Treasury were still smaller than those in previous reigns. Such a scale of expenditure could only sustain the minimum needs of the capital. In the past, whenever there was a military operation, the Ministry of Revenue, acting as the control centre of national financial resources, would always increase its expenditures in order to meet the need outside the capital, even if its revenue decreased. However, that could no longer be done during the reign of *Xianfeng* as central finance had become nothing more than "capital finance," responsible only for ensuring payments in the capital.

During reigns prior to the *Xianfeng*, most expenditures of the Silver Treasury were paid in silver, while copper coins were mainly used for soldiers' pay – according to regulations, a certain percentage of this had to be paid in copper coins. Up to 1852 the amount of copper coins used by the Silver Treasury had been quite stable, amounting to a little more than one million strings per year and accounting for about 10% of total expenditures. However, the proportion of coins in total expenditures rose sharply as from 1853, starting at about 14% in that year and rising to around 70% in the period 1855–1859. This trend continued until the last two years of *Xianfeng*, when the government had to abandon its inflationary policy and withdraw new currencies from circulation. Correspondingly, silver payments took a backseat in the expenditures of the Silver Treasury for most years during *Xianfeng*, declining to a low proportion of around 30% of total expenditures. The inversion of the proportions of silver and coins was the result of the unconventional monetary measures introduced in the *Xianfeng*, when provincial provisions to the capital were cut off by war.

The best indicator of the crisis was the proportions of actual silver in aggregate expenditures. As Table 4.10 shows, the proportions of silver were so low as to have become almost negligible. The Silver Treasury was all but an empty shell at the time and would have been bankrupted if it had not been sustained or funded by large amounts of metal tokens and paper notes. Ever since the Taiping Rebellion began there had been very limited annual provisions to the capital from the provinces and this continued even after the Ministry had adopted a new method of allocation in 1856. In 1863, this is described in an imperial edict, which stated: "For years, only Shanxi province can submit the allocated quota (of the Provisions to the capital) in time every year, while other provinces failed to meet the deadline, some of which made no submission even after the deadline"[12]. Besides, the provisions to the capital were not all actually in silver. According to regulations, official paper currencies issued inside and outside the capital were equivalent to the real amount of silver or copper coins as their face value expressed, and these were to be used for both tax payments and the submission of provisions to the capital. In practice, although these paper currencies were often rejected by local governments when people paid taxes, their use for submissions to the capital were executed to the letter. In many cases, the paper currencies submitted to the capital were purchased from the market at low prices by local authorities: "People paid 2,000 wen of copper coins to the local authorities, 800–900 wen of which will be exchanged into paper currencies for the submission to the Ministry of Revenue"[13].

The balance of the Silver Treasury during *Xianfeng* is shown in Table 4.11.

TABLE 4.11 *Revenues/expenditures and surpluses/deficits of the Silver Treasury during* Xianfeng *(in million taels)*

| Year | Aggregate revenue | Aggregate expenditure | Surplus/Deficit |
|---|---|---|---|
| 1852 | 9.79 | 11.11 | −1.32 |
| 1853 | 5.64 | 9.84 | −4.20 |
| 1854 | 10.45 | 10.47 | −0.02 |
| 1855 | (9.96) | (10.08) | −0.12 |
| 1856 | 10.66 | 9.14 | +1.52 |
| 1859 | 15.58 | 12.21 | +3.37 |
| 1860 | (9.44) | (12.84) | −3.40 |
| 1861 | 7.12 | 6.58 | +0.54 |
| Average | 9.83 | 10.28 | −0.45 |

*Source*: Based on Table A.21. Coins have been converted into taels at the rate of 1000 wen = 1 tael for 1852 and 1853, and 2000 wen = 1 tael from 1854 to 1861.

12 CSL: *Muzong Shilu*, Volume 85.

13 *Zhongguo Jindai Huobi Shi Ziliao*, p. 452.

Prior to 1853 the Silver Treasury had incurred deficits. After issuing metal tokens and paper currencies the situation improved from 1854 onwards, and surpluses returned in 1856. The deficit of 3.4 million taels in 1860 was, however, an exception, this being due to Beijing's capture by British and French allied forces at that time. On the whole there was a total net deficit of 3.63 million taels for the eight years listed in the table, i.e. on average 0.45 million taels per year.

The financial crisis in *Xianfeng* was in large part alleviated in early *Tongzhi*, as government forces began to gain the upper hand in their battles against the Taiping Army in the south. Even then, however, most provinces were still unable to submit provisions to the capital on time. According to the inventory attached to the memorial by Zao Bao in 1865, in the first 3 years of Tongzhi's reign the actual silver expenditures of the Silver Treasury were 0.194 million taels in 1862, 0.118 million taels in 1863 and 0.174 million taels in 1864, i.e. similar to those of *Xianfeng*.

Nevertheless, the crisis of the Silver Treasury generally came to an end with the crushing of the Taiping Rebellion in 1864. Table 4.12 shows the statistics of revenues/expenditures and their surpluses/deficits from 1865 to 1867.

TABLE 4.12 *Revenues/expenditures and surpluses/deficits of the Silver Treasury, 1865–1867*

| Year | Aggregate revenue | | Aggregate expenditure | | Surplus/Deficit | |
|---|---|---|---|---|---|---|
| | Silver (million taels) | Coins (million wen) | Silver (million taels) | Coins (million wen) | Silver (million taels) | Coins (million wen) |
| 1865 | 8.50 | 190 | 8.35 | 180 | +0.15 | +10 |
| 1866 | 8.58 | 140 | 8.24 | 160 | +0.34 | −20 |
| 1867 | 12.35 | 150 | 10.29 | 150 | +2.06 | 0 |
| Average | 9.81 | 160 | 8.96 | 160 | +0.85 | 0 |

*Source*: based on Table A.24.

After its victory over the Taiping rebels, the Qing Government started to restore the conventional fiscal administration systems, in order to obtain funds from provinces for the expenditures of the capital. In the 7th month of the 3rd year of *Tongzhi* (1864), when the government forces had captured Jinling (now Nanjing), the court issued an imperial edict, at the request of the Ministry of

Revenue, ordering provinces to report their military expenses during the war. It also specified in this edict: "from the 7th month of this year, all military expenses have to be paid according to regulations and follow the principle of frugality; in cases where there are no regulations or previous practices to be followed, the relevant authorities or officials have to report for filing in advance and submit detailed registers for audit afterwards"[14]. The systems of "winter estimate", "spring and autumn allocations" and submitting provincial provisions to the capital were also restored gradually from then on. From 1867 onwards, the amount of provisions to the capital that had to be paid by provinces increased from 7 million taels per year to 8 milliom taels. And after 1868, the provinces started to report the amount of *likin*, a new levy introduced in *Xianfeng*, to the Ministry of Revenue for annual payment. In addition, after the set up of new customs offices in trading ports in the early 1860s, the revenues from customs duties increased rapidly, in parallel with the development of foreign trade. Thanks to all this, together with the improvement of provincial financial situation, by the mid- to late *Tongzhi* the Silver Treasury had fully recovered from the crisis and entered a new era.

## 4.3 *Guangxu* Period

As is the case for revenue figures, only a few years of expenditure data of *Guangxu* have survived. There are shown in Table 4.13[15]:

TABLE 4.13 *Revenues/expenditures and surpluses/deficits of the Silver Treasury, 1883–1899*

| Year | Aggregate revenue | | Aggregate expenditure | | Surplus/Deficit | |
|---|---|---|---|---|---|---|
| | Silver (million taels) | Coins (million strings) | Silver (million taels) | Coins (million strings) | Silver (million taels) | Coins (million strings) |
| 1883 | 15.64 | 0.23 | 13.85 | 0.40 | +1.79 | −0.17 |
| 1891 | 19.27 | 1.39 | 17.12 | 1.59 | +2.15 | −0.20 |
| 1897 | 23.28 | 0.34 | 24.84 | 0.52 | −1.56 | −0.18 |

14 CSL: *Muzong Shilu*, Volume 108.

15 In addition to the five years shown in the table, there is also expenditure data for the 5th year of *Guangxu* (1879), but these are incomplete (data from the 11th month have been lost) and no revenue data at all can be found for it. I have therefore omitted this year in the table.

| Year | Aggregate revenue | | Aggregate expenditure | | Surplus/Deficit | |
|---|---|---|---|---|---|---|
| | Silver (million taels) | Coins (million strings) | Silver (million taels) | Coins (million strings) | Silver (million taels) | Coins (million strings) |
| 1898 | 28.80 | 0.44 | 29.20 | 0.63 | −0.40 | −0.19 |
| 1899 | 24.45 | 0.37 | 24.53 | 0.34 | −0.08 | +0.03 |
| *Average* | *22.29* | *0.55* | *21.91* | *0.70* | *+0.38* | *−0.14* |

*Source*: data in the table are all based on the four-column registers. Figures recorded in the aggregate revenue/ expenditure registers during 1897–1899 are often different from those in the four-column registers (see Appendices A and B).

Table 4.13 shows that the expenditures of the Silver Treasury in *Guangxu* differed not only from those in the *Xianfeng-Tongzhi,* but also from those in the early Qing. First, the scale of expenditures in *Guangxu* was quite different. In the early Qing, the annual amount of expenditures of the Silver Treasury was generally around 10 million taels in normal years. In the *Xianfeng-Tongzhi* period, because of the extreme financial difficulties, expenditures drawn on the Treasury were kept to a minimum, for most years even lower than those in the early Qing. In mid- and late *Guangxu,* however, expenditures doubled, reaching more than 20 million taels per year. At the same time, revenue also increased notably.

Second, the nature of expenditures had changed a lot. During the early Qing, recurrent payments of the Silver Treasury were mostly for soldiers' pay, salaries of government officials, the expenses of various *yamen* in the capital and the costs of maintenance workers and servants. All these amounted to no more than 8–9 million taels per year. Taken together with provisional expenditures, in normal years the total sum of expenditures was only about 10 million taels. By the *Guangxu,* the situation changed enormously. Table 4.14 shows various items and their four-column amounts of the Silver Treasury in 1897:

TABLE 4.14 *Items and their four-column figures for the Silver Treasury in 1897 (in taels)*

| Item | Initial balance | Revenue | Expenditure | Final balance |
|---|---|---|---|---|
| Gold | 190 | – | – | 190 |
| *Zubao* silver samples and others | 31,401 | – | – | 31.401 |

TABLE 4.14 *Items and their four-column figures for the Silver Treasury in 1897 (in taels)* (cont.)

| Item | Initial balance | Revenue | Expenditure | Final balance |
|---|---|---|---|---|
| Actual silver reserves of the inner treasury | 1,095,900 | – | – | 1,095,900 |
| Actual silver reserves of the outer treasury | 366,499 | 15,540,824 (*kuping*) | 15,142,508 (*kuping*) | 764,815 |
| 40% of import duties | 430,106 | 102,317 | 280,000 | 252,423 |
| Fund for the defence of the northeast border | 899,084 | 1,865,000 | 1,792,473 | 971,611 |
| Fund prepared for paying soldiers | 1,870,000 | 1,652,260 | 2,500,000 | 1,022,260 |
| New contribution for coastal defence | 354,654 | 944,594 | 636,091 | 663,157 |
| Silver for purchasing copper and lead | 506,883 | 274,109 | 362,000 | 418,992 |
| Income from using two different silver scales (*fang* er *liang ping kouhui* liu *fen pingyin*, 放二两平扣回六分平银) | 434,268 | 977,064 | 942,000 | 462,333 |
| New contribution for purchasing firearms | 40,000 | – | 40,000 | 0 |
| Navy fund | 41,183 | 305,511 | 316,149 | 30,544 |
| Provincial taxes and *likin* levied on domestic opium | 50,393 | 564,216 | 614,000 | 609 |
| Fund for coastal defence | 86,725 | 230,000 | 292,000 | 24,725 |
| Fund for disaster relief | 180,250 | 108,372 | 152,372 | 136,250 |
| Silver for purchasing naval warships and weapons | 556,533 | – | 556,533 | 0 |
| Railway fund | 75,000 | 310,000 | 375,000 | 10,000 |
| Fund for the *Putuoyu* tomb project | 862,437 | – | 406,000 | 456,437 |
| Fund prepared for paying soldiers | 71,929 | 209,076 | 278,563 | 2,442 |
| Monthly soldiers' pay of the newly established land army | – | 200,000 | 150,000 | 50,000 |
| Copper coins (strings) | 687,603 | 341,025 | 517,131 | 511,497 |

*Source*: see Table B.38.

In the early Qing, the content of the four-column registers was very simple: the items in it were classified only by currency type, e.g. gold, silver and copper coins (from mid-*Qianlong* to *Daoguang*, only the amounts of silver and copper coins were recorded); then, under each currency item, total amounts for the year were listed in four-columns – initial balance, total revenues, total expenditures and final balance – providing no further information. But in *Guangxu* registers, as shown in Table 4.14, in addition to the currency items, after the 1860s special capital funds allocated by the Ministry of Revenue were also listed.

In Table 4.14, the figures listed in the columns "revenue" and "expenditure" for the item "actual silver reserves of the outer treasury" give the total sum of recurrent revenues and expenditures, in which all regular provisions to the capital by provinces in the year were included in "revenue" except for the independently listed special funds; while the conventional recurrent expenditures such as soldiers' pay, salaries of government officials, expenses of various *yamen* in the capital, costs of maintenance workers and servants, and so on, were included "expenditure". As shown in the table, the amounts of traditional recurrent revenues/expenditures of the Silver Treasury were a little larger than those in the early Qing, indicating that as the level of overall expenditures in the capital rose, the scale of this part of payments also expanded. The figures of traditional revenues and expenditures of the Silver Treasury recorded in *Guangxu* registers are shown in Table 4.15.

TABLE 4.15 *Traditional revenues/expenditures of the Silver Treasury during* Guangxu (*in million* kuping *taels*)

| Year | Revenue | Expenditure | Surplus/Deficit |
|---|---|---|---|
| 1883 | 11.27 | 11.62 | −0.35 |
| 1891 | 14.25 | 13.05 | +1.20 |
| 1897 | 15.54 | 15.14 | +0.40 |
| 1898 | 18.36 | 18.01 | +0.35 |
| 1899 | 14.54 | 15.26 | −0.72 |
| Average | 14.79 | 14.62 | +0.17 |

*Source*: see Tables B.36–B.40.

Most new items were special capital funds set up after the 1860s. The main sources of these funds were new taxes levied after *Xianfeng*, such as *likin*, new maritime customs duties, taxes and *likin* levied on domestic opium. Every year, in addition to the regular provincial provisions to the capital, the Ministry of Revenue levied various special Capital funds from these new taxes. This method of funding reflected a principle of financial administration of the late Qing: that conventional revenues had to be used for supporting traditional expenditures and new expenditure items had to be funded by new revenues. Some special funds were not named after their use but after their revenue source, such as "40% of import duties", "Provincial taxes and *likin* levied on domestic opium" and some contribution of silver items.

In terms of their use, most funds were levied for national defence and military expenses, as their names indicated. In 1897, the total sum of this kind of special funds received by the Ministry of Revenue was 5.41 million taels, and their total expenditure was 6.57 million taels, accounting for 69.9% and 67.7%, respectively, of the aggregate revenues and expenditures of independently listed special funds (7.74 million taels and 9.7million taels, respectively).

There were also funds for uses other than military actions and defence. The "Fund for disaster relief" was an item of social relief. It was allocated as from 1883 with a quota of 0.12 million taels per year. The actual expenses paid from this fund were not much – from 1897 to 1899, the total sum paid out from the Silver Treasury was only 0.26 million taels. The "Railway fund" was the only one used for economic construction. Created in 1889, the initial purpose of this fund was the construction of the Lu-Han Railway (from Lugouqiao at the capital to Hankou in Hubei province), with a fixed quota of 2 million taels per year – 1.2 million taels paid by the Ministry and 0.8 million taels levied from provinces. After the suspension of the Lu-Han Railway in 1891, the fund was used for the construction of the Guandong Railway. *Fang er liang ping kouhui liu fen pingyin* (放二两平扣回六分平银) was a balance surplus created in 1894, when the Ministry of Revenue was eager to raise funds for the celebration of the 60th birthday of the Empress Dowager Cixi and to finance the First Sino-Japanese War. To this end, it began to use the capital standard scale (*jingping* 京平) to weigh silver paid out, instead of using the treasury standard scale (*kuping* 库平) which created a surplus of 6% from every tael of the silver. This deduction of balance surpluses was applied mainly to the payments of salaries and allowances of princes, nobles and government officials. It produced a total of about one million taels per year.

The "Fund for the *Putuoyu* tomb project" was used for the construction of the tomb of the Empress Dowager Cixi. According to the four-column registers, from 1897 to 1899 total payments from this fund were more than 0.85 million taels. Funds paid by the Silver Treasury for the expenses of the inner court were common to all reigns, but this phenomenon was most prominent in the

*Tongzhi* and *Guangxu* under the rule of the Empress Dowager Cixi. In the late Qing, the expenses of the inner court paid by the Silver Treasury could be either recurrent or provisional. According to Liu Yueyun's *Accounting Tables of Guangxu*, there were two such payments made as "recurrent expenditures" under the new accounting items stipulated by the Ministry of Revenue in 1884: one named "tomb supplies" (*lingqin gongying* 陵寝供应), and the other "silver handed in" (*Jiaojin yin* 交进银). During the period 1885–1894, the payment of "tomb supplies" varied from 0.03 to 0.47 million taels and totaled 1.58 million taels over the 10 years. Payments of "silver handed in" were 0.14 million taels in 1886, 0.18 million taels per year from 1887 to 1891, and 0.28 million taels per year from 1892 to 1894; for the nine years it totalled 1.88 million taels. As for provisional expenses, such as those of the wedding ceremony of Emperor Guangxu in 1888, the construction of the Summer Palace during 1886–1895, the 60th birthday celebration of the Empress Dowager Cixi in 1894, and the "fund for the *Putuoyu* tomb project" during 1895–1908, all of these had no fixed quotas, the amount depending entirely on the needs of the inner court and the ability of the Ministry of Revenue to raise more revenue. Not all the special funds for the expenses of the inner court were paid directly by the Silver Treasury. Some were allocated by the Ministry of Revenue to provinces but submitted directly to the Department of Internal Affairs, instead of to the Ministry. For example, among the special capital funds allocated by the Ministry of Revenue each year, the one called "fund for the Department of Internal Affairs" (*neiwufu jingfei* 内务府经费) was not sent to the Silver Treasury but to the Department of Internal Affairs directly. This fund was allocated from 1866 with a quota of 0.3 million taels per year at the beginning, the quota rising to 0.6 million taels after 1868 and reaching 1.1 million taels from 1894 onwards. Besides fixed funds, there were also provisional funds set up by the Ministry of Revenue but submitted to the inner court by provinces. For example, of the total of 5.5 million taels of special funds used for the wedding ceremony of the Emperor Guangxu in 1888, 2 million taels were allocated to provinces in addition to the 3.5 million taels paid by the Silver Treasury. The increasingly vague divisions between the inner court and outer authorities and increases in royal expenses were prominent features of the late Qing.

Traditional recurrent payments together with the new special funds resulted in a much higher level of expenditure of the Silver Treasury in *Guangxu*. Compared with that of the early Qing, the scale of expenditures of the Silver Treasury had roughly doubled in mid- and late *Guangxu*. As for the balance of payments at that time, since there are only five years of data surviving, it is impossible to analyse trends on the basis of these limited data. Nevertheless, from the overall picture of national balance of payments[16], I have reasons to believe, as shown in Table 4.13, that on the whole the Silver Treasury would have been able to achieve payment surpluses before the First Sino-Japanese War broke out, in 1894. After that, because of the up to 20 million taels of annual principal and interest repayments on foreign loans to finance the war effort and to pay the postwar indemnity, the central government fell into great financial difficulties and was hardly able to achieve a balance of payments ever again. In the autumn of 1899, the Ministry of Revenue reported its financial situation as follows:

> Today, there is no expenditure larger than the repayments on foreign debts and soldier's pay. The annual amount of repayments of foreign debts has been over 20 million taels in recent years. Of these, the repayments of the Franco-Russian loan and the two Anglo-German loans have already been allocated to the provinces and guaranteed by *likin* levied in seven places, and a plan has been made to compensate for the insufficiency caused by exchange rates. In addition, there are still loans borrowed from HSBC and the Cassel Bank, neither of which has been allocated nor guaranteed by reliable funds, and the shortage has been about 2 million taels per year. As for soldiers' pay, the annual amount has been about 30 million taels in recent years. Of these, except that the Green Camp Army (luying 绿营) and the provincial defence forces (*fangyong* 防勇) are supported by the provinces, the Left and the Right *Wuwei* Armies of *Beiyang* (beiyang wuwei zuo you liangjun 北洋武卫左右两军) and the *Hushen* Camp (*Hushen Ying* 虎神营), *Xiaoqi* Camp (*Xiaoqi Ying* 骁骑营) and *Hujun* Camp (*Hujun Ying* 护军营) of the capital's Eight-Banner army have been paid by the Silver Treasury monthly since their foundation. To this end, an additional annual cost of more than 3 million taels is needed[17].

To ease its financial strains, the Qing government went to all lengths to raise money after the war, such as cutting 30% of salaries and the "anti-corruption allowances" of officials, both in the capital and the provinces, drawing balancing surpluses from payments by the Silver Treasury (*fangkuan jianping* 放款减

16 According to Liu Yueyun's *Accounting Tables of Guangxu*, all the 10 years of national revenue/expenditure data surviving for the period 1885–1894 had payment surpluses, varying from 0.75 million taels to over 10 million taels annually.

17 Memorial with imperial remarks: memorial to the throne by the Ministry of Revenue on the 14th day of the 9th month of the 25th year of *Guangxu* (1899).

平), reducing clerk subsidies paid to the capital's *yamen*, downsizing the Green Camp Army and stopping the *mizhe* (米折, rice paid in silver) paid to both soldiers and officers, increasing taxes levied on salt, sugar, tea, alcohol, tobacco and domestic opium (items levied as *yanjin jiajia* (盐斤加价), *cha tang jiali* (茶糖加厘), *zhongchou yan jiu shuili* (重抽烟酒税厘) and *tuyao jiajuan* (土药加捐), implementing business contributions (*tuyao hangdian juanyin* (土药行店捐银) and *dangshang juanyin* (当商捐银), tightening up *likin* and other taxes, and so on. In 1898, in order to raise funds for indemnity payments for the First Sino-Japanese War, the Qing government issued a bond named *Zhaoxin* Stock (昭信股票), which was the second attempt of the Qing government – the first, in 1894, was *Xijie Shangkuan* (息借商款, Business Loan with Interest) – to raise funds through creating internal public debt. In the 4th month of the same year, an imperial edict was issued and all provinces were ordered to "treat the tighten up seriously, get rid of customary fees, avoid corruption and make sure every cent went to the public"[18]. Not long afterwards, Gang Yi (刚毅), the Deputy Grand Secretary (*"Xieban Da Xueshi* 协办大学士*"*) and the Ministry of Defense (*Bingbu Shangshu* 兵部尚书), were sent to the southern provinces (Jiangsu and Guangdong) to raise money. All these measures reveal just how severe the financial situation was at that time.

The more than 350 million taels (in *kuping* silver, excluding the interest) of foreign loans borrowed during and after the First Sino-Japanese War (1894–1898) were guaranteed by maritime customs duties, *likin*, salt gabelle and *likin* levied on salt (*yanli* 盐厘), all of which were important sources of revenue in the provinces, besides maritime customs duties. In order to alleviate the central government's financial burden, most of the annual repayments on these loans were allocated to provinces. Under such circumstances, the provinces had to reduce the amount of other funds submitted to the Ministry and increase their collection of taxes. In fact, after 1894, the submission of provincial provisions to the capital, as well as special funds, was often late or incomplete. According to an inventory submitted to the throne by the Ministry of Revenue in 1899, of the total 17.79 million taels of provisions to the capital, other funds allocated to provinces, and the customs for 1898, only 5.26 million taels had been submitted by the end of the year; no more than 6.44 million taels if one includes submissions that had been already underway[19]. Table 4.16

18 *Guangxu Chao Donghua Lu* (光绪朝东华录), on the 28th day of the 4th month of the 24th year of *Guangxu* (1898).

19 *Memorial copies of the Grand Council* (*junjichu lufu zouzhe* (军机处录副奏折)): inventory submitted by the Ministry of Revenue, the 25th year of *Guangxu* (1899).

shows the actual provincial submissions of special funds to the Silver Treasury during the period 1897–1899:

TABLE 4.16 *Actual provincial submissions of special funds to the Silver Treasury, 1897–1899 (in million taels)*

| Item | Allocated quota | Amount of actual submission | | | % of the allocated quota | | |
|---|---|---|---|---|---|---|---|
| | | 1897 | 1898 | 1899 | 1897 | 1898 | 1899 |
| Fund for northeastern border defence | 2.00 | 1.87 | 1.80[a] | 2.49 | 93.5 | 90.0 | 124.5 |
| Fund prepared for paying soldiers | 2.08 | 1.65 | 1.74[b] | 1.75 | 79.3 | 83.7 | 84.1 |
| Naval fund and fund for coastal defence | 4.00 | 0.54 | 0.56 | 0.50 | 13.5 | 14.0 | 12.5 |
| Fund for disaster relief | 0.12 | 0.11 | 0.16 | 0.06 | 91.7 | 133.3 | 50.0 |
| Monthly soldiers' pay of the newly established land army | 1.00 | 0.20 | 0.15 | 0.53 | 20.0 | 15.0 | 53.0 |
| Railway fund | 0.80 | 0.31 | 0.27 | 0.18[c] | 38.8 | 33.8 | 22.5 |
| Shipyard fund | 0.60 | – | 0.14 | 0.81 | – | 23.3 | 135.0 |
| Total | 10.52 | 4.68 | 4.82 | 6.32 | 44.5 | 45.8 | 60.1 |

*Source*: data of actual submission have been based on Tables B.38–B.40.
[a] Including the extra receipt of 0.08 million taels of silver dollars; [b] Including the extra receipt of 0.07 million taels of silver dollars; [c] Including the extra receipt of 0.02 million taels of silver dollars.

The high default rate of capital funds was not only due to the financial difficulties of the provinces. It also reflected the decline of central control over the provinces that accompanied an increase in the autonomy of the latter in the late Qing period.

Although the scale of revenues/expenditures of the Silver Treasury expanded greatly in the late Qing, its proportion in national aggregate revenues/expenditures dropped significantly as compared with the early Qing. In mid-*Qianlong*, the golden age of the early Qing, national aggregate revenues were no less than 40–50 million taels per year, and annual national aggregate expenditures, including provisional expenditures, were upwards of 40 million taels. The amounts of revenues/expenditures of the Silver Treasury were all about 12 million taels per year at that time. That is to say, during mid-*Qianlong*, the scale of revenues/expenditures of the Silver Treasury accounted for more than 25% of national aggregate expenditures.

On the revenue side, according to my estimate in Chapter 3, the annual revenue of the Silver Treasury accounted for only 13.7% of the actual national total revenue during the mid-*Guangxu* before 1894, and this dropped to about 12.1% after the First Sino-Japanese War. What about expenditures? According to Liu Yueyun's *Accounting Tables of Guangxu*, national expenditures varied from 72.9 million taels to 82 million taels during the period 1885–1894, averaging 77.6 million taels per year[20]. According to Jamieson's *Zhongguo Duzhi kao* (中国度支考, Examination of Fiscal Revenues and Expenditures of China), the figure was 88.98 million taels on the eve of the First Sino-Japanese War[21]. Robert Hart has put the figure at slightly above 70 million taels around 1894; after the war, since 24 million taels for repayment of foreign loans were added, the total sum of expenditures rose to about 100 million taels before 1899[22].

As I have discussed in Chapter 3, all these records or estimates do not include figures that have not been reported, and because of this, the scale of expenditures appears to more than double just a few years later after the financial cleanup was begun at the end of *Guangxu*, and no convincing explanation for the huge differences between them can be given. By my estimates, together with the unreported figures, actual national aggregate expenditures might have been no less than 140–150 million taels per year before 1894, and around 200 million taels on the eve of the Boxer Rebellion (1899). If we take the 17.12 million taels of expenditures of the Silver Treasury in 1891 as a general level (see Table 4.13), and 145 million taels as the national total, the expenditure of the Silver Treasury accounted for about 12% of the national total before 1894. For the period after 1894, if we take the average 26.19 million taels of expenditures of the Silver Treasury during 1897–1899 as the general level, and 200 million taels as the national total, the percentage was about 13%.

Compared with that in the early Qing, the proportion of revenues and expenditures of the Silver Treasury in the national totals had all decreased in the late Qing, which reflected the decline of the central finances and the concurrent formation and expansion of provincial finance.

20 Liu Yueyun (刘岳云), Chuxiang Zongbiao (出项总表, Summary Table of Expenditures), in *Guangxu Kuaiji Biao* (光绪会计表), Volume 1, pp. 3–5.

21 Jamieson: *Zhongguo Duzhi Kao* (中国度支考), p. 25.

22 See *Zhongguo Hanguan yu Yihetuan Yundong* (中国海关与义和团运动), p. 65.

CHAPTER 5

# Fluctuations in Inventories of the Silver Treasury during the Qing Dynasty

## 5.1 From *Kangxi* to *Daoguang*

The inventory of the Silver Treasury was closely related to its balance of payments. As the storage and transfer hub of the government's funds, the Silver Treasury received all monies submitted to the capital from all over the country and from them financed all central government expenses. When there was a surplus it was added to the inventory; contrarily, when deficits occurred, the existing inventory would be used as a fiscal reserve with which to make up the gap. This balancing of funds in the Silver Treasury guaranteed the stable operation of the government's finances. Changes in inventories of the Silver Treasury in a period, therefore often reflected the financial situation of the Qing government at that time. A continuously increasing inventory reflected a healthy financial state, and a large inventory made it possible to cope with unexpected setbacks. By contrast, a period in which the inventory fell sharply could put the government's finances in a tight corner or even in crisis. From the consolidation of its rule over the China proper to its final ruin, the vicissitudes of the Qing dynasty were reflected in changes in the inventory of the Silver Treasury throughout the dynasty.

Fluctuations in the inventories of the Silver Treasury from early *Kangxi* to late *Daoguang* (1667–1843) are shown in Table 5.1 and Figure 5.1.

TABLE 5.1 *Landmark inventories of the Silver Treasury from* Kangxi *to* Daoguang, *1667–1843 (in million taels)*

| Year | Inventory | Year | Inventory | Year | Inventory |
|---|---|---|---|---|---|
| 1667 | 2.49 | 1735 | 34.53 | 1796 | 56.58 |
| 1673 | 21.36 | 1736 | 33.96 | 1797 | 27.92 |
| 1678 | 3.34 | 1748 | 27.46 | 1801 | 16.93 |
| 1686 | 26.05 | 1750 | 30.80 | 1804 | 21.65 |
| 1691 | 31.85 | 1755 | 43.00 | 1820 | 31.21 |
| 1694 | 41.01 | 1758 | 36.38 | 1821 | 27.49 |
| 1719 | 47.37 | 1762 | 41.93 | 1826 | 17.58 |
| 1722 | 27.16 | 1764 | 54.27 | 1827 | 30.01 |

 | DOI 10.1163/9789004307339_007

| Year | Inventory | Year | Inventory | Year | Inventory |
|---|---|---|---|---|---|
| 1723 | 23.61 | 1765 | 60.34 | 1828 | 33.48 |
| 1724 | 31.63 | 1768 | 71.82 | 1832 | 25.69 |
| 1725 | 40.43 | 1771 | 78.94 | 1842 | 13.01 |
| 1727 | 55.25 | 1777 | 81.82 | 1843 | 9.93 |
| 1730 | 62.18 | 1795 | 69.39 | | |

*Source*: see Tables B.1 and B.42–B.45.

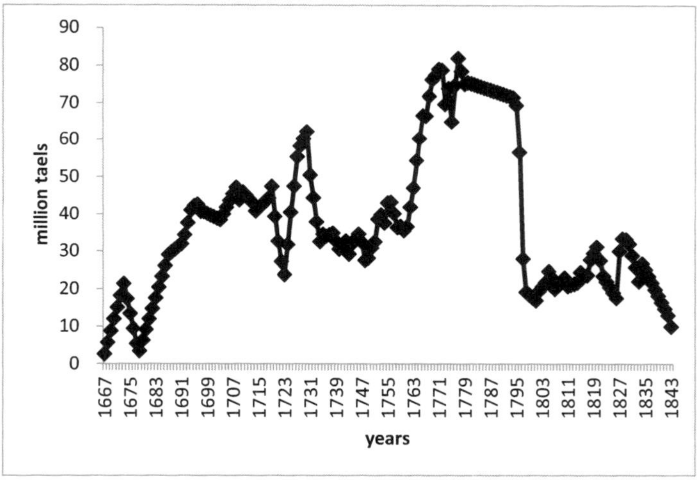


FIGURE 5.1 *Fluctuations in inventories of the Silver Treasury, 1667–1843*

Ignoring temporary fluctuations, Table 5.1 and Figure 5.1 show a generally rising trend of Silver Treasury inventories from *Kangxi* to *Qianlong* during the period 1667–1795, with approximately 80 million taels in the mid-*Qianlong* being the highest. From *Jiaqing* onwards, the trend took the opposite direction: inventories fell from approximately 70 million taels at the end of *Qianlong* to around 20–30 million taels by mid-*Daoguang*, falling to less than 10 million taels in late *Daoguang*. As for the rise and decline of the dynasty, fluctuations in inventories in the early Qing can be divided into two distinctive periods, *Kangxi-Qianlong* and *Jiaqing-Daoguang*.

The Qing dynasty established and consolidated its rule over China proper after the 18 years of fighting various Han armies that followed its invasion of the central plains of China through the *Shanhaiguan* (Shanhai Pass on the Great Wall of China) in 1644. When war ceased in early *Kangxi*, the financial condition of the Qing government began to improve, which resulted in payment surpluses for the first time since the large budget deficits suffered during *Shunzhi*. The inventory of the Silver Treasury stood at 2.49 million taels in 1667 and subsequently increased rapidly at an average rate of 3 million taels per year, reaching 21.36 million taels in 1673. This comfortable position was short-lived, however. After the rebellion of the Three Feudatories broke out in the last month of 1673, huge military expenses soon consumed most of this amount: by the end of 1678 only 3.34 million taels was left – the lowest inventory during the *Kangxi* era. In order to raise much needed funds for combatting the rebels, the Kangxi emperor had to set up several special contributions from 1675 to 1681. He sold not only nominal titles but for the first time in the Qing history also actual official posts. According to a memorial to the throne by Song Deyi, the president of the Court of Censors (*Duchayuan Zuo Duyushi* 都察院左都御史), during 1675–1677 "within three years more than 500 persons had been granted positions as magistrates through contributions"[1]. After the crushing of the revolt of the Three Feudatories and the conquest of Taiwan, the country was finally unified. By 1686, the Silver Treasury's inventories rose once more to reach 26 million taels, slightly more than before the revolt began. From then on, inventories increased significantly, reaching their highest point of 47.37 million taels in 1719. In the last years of *Kangxi*, the emperor dispatched troops to pacify Tibet and stationed massive forces in *Qinghai* to contain the Zunghar. The huge expenses of these major military actions resulted in a continuous decline in the Silver Treasury's inventories from 1720 to 1722. By the end of *Kangxi*, there was little more than 27 million taels left in the Treasury for the succeeding emperor.

In the first half of *Yongzheng*, the new emperor endeavored to deal with the messy administration and heavy corruption caused by the leniency of Kangxi in his later years. Being strict and conscientious, Yongzheng on the one hand acted vigorously against corruption and investigated all deficits, while on the other hand he made every effort to increase Treasury revenue through reforming tax collection and improving and strengthening central control over the provinces in fiscal administration. His vigorous and resolute rectification and improvements resulted in tremendous change. During the period 1724–1730, the Silver Treasury recorded continual surpluses and its annual inventories grew from around 20–30 million taels to 62.18 million taels. However, large-scale military operations against the Zunghar in the northwest, which began in

1 Song Deyi zhuan (宋德宜传, A Biography of Song Deyi), in *Qingshi Liezhuan* (清史列传), Volume 7.

1729, caused the Treasury inventory to plummet to slightly over 30 million taels by the end of the *Yongzheng* era.

For the first 20 years of *Qianlong*, inventories still stood at a level of slightly over 30 million taels. After pacifying the Zunghar in north Xinjiang and the Muslim rebellion in south Xinjiang, inventories started to grow rapidly, exceeding successively 50, 60 and 70 million taels in the 1760s. Ultimately they reached more than 78 million taels in 1771–1772. There was a transient decrease in the following two years, because of the second Jinchuan Campaign, but after that inventories rose again to reach levels of slightly over 70 - 80 million taels before the end of the reign, i.e. about twice national annual aggregate revenue and eight times annual expenditures of the Silver Treasury in normal years. Nevertheless, in the last few years of the *Qianlong*, the inventory declined somewhat, falling to 69.39 million taels in 1795 – the last year of the *Qianlong* era.

During the reigns of Kangxi, Yongzheng and Qianlong, government became more and more powerful as the economy developed and taxation increased. Because there were often payment surpluses, the inventories of the Silver Treasury grew constantly. At their highest point there was enough inventory to pay the central government's recurrent annual expenses for 7–8 years . During the three reigns, tens of major campaigns and hundreds of minor ones were pursued to expand the territory of the empire or to suppress rebellions. In addition, major engineering projects were undertaken, such as the Yellow River works, Great Canal works and Yongding River works in the north, and seawall improvements in the southeastern provinces. The expenses of all the above, together with that of disaster relief, which was needed almost every year, were very large, often consuming hundreds of thousands to tens of millions of taels. In spite of all these items, Silver Treasury inventories kept increasing without large fluctuations, except for some specific periods. This could be achieved because whenever a large provisional payment was required the government would resort to special contributions or "persuade rich merchants to donate". In addition, it would at the same time cut expenditure on regular items – together these measures ensured that financial difficulties would not affect Treasury inventories.

Of course, the prosperity of the country at that time provided it with sufficient fiscal resources and gave it many more choices should it find itself in a financial predicament. Such was the financial position that its emperors also enjoyed the luxury of frequent southern tours and grand celebrations. The abundant inventories and ample fiscal resources also allowed the Qing government to regularly exempt people from taxes during *Kangxi* and *Qianlong*. During *Kangxi*, no less than 500 exemptions were granted under various names, totaling about 140 million taels. The amount of exemptions in *Qianlong* was even greater than that in *Kangxi.* These large-scale exemptions reflected the financial situation in the country[2].

*Jiaqing-Daoguang* was an eventful period, a time in which the country was exposed to declining fortunes. During the mid- and late *Qianlong* various social contradictions came to the surface, and once exposed these contradictions intensified. One disaster appeared to followed another. Taxes became more and more difficult to collect, while contingency expenditures mounted without pauze. As a result, financial difficulties arose and the public purse became emptier by the day.

The White Lotus Rebellion consumed over 100 million taels for military expenses. Since it was impossible to raise sufficient funds for counter-insurgency operations, the Qing government had to use inventories from the Silver Treasury. At the beginning of the war, about 70 million taels were stored in the Treasury. When the war ended in 1802, however, only 19.46 million taels were left. From then on inventories remained at a level of around 20 million taels, except in the last year of *Jiaqing*, when they rose slightly to 31.2 million taels.

The inventories of the Silver Treasury decreased continually during the first few years of *Daoguang*: starting at 30 million taels in 1820 and declining to 17.58 million taels in 1826. They rose to a little more than 30 million taels during 1827–1830, then dropped back again to about 20 million taels from 1832 onwards. After the Opium War, inventories fell to 13 million taels in 1842 and further to 9.93 million taels in 1843 – the lowest figure since mid- *Kangxi.*

These figures were merely book-keeping records; the actual situation was worse. In 1843, in a scandal that shocked the whole court there were accusations that large amounts in the inventories from the Silver Treasury could not be accounted for. According to a note written by a contemporary observer the story was as follows:

> The inventories of the Silver Treasury of the Ministry of Revenue had not been cleaned up ever since Heshen ran national affairs under the reign of Qianlong. From then on, for more than 60 years generations of officials of the Treasury had managed the inventories as if they were their family property, continually embezzling large sums. Audits conducted in *Jiaqing* were all thwarted by these officials through means of bribery and so did not produce any results. Each time a censor (*yushi* 御史) sent by the

2 The detailed records on these exemptions ("mercy exemption", not the so-called disaster exemption) can be seen under the item "records of exemption" (*Ji Juanmian* 纪蠲免) in Wang Qingyun's Shiqu Yuji (石渠余纪), Volume 1.

> emperor went to check the inventories, he would be offered 3000 taels and his servants 300 taels. This had been common practice over a long period of time. When they were blackmailed by some poor officials in the capital or by candidates for imperial examinations who knew of these illegal deals, the Treasury officials would carry out an investigation into the background and personal capacity of these people and pay bribes on that basis, varying from several taels to several thousands of taels. In the 10th year of *Daoguang*, Censor Zhou Chunqi attempted to expose all the dark dealings to the throne but was dissuaded by his relative Tang Jinzhao, who told him that once the truth was exposed not only the properties of hundreds of families would be confiscated, but also hundreds of people would be killed. "It is not worth reveal such a big case just for your own reputation", he was told. And the attempt ceased. By the 23rd year (of *Daoguang*), due to internal conflicts among Treasury officials caused by unequal slicing of the "pie", the fraud could not be covered up any further and was reported to the throne at last. The Emperor was furious about it and interrogated the officials in person. Thus, all facts were brought into the open. … After a thorough audit, people knew that the actual inventory of the Silver Treasury was more than 9 million taels less than the amount recorded in the registers. On imperial orders, the missing funds were later compensated for by all officials who had served in the Silver Treasury after *Qianlong*, each paying a share according to their position.[3]

According to the report to the throne by Wei Qin, Minister of Justice and the appointed investigator of the fraud, in the books the inventory of the Silver Treasury was 12.18 million taels, while the actual amount was only 2.92 million taels, i.e. 9.25 million taels were missing[4]. This case goes to show that figures recorded in official registers are not always to be believed.

The decline of the Silver Treasury's inventories greatly weakened the ability of the Qing government to deal with contingencies. During the *Jiaqing* period, whenever provisional expenses were required, such as for the river works, large-scale disaster relief and the like, resorting to temporary contributions had become standard practice. The financial situation in *Daoguang* was even worse. Ever since putting down the Jahangir Xoja Rebellion in the 1820s with the use of contributions, the Qing government had barely maintained a balance of recurrent payments. After the Opium War, however, it could not even

---

3 Ouyang Yu (欧阳昱), *Jianwen Suolu·Qianji* (见闻琐录・前集), Volume 5.

4 Wei Qin (惟勤) et al., "Memorial to the throne on the 26th day of the 3rd month of the 23rd year of *Daoguang*" (i.e. 1843), in *Huobi Shi Ziliao*, 1–1: pp. 165–167.

make ends meet, for most of the inventories of the Silver Treasury had been consumed by that war. According to a confidential report submitted to the emperor by the Ministry of Revenue in 1850, only 1.87 million taels were left in the Treasury by the end of the 10th month of that same year[5]. This was only one month before the outbreak of the Taiping Rebellion. So, what the *Daoguang* emperor left to his son was nothing but an empty public purse.

## 5.2 *Xianfeng*, *Tongzhi* and *Guangxu*

Because many records of the Yellow Registers are missing, the surviving inventories of the Silver Treasury in the late Qing period present an incomplete picture. Related data are shown in Tables 5.2 and 5.3.

TABLE 5.2 *Inventories of the Silver Treasury in* Xianfeng

| Year | Silver (million taels) | Coins (million strings) | Total of silver and coins (million taels) | Actual Silver Reserves (million taels) |
|---|---|---|---|---|
| 1853 | 1.70 | 0.02 | 1.72 | 0.12 |
| 1854 | 1.66 | 0.03 | 1.68 | 0.13 |
| 1855 | 1.50 | 0.12 | 1.56 | 0.11 |
| 1856 | 1.46 | 0.35 | 1.64 | 0.09 |
| 1857 | – | – | – | 0.11 |
| 1858 | 2.37 | 0.40 | 2.57 | 0.05 |
| 1859 | 3.03 | 3.55 | 4.81 | 0.08 |
| 1860 | 1.18 | 0.46 | 1.41 | 0.07 |
| 1861 | 1.52 | 0.82 | 1.93 | 0.07 |

*Note*: The actual silver reserves are according to the inventory attached to the memorial of Zao Bao on the 13th day of the 3rd month of the 4th year of *Tongzhi* (1865). Strings have been converted into taels at the rate of 1:1 for 1853 and 2:1 for other years.

5 Confidential Memorial by Zhuo Bingtian (卓秉恬) on the 17th day of the 11th month of the 30th year of *Daoguang* (1850), in *Huobi Shi Ziliao*, 1–1: pp. 171–172.

TABLE 5.3 *Inventories of the Silver Treasury in* Guangxu

| Year | Inventory (million taels) | Year | Inventory (million taels) |
|---|---|---|---|
| 1882 | 8.06 | 1896 | 6.83 |
| 1883 | 9.85 | 1897 | 5.27 |
| 1890 | 8.23 | 1898 | 4.87 |
| 1891 | 10.38 | 1899 | 4.78 |

*Source*: see Table B.47.

The inventories in *Xianfeng*, as I have mentioned, were composed of actual silver, copper coins, copper and iron tokens and various paper notes denominated in silver taels or copper coins. These inventories were, therefore, far more complex than those in previous reigns.

Among the first three years of *Xianfeng*, the two years for which we have records had total payment deficits of 5.93 million taels, enough to consume the inventory resources left over from *Daoguang*. The issue of metal tokens and paper notes from 1853 onwards helped the Qing government overcome its extreme financial crisis, but greatly changed the composition of the Silver Treasury's inventories, gradually turning it into a mere "Paper Treasury". As shown in Table 5.2, from 1853 to 1856, in spite of the issue of metal tokens and paper notes, Silver Treasury inventories continued to drop year after year. After 1856, it rebounded to reach its highest point of 4.81 million taels. Then, in 1860, when Anglo-French forces captured Beijing and the *Xianfeng* emperor fled north to Jehol, the figure fell once again, sliding down to its lowest point of 1.41 million taels, although in 1861 it rebounded slightly to 1.93 million taels. During the whole period, the highest figure of actual silver stored in the Treasury was 126 thousand taels and the lowest was 50 thousand taels. Without a doubt, Silver Treasury inventories in *Xianfeng* were the lowest of all reigns in the Qing dynasty.

There are no inventory records left in the Yellow Registers of the *Tongzhi*. According to Zaobao's inventory, submitted to the throne in 1865, the actual silver reserve of the Treasury was only 50–60 thousand taels during the period 1862–1864. We do, however, know that the Silver Treasury enjoyed continuous payment surpluses from 1865 to 1867, the total sum of which was about 2.25 million taels. Combined with the fact that the financial situation had improved since the pacification of the Taiping Rebellion in 1864, I estimate that the inventories of the Silver Treasury may have been at least several million taels after mid-*Tongzhi*.

The inventories during the reign of Guangxu, as shown in Table 5.3, were about 8–9 million taels before 1894, with the highest amount being 10.38 million taels (reached in 1891). After the start of the First Sino-Japanese War, as the financial situation deteriorated, inventories fell sharply to less than 5 million taels by 1899.

During the first 20 years of *Guangxu*, central finances always showed payment surpluses. At that time, provincial provisions kept flowing to the capital, even though the provinces no longer followed orders from Beijing as closely as they had before. After the First Sino-Japanese War, however, the huge amount of repayments on foreign loans upset the balance between revenues and expenditure. And since the provinces had to bear a great part of the annual repayments, their provisions to the capital decreased correspondingly, which further worsened the imbalances of central finances. Thus, the Silver Treasury experienced continuous deficits after the war and its inventories began to fall once again.

By the time of *Guangxu*, the significance and role of the inventories of the Silver Treasury for national financial security had become far less important than in previous times. There are two reasons for this. First, in the early Qing both central and provincial finances were highly integrated, and they were managed and controlled in a unified way by the Ministry of Revenue. Under these circumstances, the Silver Treasury was not only a place where the vast majority of annual payment surpluses of the country converged, but it was also provided fiscal reserves whenever major provisional expenses were needed. Therefore, the situation of inventories of the Silver Treasury was closely related to national finance at that time. This changed in the late Qing. Ever since the *Xianfeng* and *Tongzhi* eras, with the expansion of local authority and the formation of relatively independent provincial finances, the Ministry of Revenue had gradually become a department that was only in charge of central finances. So the Silver Treasury no longer collected all provincial surpluses, and it no longer served as the national reserve.

Second, reserving large amount of real currencies in the Silver Treasury for contingencies was befitting the circumstances of the traditional metal-based economy of the early Qing. At that time, due to the lack of modern credit systems and paper money, it was impossible for national government finances to operate without a physical silver and copper treasury for handling government funds. But in the late Qing, modern banks of Western countries had already been set up everywhere in treaty ports, and native banks handling money deposits, loans and remittances, such as *qianzhuang* (钱庄, bank for cash) and *piaohao* (票号, bank for drafts), were prospering. Especially during *Guangxu*, the Qing government started to use some of these modern financial institutions for some aspects such as remitting government funds through *piaohao*, borrowing money from foreign banks and firms or from domestic banks (*qianzhuang* and *piaohao*). The fact that both the military funds for the First Sino-Japanese War and the enormous postwar indemnity payments were paid mainly from foreign loans rather than from the inventories of the Silver Treasury was clear proof that the Treasury was no longer the only guarantee of government financial security at that time.

By 1904, the Qing Government decided to establish its first official bank, named *Hubu Yinhang* (户部银行, Ministry of Revenue Bank). In 1908, it was renamed The Da Qing Bank. As the "confluence of circulation of fiscal funds"[6], according to the regulations of the *Hubu* Bank, the activities of this new financial institution would include not only issuing paper notes and national currencies, as well as the handling of government deposits and loans, but it was also to manage the national treasury. Although the reform eventually failed, because of a strong boycott by vested interests within the Silver Treasury, it further reduced the influence of the Treasury in national finances. In 1902, with the abolishment of *Guanku Dachen* (管库大臣) the independent status of the "Three Stores" ended and they were placed under the management of the Ministry of Revenue once more. In 1906, the Silver Treasury was renamed *Jinyin Ku* (金银库, the Gold and Silver Treasury), under the authority of the Ministry of Finance. During this period, its role as the manager of national revenues and expenditures had been partially replaced by the *Hubu* Bank, and the time of the Silver Treasury was gone forever[7].

6 Liu Jinzao: *Qingchao Xu Wenxian Ttongkao*, p. 8125.

7 When the *Hubu* Bank was renamed the Da Qing Bank in 1908, the deposits of the Ministry of Finance in it were more than 10 million taels, twice as much as the inventories of the Silver Treasury at that time; see *Daqing Yinhang Shimo Ji*, p. 178.

# *Appendices*

# Appendix A: Tables of Aggregate Revenue/ Expenditure of the Silver Treasury

TABLE A.1 *Amounts of gold, silver and copper coins in the Silver Treasury of the 44th year of* Kangxi, *1705*

| Item | Initial balance | Revenue | Expenditure | Final balance | Remarks |
|---|---|---|---|---|---|
| Gold (taels) | – | 5.195 | 5.195 | – | – Data of "initial balance" and "final balance" are missing in the register.<br>– The revenue and expenditure of amber, mercury and ladybell in the register are not included in this table. |
| Silver (taels) | – | 9,101,748.050 | 7,474,582.125 | – | |
| Impure silver (taels) | – | 1,116.576 | 750.000 | – | |
| Copper coins (strings) | – | 379,604.002 | 345,031.777 | – | |

*Source*: based on the Kangxi Sishisi Nianfen Qianliang Shumu Ce (康熙四十四年分钱粮数目册, register for amount of money and grain of the 44th year of Kangxi), The Yellow Registers (The Silver Treasury of the Ministry of Revenue), Volume 35.

TABLE A.2 *Payment surpluses/deficits of the Silver Treasury of the 44th year of* Kangxi, *1705*

| Revenue | | Expenditure | | Surplus/Deficit (+/-) | |
|---|---|---|---|---|---|
| Silver (taels) | Copper coins (strings) | Silver (taels) | Copper coins (strings) | Silver (taels) | Copper coins (strings) |
| 9,102,865 | 379,604 | 7,475,332 | 345,032 | +1,627,533 | +34,572 |

*Source*: based on Table A.1. The silver figures included impure silver.

 | DOI 10.1163/9789004307339_008

TABLE A.3 *Aggregate revenues of the Silver Treasury during* Yongzheng, *1723–1735*

| Year | Silver (taels) | Copper coins (strings) | Others | Remarks |
|---|---|---|---|---|
| *1st year (1723)* | *9,401,510** | *486,987** | – | |
| *2nd year (1724)* | *18,013,925* | *615,210* | – *Gold 619 taels*<br>– *Mercury 48 catties and 10 taels* | *The amount of copper coins is the total of large and small coins.* |
| 1st month | 1,090,657.024 | – | – | |
| 2nd month | 1,518,658.571 | 165.400 | – | Large and small coins |
| 3rd month | 1,002,473.188 | 62,275.200 | – | Large coins |
| 4th month | 1,130,623.857 | 61,525.200 | – | Large coins |
| Leap month | 1,104,564.459 | 15.698 | – | Large and small coins |
| 5th month | 271,388.511 | – | Gold 97 taels | |
| 6th month | 634,191.268 | 71,964.188 | Gold 522 taels | Large coins |
| 7th month | 2,700,973.694 | 1,227.612 | Mercury 48 catties and 10 taels | |
| 8th month | 1,111,002.478 | 111,236.709 | – | Large coins |
| 9th month | 2,273,715.174 | 53,508.590 | – | Large coins |
| 10th month | 462,649.996 | 70,629.661 | – | Large coins |
| 11th month | 1,999,700.762 | 69.600 | – | Large coins |
| 12th month | 2,713,325.562 | 182,591.839 | – | |
| *3rd year (1725)* | *17,044,450* | *536,633* | – *Gold 105.131 taels*<br>– *Impure–silver seals 8, total 520 taels*<br>– *Mercury 48 catties and 10 taels* | *The amount of coins if the total of large and small coins.* |
| 1st month | 1,233,861.681 | 20.800 | – | Large coins |
| 2nd month | 978,759.150 | 51,396.000 | – | Large coins |
| 3rd month | 508,309.582 | 37.045 | – *Gold 105.131 taels*<br>– *Impure–silver seal 1, 65 taels* | Large coins |
| 4th month | 1,355,727.551 | 70,273.552 | Impure–silver seals 2, total 99 taels | Large coins |
| 5th month | 2,147,063.656 | 10,205.065 | | Large coins |

| Year | Silver (taels) | Copper coins (strings) | Others | Remarks |
|---|---|---|---|---|
| 6th month | 1,547,195.955 | 62,698.677 | Impure–silver seal 1, 59 taels | Large and small coins |
| 7th month | 793,900.413 | 751.250 | Impure–silver seal 1, 108 taels | Large coins |
| 8th month | 446,563.541 | 166,352.321 | Mercury 48 catties and 10 taels | |
| 9th month | 2,391,031.923 | 2,389.328 | Impure–silver seal 1, 60 taels | |
| 10th month | 1,571,672.789 | 74,111.120 | Impure–silver seals 2, total 129 taels | Large coins |
| 11th month | 705,904.447 | 18.375 | – | |
| 12th month | 3,364,459.121 | 98,379.337 | – | Large coins |
| *5th year (1727)* | *16,861,818* | *479,505* | – *Gold 57.2 taels*<br>– *Impure–silver seals 2, total 148.5 taels*<br>– *Mercury 48 catties and 10 taels* | |
| 1st month | 1,992,149.221 | – | – | |
| 2nd month | 1,429,023.563 | 5.460 | – | |
| 3rd month | 117,580.678 | – | – | |
| Leap month | 892,164.627 | 10,859.998 | – | |
| 4th month | 1,829,080.542 | 66,699.722 | Mercury 48 catties and 10 taels | |
| 5th month | 2,340,004.348 | 164.575 | – | |
| 6th month | 895,800.117 | 66,479.694 | – | |
| 7th month | 689,002.693 | 42.150 | – | |
| 8th month | 986,286.243 | – | – | |
| 9th month | 1,154,096.433 | 4,511.550 | – | |
| 10th month | 595,816.776 | 66,406.142 | Impure–silver seal 1, 92 taels | |
| 11th month | 1,715,918.882 | 140,266.962 | Gold 57.2 taels | |
| 12th month | 2,224,893.476 | 124,069.240 | Impure–silver seal 1, 56.5 taels | |
| *7th year (1729)* | *17,964,254* | *660,988* | – *Gold 4,328.24 taels*<br>– *Impure–silver seals 7, total 648 taels*<br>– *Mercury 48 cattiesand 10 taels* | |

TABLE A.3 *Aggregate revenues of the Silver Treasury during* Yongzheng, *1723–1735* (cont.)

| Year | Silver (taels) | Copper coins (strings) | Others | Remarks |
|---|---|---|---|---|
| 1st month | 882,954.278 | 3.600 | – | |
| 2nd month | 1,575,190.773 | 69,484.553 | – | |
| 3rd month | 810,449.178 | 19,770.913 | Impure–silver seal1, 124 taels | |
| 4th month | 715,141.553 | 163.100 | Impure–silver seals 4, total 354 taels | |
| 5th month | 3,136,929.231 | 64,912.255 | – *Gold 4,157.840 taels*<br>– *Mercury 48 catties and 10 taels* | |
| 6th month | 2,138,152.319 | 1,231.065 | Impure–silver seal 1, 103 taels | |
| 7th month | 2,045,856.448 | 18,850.277 | Gold 7 taels | |
| Leap month | 428,708.395 | 66,530.395 | – | |
| 8th month | 847,404.023 | 66,330.675 | – | |
| 9th month | 290,172.190 | 64,545.213 | – | |
| 10th month | 757,094.957 | 64,461.405 | – | |
| 11th month | 1,884,558.661 | 66,494.935 | Gold 163.4 taels | |
| 12th month | 2,451,641.574 | 158,209.483 | Impure–silver seal 1, 67 taels | |
| *9th year (1731)* | *9,964,312* | *622,314* | – *Gold 233.5 taels*<br>– *Mercury 48 catties and 10 taels* | |
| 1st month | 158,781.494 | – | | |
| 2nd month | 1,373,998.718 | 20,425.907 | Gold 52 taels | |
| 3rd month | 1,996,980.799 | 24,461.717 | Gold 76.5 taels | |
| 4th month | 426,435.751 | 1,037.060 | Gold 5 taels | |
| 5th month | 790,237.425 | 7.900 | – | |
| 6th month | 141,473.564 | 224,893.156 | – | |
| 7th month | 233,528.024 | 4,050.580 | – | |
| 8th month | 780,884.780 | 74,917.732 | Mercury 48 catties and 10 taels | |
| 9th month | 563,621.475 | 3,007.876 | Gold 100 taels | |
| 10th month | 892,700.460 | 59,411.240 | – | |
| 11th month | 1,758,047.445 | 94,067.928 | – | |
| 12th month | 847,622.503 | 116,032.502 | – | |

| Year | Silver (taels) | Copper coins (strings) | Others | Remarks |
|---|---|---|---|---|
| *10th year (1732)* | *11,656,097* | *989,864* | *– Gold 289.2 taels*<br>*– Impure–silver seals 10, total 812.5 taels* | |
| 1st month | 168,948.242 | 201.440 | – | |
| 2nd month | 1,512,399.386 | 62,601.556 | Impure–silver seals 3, total 269.3 taels | |
| 3rd month | 557,091.702 | 102,353.280 | Impure–silver seals 4, total 280.2 taels | |
| 4th month | 499,977.456 | 105,930.728 | – | |
| 5th month | 548,050.831 | 83,505.237 | – | |
| Leap month | 1,208,762.141 | 74,292.625 | – | The amount of coins included 750 wen of small coins |
| 6th month | 605,141.995 | 108,997.077 | Impure silver seals 3, total 263 taels | |
| 7th month | 1,364,994.825 | 99,300.906 | – | |
| 8th month | 470,005.559 | 67,779.580 | – | |
| 9th month | 534,803.012 | 49,744.392 | – | |
| 10th month | 792,361.029 | 75,228.974 | – | |
| 11th month | 684,046.514 | 37,106.849 | Gold 289.2 taels | |
| 12th month | 2,709,514.285 | 122,821.607 | – | |
| *11th year (1733)* | *11,709,139* | *638,455* | *Gold 565.872 taels* | |
| 1st month | 1,003,643.059 | – | – | |
| 2nd month | 1,138,828.213 | 29,663.998 | Gold 405.352 taels | |
| 3rd month | 542,328.248 | 49,901.142 | Gold 44.8 taels | |
| 4th month | 939,289.659 | 30,369.096 | – | |
| 5th month | 963,795.970 | 45,227.601 | – | |
| 6th month | 1,075,998.744 | 49,259.664 | – | |
| 7th month | 362,499.647 | 21,091.569 | – | |
| 8th month | 219,868.726 | 132,575.775 | Gold 115.720 taels | |
| 9th month | 864,504.265 | 27,889.015 | – | |
| 10th month | 560,123.725 | 39,020.652 | – | |
| 11th month | 1,518,018.529 | 41,525.589 | – | |
| 12th month | 2,520,239.824 | 171,930.509 | – | |

TABLE A.3 *Aggregate revenues of the Silver Treasury during* Yongzheng, *1723–1735* (cont.)

| Year | Silver (taels) | Copper coins (strings) | Others | Remarks |
|---|---|---|---|---|
| *13th year (1735)* | *16,062,619* | *480,224* | – *Gold 325.66 taels*<br>– *Impure–silver seals 2, total 99.8 taels* | |
| 1st month | 774,601.413 | 640.264 | – | |
| 2nd month | 103,330.249 | 3,156.468 | – | |
| 3rd month | 1,217,219.246 | 5,546.988 | – | |
| 4th month | 465,123.419 | 38,613.584 | – | |
| Leap month | 2,519,352.472 | 37,944.501 | – | |
| 5th month | 1,296,229.469 | 37,878.091 | Impure–silver seal 1, 43.8 taels | |
| 6th month | 1,184,450.696 | 41,844.909 | – | |
| 7th month | 1,151,755.726 | 35,797.228 | – | |
| 8th month | 1,062,909.961 | 72,922.865 | – | |
| 9th month | 1,730,886.832 | 38,306.517 | – | |
| 10th month | 2,049,888.393 | 36,326.231 | Gold 323.7 taels | |
| 11th month | 71,851.739 | 38,190.308 | Gold 1.960 taels | |
| 12th month | 2,435,019.415 | 93,056.530 | Impure–silver seal 1, 56 taels | |
| *Average of* Yongzheng | *14,297,569* | *612,242* | – | |

*Source*: figures marked with * are from the four-column register of the 1st year of Yongzheng (see Table B.2 for details), others are based on aggregate revenue registers of Yongzheng, The Yellow Registers (The Silver Treasury of the Ministry of Revenue), Volume 1.

TABLE A.4 *Aggregate expenditures of the Silver Treasury during* Yongzheng, *1723–1733*

| Year | Silver (taels) | Copper coins (strings) | Others | Remarks |
|---|---|---|---|---|
| *1st year (1723)* | *10,351,722** | *471,152** | – | |
| *3rd year (1725)* | *8,661,550* | *618,553* | *Mercury 5 catties and 10.24 taels* | |
| 1st month | 109,125.958 | – | – | |

| Year | Silver (taels) | Copper coins (strings) | Others | Remarks |
|---|---|---|---|---|
| 2nd month | 912,625.569 | 165,702.589 | – | |
| 3rd month | 714,658.279 | 1,056.000 | – | |
| 4th month | 1,204,884.892 | 70,659.977 | – | |
| 5th month | 417,614.627 | 1,761.000 | – | |
| 6th month | 346,018.515 | 70,872.091 | – | |
| 7th month | 444,940.044 | 981.000 | – | |
| 8th month | 1,070,753.129 | 164,291.961 | Mercury 5 catties and 10.24 taels | |
| 9th month | 575,901.946 | 1,257.000 | – | |
| 10th month | 945,454.688 | 70,300.753 | – | |
| 11th month | 543,839.857 | 1,299.000 | – | |
| 12th month | 1,375,732.646 | 70,371.537 | – | |
| *7th year* (1729) | *16,291,286* | *828,140* | *Mercury 8 catties and 6.28 taels* | |
| 1st month | 1,012,204.747 | 72.000 | – | |
| 2nd month | 3,569,272.813 | 67,037.472 | Mercury 6 catties and 14 taels | |
| 3rd month | 536,871.016 | 65,091.100 | – | |
| 4th month | 683,601.390 | 65,762.566 | – | |
| 5th month | 2,338,451.582 | 65,814.038 | – | |
| 6th month | 1,106,709.998 | 65749.463 | – | |
| 7th month | 485,288.861 | 65,669.632 | – | |
| Leap month | 1,365,026.558 | 65,671.545 | – | |
| 8th month | 1,444,628.579 | 65,641.875 | – | |
| 9th month | 745,779.630 | 65,707.397 | Mercury 1 catty and 8.28 taels | |
| 10th month | 635,945.734 | 65,766.105 | – | |
| 11th month | 1,475,352.168 | 65,778.435 | – | |
| 12th month | 892,153.073 | 104,378.435 | – | |
| *8th year* (1730) | *12,958,261* | *482,661* | – *Gold 4 taels*<br>– *Mercury 8 catties and 5.972 taels* | |
| 1st month | 1,355,004.959 | – | – | |
| 2nd month | 924,086.933 | 33,458.161 | – | |
| 3rd month | 1,291,315.397 | 33,467.467 | – | |
| 4th month | 1,101,314.076 | 33,801.777 | – | |

TABLE A.4 *Aggregate expenditures of the Silver Treasury during* Yongzheng, *1723–1733* (cont.)

| Year | Silver (taels) | Copper coins (strings) | Others | Remarks |
|---|---|---|---|---|
| 5th month | 358,477.217 | 33,847.929 | – | |
| 6th month | 1,065,680.523 | 33,854.892 | – Gold 2 taels<br>– Mercury 3 catties and 1.8 taels | |
| 7th month | 503,475.585 | 33,837.765 | – | |
| 8th month | 1,082,830.164 | 33,908.202 | – | |
| 9th month | 982,924.144 | 40,201.806 | – | |
| 10th month | 780,136.054 | 99,426.951 | Mercury 2 catties and 2.372 taels | |
| 11th month | 1,032,140.579 | 33,944.063 | – Gold 2 taels<br>– Mercury 10 taels | |
| 12th month | 2,480,875.738 | 72,912.142 | Mercury 2 catties and 7.8 taels | |
| *9th year (1731)* | *24,109,615* | *692,426* | – *Gold 2026.611 taels*<br>– *Mercury 1 catty and 5 taels* | *The 1st month data are missing in the original register* |
| 2nd month | 1,194,334.867 | 66,543.328 | – Gold 102 taels<br>– Mercury 10 taels | |
| 3rd month | 5,769,866.232 | 33,906.838 | Gold 500 taels | |
| 4th month | 2,283,885.851 | 1,190.000 | Gold 500 taels | |
| 5th month | 571,312.586 | 41,295.210 | Gold 500 taels | |
| 6th month | 946,745.851 | 43,777.430 | – | |
| 7th month | 2,839,198.785 | 73,235.559 | – | |
| 8th month | 2,200,845.673 | 65,185.118 | – | |
| 9th month | 881,746.796 | 65,548.110 | Gold 424..611 taels | |
| 10th month | 1,848,085.228 | 65,420.987 | – | |
| 11th month | 2,335,518.117 | 65,331.152 | Mercury 11 taels | |
| 12th month | 3,238,075.005 | 170,991.942 | – | |
| *11th year (1733)* | *18,168,240* | *541,957* | – *Gold 1,501.7618 taels*<br>– *Mercury 569 catties and 9.72804 taels* | *The amount of coins are the total of large and small coins.* |
| 1st month | 1,370,013.911 | 2,000.000 | – | |

| Year | Silver (taels) | Copper coins (strings) | Others | Remarks |
|---|---|---|---|---|
| 2nd month | 2,787,064.679 | 38,684.659 | – | |
| 3rd month | 1,082,401.004 | 38,839.790 | Mercury 569 catties and 9.72804 taels | The amount of coins included 750 wen of small coins |
| 4th month | 489,087.281 | 38,733.671 | Gold 502.62 taels | |
| 5th month | 1,684,033.375 | 40,646.361 | – | |
| 6th month | 538,369.516 | 38,729.666 | – | |
| 7th month | 1,775,800.235 | 38,692.979 | – | |
| 8th month | 2,114,054.187 | 112,075.777 | – | |
| 9th month | 597,281.404 | 38,278.951 | Gold 98.8018 taels | |
| 10th month | 462,068.809 | 38,038.606 | Gold 142.1 taels | |
| 11th month | 558,447.072 | 38,338.229 | Gold 758.24 taels | |
| 12th month | 4,709,618.272 | 78,898.771 | – | |
| *Average of* Yongzheng | *15,090,112* | *605,815* | – | |

*Source*: figures marked with * are from the four-column register of the 1st year of Yongzheng (see Table B.2 for details), others are based on aggregate expenditure registers of Yongzheng, The Yellow Registers (The Silver Treasury of the Ministry of Revenue), Volume 13.

TABLE A.5 *Payment surpluses/deficits of the Silver Treasury during* Yongzheng, *1723–1733* (*1*)

| Year | Aggregate revenue | | Aggregate expenditure | | Surplus/Deficit (+/–) | |
|---|---|---|---|---|---|---|
| | Silver (taels) | Copper coins (strings) | Silver (taels) | Copper coins (strings) | Silver (taels) | Copper coins (strings) |
| 1st year (1723) | 9,401,510* | 486,987* | 10,351,722* | 471,152* | –950,212 | +15,835 |
| 3rd year (1725) | 17,044,450 | 536,633 | 8,661,550 | 618,553 | +8,382,900 | –81,920 |
| 7th year (1729) | 17,964,254 | 660,988 | 16,291,286 | 828,140 | +1,672,968 | –167,152 |
| 9th year (1731) | 9,964,312 | 622,314 | 24,109,615 | 692,426 | –14,145,303 | –70,112 |
| 11th year (1733) | 11,709,139 | 638,455 | 18,168,240 | 541,957 | –6,459,101 | +96,498 |

TABLE A.5 *Payment surpluses/deficits of the Silver Treasury during* Yongzheng, *1723–1733* (*1*) (cont.)

| Year | Aggregate revenue | | Aggregate expenditure | | Surplus/Deficit (+/–) | |
|---|---|---|---|---|---|---|
| | Silver (taels) | Copper coins (strings) | Silver (taels) | Copper coins (strings) | Silver (taels) | Copper coins (strings) |
| *average of* Yongzheng | *13,216,733* | *589,075* | *15,516,483* | *630,446* | *–2,299,750* | *–41,371* |

*Source*: based on Tables A.3 and A.4.

TABLE A.6 *Payment surpluses/deficits of the Silver Treasury during* Yongzheng, *1723–1735* (*2*)

| Year | Aggregate revenue (million taels) | Aggregate expenditure (million taels) | Surplus/Deficit (million taels) | Year–end inventories on 1775 list (million taels) |
|---|---|---|---|---|
| 1st year (1723) | 9.40 | 10.35 | –0.95 | 23.61 |
| 2nd year (1724) | 18.01 | (9.99) | +8.02 | 31.63 |
| 3rd year (1725) | 17.04 | 8.66 | +8.38 | 40.43[a] |
| 4th year (1726) | – | – | +6.98 | 47.41 |
| 5th year (1727) | 16.86 | (9.02) | +7.84 | 55.25 |
| 6th year (1728) | – | – | +2.99 | 58.24 |
| 7th year (1729) | 17.96 | 16.29 | +1.67 | 60.25[b] |
| 8th year (1730) | (14.89) | 12.96 | +1.93 | 62.18 |
| 9th year (1731) | 9.96 | 24.11 | –14.15 | 50.38[c] |
| 10th year (1732) | 11.66 | (17.65) | –5.69 | 44.39[d] |
| 11th year (1733) | 11.71 | 18.17 | –6.46 | 37.93 |

| Year | Aggregate revenue (million taels) | Aggregate expenditure (million taels) | Surplus/Deficit (million taels) | Year–end inventories on 1775 list (million taels) |
|---|---|---|---|---|
| 12th year (1734) | – | – | –5.43 | 32.50 |
| 13thyear (1735) | 16.06 | (14.03) | +2.03 | 34.53 |
| *average of* Yongzheng | *14.36* | *14.12* | *+0.55*[e] *+0.24*[f] | |

*Source*: based on Tables A.3, A.4 and B.42. Figures in parentheses have been calculated on the basis of the aggregate revenues/expenditures of the year and the inventory of the year, and that of the previous year. Surplus/deficit figures of the years without revenue/expenditure data have been obtained by calculating the inventory differences of the year and the previous year. [a] Calculated on the basis of the surplus of the year, the inventory figure ought to be 40.01 million taels; [b] Calculated on the basis of the surplus of the year, the inventory figure ought to be59.91 million taels; [c] Calculated on the basis of the deficit of the year, the inventory figure ought to be 48.03 million taels; [d] Calculated on the basis of the deficit of the year, the inventory figure ought to be 44.69 million taels; [e] The figure is obtain by calculating on the basis of all the surplus/deficit figures listed in the column; [f] The figure is obtain by calculating the difference between the average revenue and expenditure figures.

TABLE A.7 *Aggregate revenues of the Silver Treasury during* Qianlong, *1736–1795*

| Year | Silver (taels) | Copper coins (strings) | Others | Remarks |
|---|---|---|---|---|
| *1st year (1736)* | *14,789,281* | *645,172* | *Gold 0.7 taels* | |
| 1st month | 372,236.224 | 798.324 | – | |
| 2nd month | 2,351,908.848 | 74,628.274 | – | |
| 3rd month | 459,561.925 | 33,510.673 | – | |
| 4th month | 245,230.890 | 20,720.937 | – | |
| 5th month | 616,730.323 | 53,901.584 | – | |
| 6th month | 2,559,496.721 | 49,326.667 | – | |
| 7th month | 1,342,259.853 | 40,051.857 | – | |
| 8th month | 486,006.300 | 77,305.097 | Gold 0.7 taels | |
| 9th month | 1,645,159.444 | 70,963.614 | – | |
| 10th month | 797,268.517 | 62,200.297 | – | |
| 11th month | 546,067.527 | 64,062.717 | – | |

TABLE A.7 *Aggregate revenues of the Silver Treasury during* Qianlong, *1736–1795* (cont.)

| Year | Silver (taels) | Copper coins (strings) | Others | Remarks |
|---|---|---|---|---|
| 12th month | 3,367,354.217 | 97,701.636 | – | |
| *2nd year (1737)* | *14,733,557* | *586,856* | – *Gold 118.6 taels*<br>– *Silver seals 10, total 633.5 taels*<br>– *Impure–silver seals 11, total 711 taels* | |
| 1st month | 1,238,353.630 | 1,014.022 | – | |
| 2nd month | 1,882,002.279 | 61,123.989 | – | |
| 3rd month | 309,301.674 | 11,186.439 | Gold 73 taels | |
| 4th month | 91,265.038 | 30,946.106 | – | |
| 5th month | 528,001.811 | 43,685.405 | Gold 45.6 taels | |
| 6th month | 1,633,636.451 | 19,238.865 | – | |
| 7th month | 895,097.537 | 39,788.855 | Silver seals 10, total 633.5 taels | |
| 8th month | 803,143.680 | 62,867.968 | Impure–silver seals 8, total 491 taels | |
| 9th month | 912,212.917 | 33,675.237 | – | |
| Leap month | 1,334,780.233 | 47,445.179 | – | |
| 10th month | 332,186.892 | 59,340.507 | – | |
| 11th month | 2,004,627.492 | 59,871.178 | Old impure–silver seals 3, total 220 taels | |
| 12th month | 2,768,947.127 | 116,672.713 | – | |
| *3rd year (1738)* | *10,427,790* | *65,3604* | *Impure–silver seals 19, total 1,385 taels* | |
| 1st month | 899,820.274 | 0.600 | – | |
| 2nd month | 1,408,449.303 | 48,071.990 | – | |
| 3rd month | 263,604.899 | 36,265.124 | Impure–silver seals 11, total 815.5 taels | |
| 4th month | 153,020.735 | 27,959.244 | Impure–silver seals 8, total 569.5 taels | |

| Year | Silver (taels) | Copper coins (strings) | Others | Remarks |
|---|---|---|---|---|
| 5th month | 207,948.286 | 26,835.329 | – | |
| 6th month | 699,761.335 | 58,708.421 | – | |
| 7th month | 1,216,567.342 | 64,596.449 | – | |
| 8th month | 669,334.631 | 114,870.036 | – | |
| 9th month | 982,436.117 | 38,943.925 | – | |
| 10th month | 578,430.758 | 38,685.855 | – | |
| 11th month | 1,168,546.388 | 69,701.093 | – | |
| 12th month | 2,179,870.240 | 128,966.034 | – | |
| *5th year (1740)* | *8,240,136* | *1,006,283* | – | *Original note: "The total revenues of copper coins are 1,006,283.294 strings." There are no monthly totals of copper coins this year.* |
| 1st month | 193,566.020 | – | – | |
| 2nd month | 406,244.984 | – | – | |
| 3rd month | 568,408.011 | – | – | |
| 4th month | 171,423.446 | – | – | |
| 5th month | 542,999.225 | – | – | |
| 6th month | 574,769.815 | – | – | |
| Leap month | 679,334.493 | – | – | |
| 7th month | 893,070.341 | – | – | |
| 8th month | 744,748.703 | – | – | |
| 9th month | 838,857.586 | – | – | |
| 10th month | 628,273.985 | – | – | |
| 11th month | 696,318.293 | – | – | |
| 12th month | 1,302,120.903 | – | – | |
| *9th year (1744)* | *13,459,941* | *1,138,259* | *Impure silver seals 9, total 597.5 taels* | |
| 1st month | 1,059,234.348 | 5.850 | – | |
| 2nd month | 1,253,577.500 | 104,122.403 | – | |
| 3rd month | 1,139,859.963 | 73,475.384 | – | |
| 4th month | 281,764.162 | 109,138.615 | – | |
| 5th month | 296,418.390 | 109,985.934 | – | |
| 6th month | 964,411.158 | 73,786.950 | – | |

TABLE A.7 *Aggregate revenues of the Silver Treasury during* Qianlong, *1736–1795* (cont.)

| Year | Silver (taels) | Copper coins (strings) | Others | Remarks |
| --- | --- | --- | --- | --- |
| 7th month | 764,806.703 | 74,693.360 | Impure silver seals 9, total 597.5 taels | |
| 8th month | 1,092,306.212 | 145,950.171 | – | |
| 9th month | 538,357.780 | 110,411.439 | – | |
| 10th month | 827,646.655 | 114,785.309 | – | |
| 11th month | 801,940.321 | 73,794.021 | – | |
| 12th month | 4,439,618.177 | 148,109.653 | – | |
| *11th year (1746)* | *10,618,227* | *1,020,643* | – *Gold 7.487 taels*<br>– *Silver seals 16, total 1,362 taels* | |
| 1st month | 665,821.672 | 203.450 | – | |
| 2nd month | 745,364.515 | 109,250.580 | – | |
| 3rd month | 556,801.265 | 73,778.218 | – | |
| Leap month | 660,582.393 | 74,334.549 | – | |
| 4th month | 230,546.895 | 109,663.738 | Silver seals 15, total 1,233 taels | |
| 5th month | 523,805.778 | 11,110.238 | | |
| 6th month | 672,265.495 | 74,507.182 | Old seal 1, 129 taels | |
| 7th month | 1,152,428.867 | 76,213.148 | Gold 7.487 taels | |
| 8th month | 368,366.301 | 109,748.358 | – | |
| 9th month | 621,563.351 | 75,216.095 | – | |
| 10th month | 431,169.787 | 74,642.532 | – | |
| 11th month | 110,270.603 | 79,529.619 | – | |
| 12th month | 3,879,239.992 | 152,445.659 | – | |
| *13th year (1748)* | *8,187,984** | *1,017,312** | – | |
| *14th year (1749)* | *10,104,020* | *980,102* | – | |
| 1st month | 953,804.962 | 15.000 | – | |
| 2nd month | 398,484.809 | 109,598.527 | – | |
| 3rd month | 348,215.431 | 73,347.280 | – | |

| Year | Silver (taels) | Copper coins (strings) | Others | Remarks |
|---|---|---|---|---|
| 4th month | 216,558.488 | 75,003.399 | – | |
| 5th month | 1,165,339.232 | 109,270.092 | – | |
| 6th month | 227,921.820 | 75,099.406 | – | |
| 7th month | 384,515.634 | 77,978.074 | – | |
| 8th month | 332,216.010 | 106,622.531 | – | |
| 9th month | 1,008,000.706 | 74,986.623 | – | |
| 10th month | 416,937.642 | 75,924.756 | – | |
| 11th month | 1,366,830.097 | 44,157.967 | – | |
| 12th month | 3,285,195.336 | 158,097.874 | – | |
| *16th year (1751)* | *9,348,951* | *913,510* | – *Gold 35.373 taels*<br>– *Old silver seals 89, total 7,872.6 taels* | *Data of the 12th month are missing.* |
| 1st month | 967,533.640 | 809.035 | – | |
| 2nd month | 1,334,487.165 | 73,035.167 | – | |
| 3rd month | 893,457.038 | 72,811.654 | – | |
| 4th month | 422,756.536 | 74,750.339 | – | |
| 5th month | 177,657.141 | 74,731.298 | – Gold 35.373 taels<br>– Old silver seals 89, total 7,872.6 taels | |
| Leap month | 1,354,299.228 | 74,895.406 | – | |
| 6th month | 1,939,330.902 | 74,084.713 | – | |
| 7th month | 395,428.661 | 114,575.980 | – | |
| 8th month | 433,124.355 | 107,667.253 | – | |
| 9th month | 388,531.819 | 75,519.296 | – | |
| 10th month | 464,450.297 | 82,029.886 | – | |
| 11th month | 577,894.666 | 88,600.333 | – | |
| *18th year (1753)* | *11,619,370* | *1,077,567* | *old silver seals 30, total 2,613.5 taels* | *According to the four-column register, the amount of old seals received in the year is 43, total 1613.350 taels.* |
| 1st month | 617,603.497 | 120.610 | – | |
| 2nd month | 1,789,288.637 | 110,009.631 | – | |
| 3rd month | 341,861.619 | 72,720.320 | – | |
| 4th month | 279,735.872 | 74,952.071 | – | |

TABLE A.7 *Aggregate revenues of the Silver Treasury during* Qianlong, *1736–1795* (cont.)

| Year | Silver (taels) | Copper coins (strings) | Others | Remarks |
| --- | --- | --- | --- | --- |
| 5th month | 1,246,468.748 | 75,541.310 | Old silver seals 25, total 2,215 taels | |
| 6th month | 1,001,655.389 | 81457.489 | – | |
| 7th month | 714,993.199 | 85,551.812 | Old silver seal 1, 51.5 taels | |
| 8th month | 1,467,281.385 | 113,587.153 | – | |
| 9th month | 482,508.536 | 77,874.849 | Old silver seals 4, total 347 taels | |
| 10th month | 801,034.528 | 79,159.362 | – | |
| 11th month | 435,880.860 | 81,443.773 | – | |
| 12th month | 2,441,058.107 | 225,148.697 | – | |
| *19th year (1754)* | *14,248,869* | *1,131,093* | *Old silver seals 2, total 153 taels* | |
| 1st month | 516,163.771 | 9.000 | – | |
| 2nd month | 593,435.245 | 119,093.283 | – | |
| 3rd month | 777,476.219 | 76,336.533 | – | |
| 4th month | 247,624.321 | 77,452.655 | – | |
| Leap month | 317,323.402 | 77,763.494 | Old silver seals 2, total 153 taels | |
| 5th month | 2,700,373.015 | 80,063.619 | – | |
| 6th month | 1,485,250.166 | 79,111.354 | – | |
| 7th month | 103,283.971 | 76,986.712 | – | |
| 8th month | 637,049.848 | 133,916.778 | – | |
| 9th month | 637,108.859 | 78,987.471 | – | |
| 10th month | 419,106.325 | 78,960.388 | – | |
| 11th month | 124,695.183 | 87,752.431 | – | |
| 12th month | 5,689,979.031 | 164,659.623 | – | |
| *20th year (1755)* | *15,639,475* <br> *15,639,465** | *1,086,862* | – | |
| 1st month | 1,153,836.435 | 41,350.404 | – | |
| 2nd month | 1,059,898.868 | 113,973.347 | – | |
| 3rd month | 3,139,769.101 | 77,181.200 | – | |
| 4th month | 434,478.585 | 81,336.879 | – | |
| 5th month | 394,446.093 | 76,977.551 | – | |

| Year | Silver (taels) | Copper coins (strings) | Others | Remarks |
|---|---|---|---|---|
| 6th month | 1,310,487.078 | 77,120.200 | – | |
| 7th month | 1,065,227.431 | 82,255.633 | – | |
| 8th month | 1,954,644.350 | 76,525.247 | – | |
| 9th month | 791,818.653 | 78,201.996 | – | |
| 10th month | 1,099,509.262 | 78,612.786 | – | |
| 11th month | 557,147.666 | 78,431.815 | – | |
| 12th month | 2,678,211.401 | 224,894.955 | – | |
| *22nd year (1757)* | *9,318,433** | *1,203,957** | – | |
| *25th year (1760)* | *10,336,272* | *1,560,585* | *Old silver seals 18, total 1,922.890 taels* | |
| 1st month | 65,253.237 | 41,675.076 | – | |
| 2nd month | 490,661.044 | 121,503.277 | – | |
| 3rd month | 547,125.944 | 104,213.594 | Old silver seals 2, total 165 taels | |
| 4th month | 642,468.320 | 89,230.271 | – | |
| 5th month | 417,870.346 | 110,997.367 | Old seals 14, total 1,621.99 taels | |
| 6th month | 869,420.467 | 148,198.148 | – | |
| 7th month | 712,513.843 | 116,651.334 | Old silver seals 2, total 135.9 taels | |
| 8th month | 1,543,300.084 | 168,090.927 | – | |
| 9th month | 1,329,307.951 | 146,085.705 | – | |
| 10th month | 311,480.264 | 139,444.595 | – | |
| 11th month | 109,520.104 | 144,959.983 | – | |
| 12th month | 3,297,350.096 | 229,534.784 | – | |
| *26th year (1761)* | *11,442,266* | *1,197,764* | – | |
| 1st month | 423,223.527 | 41,720.915 | – | |
| 2nd month | 1,605,544.717 | 123,494.781 | – | |
| 3rd month | 1,673,116.108 | 90,794.045 | – | |
| 4th month | 401,987.213 | 86,494.748 | – | |
| 5th month | 633,710.235 | 91,184.519 | – | |
| 6th month | 1,181,678.774 | 86,119.353 | – | |

TABLE A.7 *Aggregate revenues of the Silver Treasury during* Qianlong, *1736–1795* (cont.)

| Year | Silver (taels) | Copper coins (strings) | Others | Remarks |
|---|---|---|---|---|
| 7th month | 744,762.174 | 92,545.588 | – | |
| 8th month | 694,183.415 | 84,616.675 | – | |
| 9th month | 1,383,746.989 | 84,616.675 | – | |
| 10th month | 658,209.950 | 87,075.220 | – | |
| 11th month | 176,946.382 | 87,301.954 | – | |
| 12th month | 1,865,156.654 | 241,799.374 | – | |
| *28th year (1763)* | *14,669,589* | *1,137,386* | – | |
| 1st month | 351,647.425 | 42,084.333 | – | |
| 2nd month | 413,922.889 | 120,760.065 | – | |
| 3rd month | 2,065,473.227 | 87,841.370 | – | |
| 4th month | 1,605,708.423 | 69,192.012 | – | |
| 5th month | 205,080.390 | 106,210.665 | – | |
| 6th month | 1,459,637.570 | 73,216.628 | – | |
| 7th month | 2,910,988.434 | 70,577.731 | – | |
| 8th month | 1,513,341.178 | 103,261.434 | – | |
| 9th month | 262,323.271 | 71,573.377 | – | |
| 10th month | 227,620.403 | 73,038.499 | – | |
| 11th month | 203,005.852 | 84,586.495 | – | |
| 12th month | 3,450,839.656 | 235,043.036 | – | |
| *29th year (1764)* | *16,868,335* | *1,245,961* | – | |
| 1st month | 636,905.631 | 41,948.286 | – | |
| 2nd month | 1,601,291.334 | 122,106.362 | – | |
| 3rd month | 2,852,787.780 | 83,070.885 | – | |
| 4th month | 1,095,090.597 | 85,479.737 | – | |
| 5th month | 842,999.498 | 89,107.762 | – | |
| 6th month | 841,660.012 | 89,405.718 | – | |
| 7th month | 2,505,481.144 | 85,925.314 | – | |
| 8th month | 2,211,645.948 | 119,796.674 | – | |
| 9th month | 1,070,758.239 | 84,230.289 | – | |
| 10th month | 113,987.903 | 85,678.025 | – | |
| 11th month | 224,209.476 | 85,066.125 | – | |

| Year | Silver (taels) | Copper coins (strings) | Others | Remarks |
|---|---|---|---|---|
| 12th month | 2,871,517.702 | 274,145.609 | – | |
| *30th year (1765)* | *15,417,601* | *1,315,785* | – | |
| 1st month | 835,107.708 | – | – | |
| 2nd month | 2,994,456.917 | 127,337.394 | – | |
| Leap month | 2,705,270.382 | 89,359.353 | – | |
| 3rd month | 532,860.384 | 86,990.234 | – | |
| 4th month | 147,148.314 | 85,337.813 | – | |
| 5th month | 17,492.651 | 85,142.967 | – | |
| 6th month | 38,736.126 | 86,277.431 | – | |
| 7th month | 2,379,733.826 | 88,047.550 | – | |
| 8th month | 1,299,211.437 | 125,414.344 | – | |
| 9th month | 2,034,772.008 | 84,996.399 | – | |
| 10th month | 699,463.548 | 92,362.269 | – | |
| 11th month | 300,570.507 | 85,680.125 | – | |
| 12th month | 1,432,777.102 | 278,839.177 | – | |
| *35th year (1770)* | *10,978,839* | *1,384,474* | – | |
| 1st month | 82,933.825 | 50.000 | – | |
| 2nd month | 511,753.533 | 128,117.370 | – | |
| 3rd month | 1,438,260.062 | 84,472.698 | – | |
| 4th month | 398,800.950 | 83,593.887 | – | |
| 5th month | 907,070.694 | 83,883.513 | – | |
| Leap month | 805,011.635 | 82,870.872 | – | |
| 6th month | 437,270.070 | 83,584.918 | – | |
| 7th month | 1,078,886.071 | 85,237.174 | – | |
| 8th month | 1,298,815.744 | 123,290.053 | – | |
| 9th month | 638,989.069 | 85,817.914 | – | |
| 10th month | 523,296.277 | 85,566.784 | – | |
| 11th month | 394,763.902 | 86,126.953 | – | |
| 12th month | 2,462,986.670 | 371,862.351 | – | |
| *37th year (1772)* | *11,871,843* | *1,178,843* | – | |
| 1st month | 85,548.798 | 3.000 | – | |
| 2nd month | 955,553.424 | 120,885.131 | – | |

TABLE A.7 *Aggregate revenues of the Silver Treasury during* Qianlong, *1736–1795* (cont.)

| Year | Silver (taels) | Copper coins (strings) | Others | Remarks |
|---|---|---|---|---|
| 3rd month | 113,407.525 | 85,998.277 | – | |
| 4th month | 1,036,312.080 | 82,258.125 | – | |
| 5th month | 2,141,182.305 | 84,955.573 | – | |
| 6th month | 778,564.941 | 83,039.241 | – | |
| 7th month | 927,592.373 | 84,705.849 | – | |
| 8th month | 368,216.247 | 118,872.706 | – | |
| 9th month | 974,685.307 | 82,486.585 | – | |
| 10th month | 836,353.310 | 83,189.878 | – | |
| 11th month | 432,509.434 | 83,077.839 | – | |
| 12th month | 3,221,917.211 | 269,371.199 | – | |
| *38th year (1773)* | *8,966,307** | *1,277,811** | – | |
| *39th year (1774)* | *17,587,994* | *1,185,825* | – | |
| 1st month | 213,400.754 | 113.000 | – | |
| 2nd month | 402,771.423 | 122,212.762 | – | |
| 3rd month | 392,159.731 | 85,509.368 | – | |
| 4th month | 465,059.965 | 85,163.609 | – | |
| 5th month | 351,127.714 | 84,282.948 | – | |
| 6th month | 1,216,815.969 | 86,199.873 | – | |
| 7th month | 171,200.285 | 83,775.420 | – | |
| 8th month | 701,175.420 | 118,789.663 | – | |
| 9th month | 47,578.590 | 82,764.391 | – | |
| 10th month | 1,122,200.495 | 82,632.224 | – | |
| 11th month | 940,130.290 | 83,769.975 | – | |
| 12th month | 11,564,373.674 | 270,611.821 | – | |
| *40th year (1775)* | *14,134,913** | *1,254,947** | – | |
| *41st year (1776)* | *18,711,298* | *1,019,360*<br>*1,294,815** | – | |
| 1st month | 74,515.997 | 128.300 | – | |
| 2nd month | 1,025,810.714 | 122,225.124 | – | |
| 3rd month | 362,194.877 | 84,689.403 | – | |

| Year | Silver (taels) | Copper coins (strings) | Others | Remarks |
|---|---|---|---|---|
| 4th month | 453,265.797 | 83,384.844 | – | |
| 5th month | 1,219,916.382 | 84,210.433 | – | |
| 6th month | 1,083,856.720 | 85,679.743 | – | |
| 7th month | 709,742.519 | 180,860.153 | – | |
| 8th month | 2,532,730.764 | 121,130.774 | – | |
| 9th month | 929,891.451 | 86,481.954 | – | |
| 10th month | 755,937.777 | 84,557.570 | – | |
| 11th month | 1,438,129.904 | 86,012.017 | – | |
| 12th month | 8,125,305.220 | 275,454..893 | – | |
| *42nd year (1777)* | *18,117,732** | *1,203,459** | – | |
| *43rd year (1778)* | *11,477,632* | *1,284,266* | – | |
| 1st month | 597,150.635 | 219.000 | – | |
| 2nd month | 702,635.896 | 123,143.720 | – | |
| 3rd month | 337,826.386 | 85,547.805 | – | |
| 4th month | 1,380,660.024 | 85,730.590 | – | |
| 5th month | 909,104.415 | 83,263.731 | – | |
| 6th month | 944,931.594 | 86,175.320 | – | |
| Leap month | 619,818.997 | 84,358.787 | – | |
| 7th month | 67,747.484 | 85,363.384 | – | |
| 8th month | 493,050.913 | 123,100.986 | – | |
| 9th month | 241,035.672 | 82,917.169 | – | |
| 10th month | 880,031.504 | 84,826.253 | – | |
| 11th month | 1,878,841.863 | 86,230.410 | – | |
| 12th month | 2,424,796.317 | 273,389.043 | – | |
| *45th year (1780)* | *10,567,108** | *1,193,808** | – | |
| *46th year (1781)* | *13,930,618* | *1,285,728* | – | |
| 1st month | 1,402,961.273 | 76.910 | – | |
| 2nd month | 1,439,620.211 | 122,551.143 | – | |
| 3rd month | 904,508.693 | 86,917.651 | – | |
| 4th month | 702,612.861 | 82,700.439 | – | |
| 5th month | 757,112.912 | 85,227.572 | – | |

TABLE A.7 *Aggregate revenues of the Silver Treasury during* Qianlong, *1736–1795* (cont.)

| Year | Silver (taels) | Copper coins (strings) | Others | Remarks |
|---|---|---|---|---|
| Leap month | 1,081,668.913 | 84,612.178 | – | |
| 6th month | 1,132,964.461 | 84,749.227 | – | |
| 7th month | 766,263.059 | 84,494.757 | – | |
| 8th month | 973,814.668 | 122,428.391 | – | |
| 9th month | 587,288.698 | 84,721.731 | – | |
| 10th month | 330,425.584 | 87,540.018 | – | |
| 11th month | 1,381,562.699 | 84,980.088 | – | |
| 12th month | 2,469,813.842 | 274,727.943 | – | |
| *47th year (1782)* | *13,657,359* | *1,206,487* | – | |
| 1st month | 700,389.511 | 107.880 | – | |
| 2nd month | 1,313,998.022 | 122,334.665 | – | |
| 3rd month | 1,196,798.243 | 86,555.497 | – | |
| 4th month | 927,305.283 | 85,698.212 | – | |
| 5th month | 8,895.477 | 86,864.348 | – | |
| 6th month | 435,714.868 | 85,084.245 | – | |
| 7th month | 1,508,012.050 | 84,998.356 | – | |
| 8th month | 1,440,089.657 | 120,971.865 | – | |
| 9th month | 775,036.170 | 85,136.073 | – | |
| 10th month | 602,298.000 | 86,587.947 | – | |
| 11th month | 1,188,553.411 | 88,887.745 | – | |
| 12th month | 3,560,268.508 | 273,260.400 | – | |
| *48th year (1783)* | *6,941,275* | *922,104* | – | *Data of the 12th month are missing.* |
| 1st month | 500,668.969 | 1,057.021 | – | |
| 2nd month | 1,415,421.742 | 117,254.821 | – | |
| 3rd month | 436,394.621 | 81,756.413 | – | |
| 4th month | 63,134.659 | 84,602.143 | – | |
| 5th month | 542,599.913 | 86,105.300 | – | |
| 6th month | 164,833.061 | 86,163.159 | – | |
| 7th month | 323,555.342 | 85,331.627 | – | |
| 8th month | 867,556.934 | 122,071.125 | – | |
| 9th month | 731,943.484 | 84,708.955 | – | |
| 10th month | 1,381,598.531 | 85,565.906 | – | |

| Year | Silver (taels) | Copper coins (strings) | Others | Remarks |
|---|---|---|---|---|
| 11th month | 513,567.975 | 87,487.356 | – | |
| *49th year (1784)* | *12,407,397* | *1,382,518* | – | |
| 1st month | 1,063,921.367 | 1,367.125 | – | |
| 2nd month | 531,476.999 | 119,186.859 | – | |
| 3rd month | 589,030.270 | 83,881.873 | – | |
| Leap month | 102,982.203 | 82,128.596 | – | |
| 4th month | 419,714.507 | 88,106.567 | – | |
| 5th month | 604,337.265 | 83,037.652 | – | |
| 6th month | 94,477.731 | 84,708.583 | – | |
| 7th month | 621,560.023 | 89,316.270 | – | |
| 8th month | 682,043.565 | 124,564.394 | – | |
| 9th month | 2,327,765.256 | 86,404.407 | – | |
| 10th month | 254,664.156 | 122,942.627 | – | |
| 11th month | 1,377,822.519 | 133,489.313 | – | |
| 12th month | 373,7601.043 | 283,384.085 | – | |
| *50th year (1785)* | *11,466,163* | *1,231,695* | – | |
| 1st month | 405,512.095 | 213.000 | – | |
| 2nd month | 592,157.709 | 135,479.172 | – | |
| 3rd month | 588,309.123 | 91,071.705 | – | |
| 4th month | 1,047,242.107 | 84,848.566 | – | |
| 5th month | 373,048.764 | 85,475.072 | – | |
| 6th month | 1,242,973.604 | 90,721.431 | | |
| 7th month | 200,517.931 | 84,903.988 | – | |
| 8th month | 382,703.238 | 119,255.837 | – | |
| 9th month | 1,903,727.782 | 87,421.036 | – | |
| 10th month | 975,196.531 | 85,581.537 | – | |
| 11th month | 437,810.198 | 84,565.944 | – | |
| 12th month | 3,316,963.752 | 282,158.205 | – | |
| *51st year (1786)* | *7,461,334* | *1,301,573* | – | |
| 1st month | 536,103.430 | 4,942.000 | – | |
| 2nd month | 530,444.027 | 120,280.635 | – | |
| 3rd month | 230,710.042 | 82,344.138 | – | |

TABLE A.7 *Aggregate revenues of the Silver Treasury during* Qianlong, *1736–1795* (cont.)

| Year | Silver (taels) | Copper coins (strings) | Others | Remarks |
|---|---|---|---|---|
| 4th month | 272,164.976 | 82,460.449 | – | |
| 5th month | 217,213.510 | 89,362.269 | – | |
| 6th month | 263,815.944 | 84,575.742 | – | |
| 7th month | 185,425.887 | 84,945.274 | – | |
| Leap month | 383,677.735 | 90,408.546 | – | |
| 8th month | 246,736.959 | 122,349.022 | – | |
| 9th month | 92,530.547 | 84,646.198 | – | |
| 10th month | 75,379.746 | 82,552.823 | – | |
| 11th month | 798,822.466 | 89,025.978 | – | |
| 12th month | 3,628,309.004 | 283,679.618 | – | |
| *55th year (1790)* | *16,230,598* | *1,219,814* | – | |
| 1st month | 536,103.430 | 4,942.000 | – | |
| 2nd month | 1,330,771.093 | 122,272.111 | – | |
| 3rd month | 640,541.578 | 84,970.640 | – | |
| 4th month | 1,111,276.654 | 84,217.898 | – | |
| 5th month | 1,260,710.405 | 84,458.255 | – | |
| 6th month | 1,594,113.198 | 83,965.305 | – | |
| 7th month | 212,188.074 | 88,798.196 | – | |
| 8th month | 754,463.883 | 150,687.633 | – | |
| 9th month | 922,025.310 | 56,178.689 | – | |
| 10th month | 1,699,335.330 | 85,315.884 | – | |
| 11th month | 1,750,072.248 | 91,064.703 | – | |
| 12th month | 4,418,997.257 | 282,943.119 | – | |
| *57th year (1792)* | *8,762,067* | *1,301,334* | – | |
| 1st month | 84,294.093 | 17.000 | – | |
| 2nd month | 1,196,599.320 | 122,520.961 | – | |
| 3rd month | 38,687.185 | 86,088.490 | – | |
| 4th month | 214,967.314 | 86,553.304 | – | |
| Leap month | 106,325.193 | 85,779.460 | – | |
| 5th month | 297,507.958 | 85,854.092 | – | |
| 6th month | 148,899.776 | 86,288.914 | – | |
| 7th month | 1,213,607.978 | 89,145.352 | – | |

| Year | Silver (taels) | Copper coins (strings) | Others | Remarks |
|---|---|---|---|---|
| 8th month | 580,029.548 | 120,414.489 | – | |
| 9th month | 102,131.198 | 88,493.195 | – | |
| 10th month | 584,141.348 | 85,623.212 | – | |
| 11th month | 590,102.058 | 87,401.214 | – | |
| 12th month | 3,604,774.431 | 277,154.238 | – | |
| *58th year (1793)* | *10,111,935* | *1,213,081* | – | |
| 1st month | 3,516.204 | – | – | |
| 2nd month | 392,829.452 | 123,915.418 | – | |
| 3rd month | 871,560.105 | 85,322.938 | – | |
| 4th month | 32,809.316 | 86,526.017 | – | |
| 5th month | 1,209,797.190 | 86,261.348 | – | |
| 6th month | 947,294.131 | 85,580.483 | – | |
| 7th month | 1,038,907.583 | 85,197.522 | – | |
| 8th month | 541,125.503 | 123,312.859 | – | |
| 9th month | 212,787.562 | 85,890.860 | – | |
| 10th month | 334,723.152 | 86,377.897 | – | |
| 11th month | 1,133,413.407 | 86,706.104 | – | |
| 12th month | 3,393,171.571 | 277,989.559 | – | |
| *59th year (1794)* | *9,179,009* | *517,268* | – | |
| 1st month | 103,863.636 | – | – | |
| 2nd month | 655,707.100 | 124,060.039 | – | |
| 3rd month | 497,532.299 | 86,023.761 | – | |
| 4th month | 468,446.010 | 86,257.888 | – | |
| 5th month | 54,805.338 | 96,288.957 | – | |
| 6th month | 37,797.325 | 85,017.700 | – | |
| 7th month | 1,108,846.250 | 815.500 | – | |
| 8th month | 771,289.470 | 103.000 | – | |
| 9th month | 701,335.719 | 76.000 | – | |
| 10th month | 1,049,359.818 | 7,600.791 | – | |
| 11th month | 424,335.183 | 16,873.172 | – | |
| 12th month | 3,305,690.713 | 14,150.969 | – | |
| *60th year (1795)* | *8,665,152* | *142,656* | – | |

TABLE A.7 *Aggregate revenues of the Silver Treasury during* Qianlong, *1736–1795* (cont.)

| Year | Silver (taels) | Copper coins (strings) | Others | Remarks |
|---|---|---|---|---|
| 1st month | 10,448.789 | 180.000 | – | |
| 2nd month | 368,792.424 | 10,156.709 | – | |
| Leap month | 621,630.694 | 11,202.666 | – | |
| 3rd month | 24,272.170 | 8,336.700 | – | |
| 4th month | 219,558.380 | 15,750.776 | – | |
| 5th month | 60,253.825 | 9,448.194 | – | |
| 6th month | 136,441.514 | 17,258.380 | – | |
| 7th month | 254,085.791 | 9,345.406 | – | |
| 8th month | 488,714.439 | 8,904.783 | – | |
| 9th month | 632,622.624 | 10,529.076 | – | |
| 10th month | 58,363.465 | 9,835.564 | – | |
| 11th month | 895,429.186 | 14,633.863 | – | |
| 12th month | 4,894,538.846 | 17,074.061 | – | |
| *Average of* Qianlong | *12,123,597* | *1,102,663* | – | |

*Source*: figures marked with * are from four-column registers of each of the years; data of the 3rd year are from the aggregate revenue register of the same year kept by FHAC; others are based on aggregate revenue registers of Qianlong, The Yellow Registers · The Silver Treasury of the Ministry of Revenue, Volumes 2–7. In calculating the averages, the figure of silver of the 20th year is based on the record of the aggregate revenue register and that of copper coins of the 41st year is based on the four-column register.

TABLE A.8 *Aggregate expenditures of the Silver Treasury during* Qianlong, *1736–1795*

| Year | Silver (taels) | Copper coins (strings) | Others | Remarks |
|---|---|---|---|---|
| *1st year* (1736) | *15,400,142* | *1,120,449* | *Gold 1,059.143 taels* | |
| 1st month | 222,764.500 | 11.815 | – | |
| 2nd month | 990,318.378 | 73,979.058 | Gold 14.81 taels | |
| 3rd month | 944,896.439 | 37,740.213 | Gold 172.889 taels | |
| 4th month | 826,514.694 | 33,161.045 | – | |
| 5th month | 547,658.969 | 539,121.154 | – | |
| 6th month | 481,243.427 | 49,004.025 | – | |

| Year | Silver (taels) | Copper coins (strings) | Others | Remarks |
|---|---|---|---|---|
| 7th month | 901,215.837 | 39,075.468 | Gold 6.385 taels | |
| 8th month | 5,940,080.489 | 76,405.096 | Gold 42.3 taels | |
| 9th month | 646,518.922 | 62,801.061 | Gold 802.192 taels | |
| 10th month | 559,899.269 | 72,415.589 | – | |
| 11th month | 844,108.785 | 63,566.430 | Gold 5.183 taels | |
| 12th month | 2,494,921.985 | 73,168.165 | Gold 15.384 taels | |
| *3rd year (1738)* | *9,954,450* | *675,705* | – *Gold 1,925.935 taels*<br>– *Impure–silver seals 43, total 2,884.3 taels* | |
| 1st month | 214,139.344 | 3,000.000 | – | |
| 2nd month | 1,664,417.712 | 59,599.741 | – | |
| 3rd month | 1,055,305.384 | 35,614.203 | Impure–silver seals 24, total 1,499.3 taels | |
| 4th month | 9,112,04.456 | 30,545.020 | – | |
| 5th month | 448,637.407 | 30,598.626 | – | |
| 6th month | 470,930.699 | 52,513.886 | Gold 30.7 taels | |
| 7th month | 447,336.088 | 63,096.208 | Gold 366.8 taels | |
| 8th month | 970,868.066 | 115,441.038 | Gold 500 taels | |
| 9th month | 705,690.086 | 39,352.634 | Gold 90.468 taels | |
| 10th month | 710,283.083 | 39,366.842 | – Gold 396.518 taels<br>– Impure–silver seals 19, total 1,385 taels | |
| 11th month | 1,174,186.159 | 77,159.779 | Gold 506.049 taels | |
| 12th month | 1,181,451.964 | 129,417.256 | Gold 35.4 taels | |
| *5th year (1740)* | *10,337,236* | *993,209* | *Gold 318.032 taels* | |
| 1st month | 177,466.078 | – | – | |
| 2nd month | 1,101,292.370 | 84,526.751 | – | |
| 3rd month | 1,451,392.606 | 42,908.036 | Gold 4.117 taels | |
| 4th month | 678,493.986 | 84,573.927 | – | |
| 5th month | 424,141.093 | 84,908.806 | – | |
| 6th month | 445,508.579 | 104,696.729 | – | |
| Leap month | 465,598.042 | 84,505.681 | – | |
| 7th month | 523,053.822 | 84,769.656 | – | |
| 8th month | 999,969.597 | 83,340.902 | – | |
| 9th month | 506,321.380 | 83,270.397 | – | |

TABLE A.8 *Aggregate expenditures of the Silver Treasury during* Qianlong, *1736–1795* (cont.)

| Year | Silver (taels) | Copper coins (strings) | Others | Remarks |
|---|---|---|---|---|
| 10th month | 672,541.188 | 42,145.867 | – | |
| 11th month | 550,737.766 | 83,135.841 | – | |
| 12th month | 2,340,719.727 | 130,426.353 | Gold 313.915 taels | |
| *8th year (1743)* | *11,638,228* | *1,383,044* | *Gold 0.539 taels* | |
| 1st month | 795,112.951 | 9.000 | – | |
| 2nd month | 1,188,367.470 | 111,785.590 | – | |
| 3rd month | 684,990.532 | 75,329.625 | – | |
| 4th month | 787,236.139 | 111,629.863 | – | |
| Leap month | 886,911.031 | 111,337.472 | Gold 0.539 tael | |
| 5th month | 602,524.621 | 115,944.772 | – | |
| 6th month | 836,583.210 | 116,452.430 | – | |
| 7th month | 926,868.487 | 113,169.269 | – | |
| 8th month | 750,372.409 | 141,078.327 | – | |
| 9th month | 527,300.818 | 74,711.892 | – | |
| 10th month | 370,357.030 | 75,156.050 | – | |
| 11th month | 499,637.292 | 111,965.948 | – | |
| 12th month | 2,781,965.574 | 224,473.519 | – | |
| *9th year (1744)* | *5,315,454* | *701,882* | *Gold 5.768 taels* | *The monthly totals from the 9th to the 12th months are missing in the original register* |
| 1st month | 226,557.585 | | – | |
| 2nd month | 1,157,342.360 | 110,643.906 | – | |
| 3rd month | 756,646.194 | 74,533.649 | Gold 3.918 taels | |
| 4th month | 410,439.033 | 110,576.337 | Gold 1.85 taels | |
| 5th month | 409,497.863 | 110,510.655 | – | |
| 6th month | 823,121.453 | 74,459.763 | – | |
| 7th month | 508,541.149 | 74,494.234 | – | |
| 8th month | 1,023,307.979 | 146,663.331 | – | |
| *13th year (1748)* | *13,087,744** | *1,013,387** | – | |

| Year | Silver (taels) | Copper coins (strings) | Others | Remarks |
|---|---|---|---|---|
| *14th year (1749)* | *6,871,618* | *829,375* | – | *Data of the 12th month are missing in the original register* |
| 1st month | 136,588.911 | | – | |
| 2nd month | 1,034,204.473 | 111,316.940 | – | |
| 3rd month | 757,609.223 | 75,226.354 | – | |
| 4th month | 500,617.927 | 75,196.046 | – | |
| 5th month | 444,728.537 | 111,457.197 | – | |
| 6th month | 806,011.610 | 77,947.933 | – | |
| 7th month | 487,247.096 | 77,101.971 | – | |
| 8th month | 834,262.637 | 10,7081.649 | – | |
| 9th month | 840,595.576 | 75,369.737 | – | |
| 10th month | 431,044.629 | 75,024.980 | – | |
| 11th month | 598,707.001 | 43,651.882 | – | |
| *15th year (1750)* | *6,965,567* | *822,984* | *Old silver seals 170, total 16,888.6 taels* | *Data of the 12th month are missing in the original register* |
| 1st month | 245,668.517 | 2,902.890 | – | |
| 2nd month | 1,177,855.432 | 110,553.984 | – | |
| 3rd month | 534,809.062 | 74,795.214 | – | |
| 4th month | 617,753.763 | 74,661.347 | – | |
| 5th month | 455,078.515 | 110,647.702 | – | |
| 6th month | 450,522.033 | 75,002.761 | – | |
| 7th month | 718,489.810 | 75,047.337 | – | |
| 8th month | 1,108,473.089 | 111,285.083 | Old silver seals 89, Impure–silver 8,609.5 taels | |
| 9th month | 532,740.042 | 74,971.324 | – | |
| 10th month | 560,630.201 | 74,705.623 | Oldsilver seals 81, total 8,279.1 taels | |
| 11th month | 563,546.256 | 38,411.203 | – | |
| *17th year (1752)* | *8,585,428* | *790,408* | – | *Data of the 12th month are missing in the original register* |
| 1st month | 345,762.606 | – | – | |
| 2nd month | 1,311,345.042 | 74,503.920 | – | |
| 3rd month | 725,825.157 | 74,856.196 | – | |

TABLE A.8 *Aggregate expenditures of the Silver Treasury during* Qianlong, *1736–1795* (cont.)

| Year | Silver (taels) | Copper coins (strings) | Others | Remarks |
|---|---|---|---|---|
| 4th month | 608,434.404 | 74,665.054 | – | |
| 5th month | 455,384.697 | 74,699.144 | – | |
| 6th month | 775,538.688 | 74,753.207 | – | |
| 7th month | 693,190.280 | 79,625.493 | – | |
| 8th month | 858,867.989 | 108,664.730 | – | |
| 9th month | 498,648.946 | 75,261.206 | – | |
| 10th month | 493,869.097 | 78,542.995 | – | |
| 11th month | 1,818,561.412 | 74,835.988 | – | |
| *18th year (1753)* | *10,379,263* | *1,075,730* | *Old silver seals 43, total 3,613.35 taels* | |
| 1st month | 142,750.620 | 6.000 | – | |
| 2nd month | 1,196,801.426 | 110,864.694 | – | |
| 3rd month | 909,183.875 | 74,842.900 | – | |
| 4th month | 759,009.323 | 75,767.867 | – | |
| 5th month | 589,621.645 | 76,025.544 | – | |
| 6th month | 476,897.331 | 80,004.754 | – | |
| 7th month | 449,366.257 | 85,968.282 | – | |
| 8th month | 1,027,115.678 | 115,122.507 | – | |
| 9th month | 571,043.078 | 77,962.174 | – | |
| 10th month | 422,028.964 | 77,864.204 | Old silver seals 43, total 3,613.35 taels | |
| 11th month | 2,480,767.991 | 82,963.411 | – | |
| 12th month | 1,354,677.139 | 218,337.485 | – | |
| *20th year (1755)* | *10,247,839** | *1,086,942** | – | |
| *22nd year (1757)* | *12,388,209* | *1,214,285*<br>*1,214,283** | – | |
| 1st month | 343,374.805 | 47,565.314 | – | |
| 2nd month | 857,518.970 | 121,759.293 | – | |
| 3rd month | 512,488.130 | 89,192.893 | – | |
| 4th month | 486,708.152 | 84,614.542 | – | |
| 5th month | 457,750.716 | 84,582.462 | – | |
| 6th month | 594,154.823 | 85,479.130 | – | |

| Year | Silver (taels) | Copper coins (strings) | Others | Remarks |
|---|---|---|---|---|
| 7th month | 985,038.143 | 85,822.599 | – | |
| 8th month | 762,102.494 | 122,311.351 | – | |
| 9th month | 3,500,286.523 | 85,001.631 | – | |
| 10th month | 411,533.800 | 90,234.279 | – | |
| 11th month | 2,312,037.977 | 90,051.388 | – | |
| 12th month | 1,165,214.322 | 2,27,669.743 | – | |
| *23rd year (1758)* | *8,951,247* | *1,001,869* | *Old silver seals 13, total 1,339.780 taels* | *Data of the 12th month are missing in the original register* |
| 1st month | 218,169.599 | 41,750.647 | – | |
| 2nd month | 937,401.563 | 122,157.348 | – | |
| 3rd month | 715,298.572 | 82,352.344 | Old silver seals 13, total 1,339.780 taels | |
| 4th month | 504,000.052 | 82,283.072 | – | |
| 5th month | 547,780.853 | 82,607.242 | – | |
| 6th month | 915,167.714 | 83,156.618 | – | |
| 7th month | 817,622.940 | 89,365.203 | – | |
| 8th month | 766,425.972 | 120,427.245 | – | |
| 9th month | 684,909.795 | 83,743.399 | – | |
| 10th month | 479,081.138 | 85,396.909 | – | |
| 11th month | 2,365,388.361 | 128,629.417 | – | |
| *25th year (1760)* | *11,572,236* | *1,750,059* | *Old silver seals 32, total 308.29 taels* | |
| 1st month | 266,698.945 | 121,142.217 | – | |
| 2nd month | 843,634.237 | 104,766.906 | – | |
| 3rd month | 697,883.817 | 89,295.079 | – | |
| 4th month | 2,451,402.039 | 90,038.998 | – | |
| 5th month | 470,070.780 | 139,763.168 | – | |
| 6th month | 552,270.120 | 139,806.830 | – | |
| 7th month | 1184,856.499 | 169,132.609 | – | |
| 8th month | 1,173,978.622 | 148,559.708 | Old silver seals 32, total 308.29 taels | |
| 9th month | 425,827.213 | 139,556.317 | – | |
| 10th month | 458,710.823 | 144,946.902 | – | |
| 11th month | 2,051,359.128 | 231,525.380 | – | |

TABLE A.8 *Aggregate expenditures of the Silver Treasury during* Qianlong, *1736–1795* (cont.)

| Year | Silver (taels) | Copper coins (strings) | Others | Remarks |
|---|---|---|---|---|
| 12th month | 995,543.322 | 231,525.380 | – | |
| *26th year (1761)* | *10,300,595* | *1,235,693* | *Old silver seals 2, total 135.9 taels* | |
| 1st month | 284,454.634 | 41,732.842 | – | |
| 2nd month | 799,316.840 | 124,041.268 | – | |
| 3rd month | 595,966.523 | 90,337.499 | Old silver seals 2, total 135.9 taels | |
| 4th month | 493,246.293 | 87,048.796 | – | |
| 5th month | 834,332.822 | 91,049.207 | – | |
| 6th month | 518,519.311 | 86,216.557 | – | |
| 7th month | 634,202.153 | 92,995.688 | – | |
| 8th month | 1,820,641.440 | 121,736.874 | – | |
| 9th month | 488,381.965 | 85,936.306 | – | |
| 10th month | 640,811.857 | 86,944.703 | – | |
| 11th month | 536,111.611 | 86,676.079 | – | |
| 12th month | 2,654,609.913 | 240,976.829 | – | |
| *27th year (1762)* | *10,365,967* | *1,515,125* | – | |
| 1st month | 285,279.238 | 72,303.247 | – | |
| 2nd month | 805,112.520 | 142,494.054 | – | |
| 3rd month | 542,627.605 | 83,584.869 | – | |
| 4th month | 538,803.894 | 84,303.785 | – | |
| 5th month | 502,376.171 | 83,087.696 | – | |
| Leap month | 408,998.123 | 83,788.693 | – | |
| 6th month | 597,033.242 | 84,759.531 | – | |
| 7th month | 1,389,010.695 | 101,404.704 | – | |
| 8th month | 529,145.770 | 177,242.770 | – | |
| 9th month | 1,521,240.530 | 72,131.062 | – | |
| 10th month | 412,001.569 | 124,239.342 | – | |
| 11th month | 559,559.029 | 87,042.103 | – | |
| 12th month | 2,274,778.664 | 318,743.313 | – | |
| *28th year (1763)* | *9,533,903** | *1,138,024** | – | |

| Year | Silver (taels) | Copper coins (strings) | Others | Remarks |
|---|---|---|---|---|
| *29th year (1764)* | *9,658,131* | *1,244,955* | – | |
| 1st month | 259,803.037 | 41,514.444 | – | |
| 2nd month | 931,220.945 | 121,069.685 | – | |
| 3rd month | 840,116.517 | 84,251.775 | – | |
| 4th month | 519,357.051 | 85,249.317 | – | |
| 5th month | 532,574.588 | 88,854.374 | – | |
| 6th month | 459,378.476 | 88,818.334 | – | |
| 7th month | 621,591.882 | 86,165.114 | – | |
| 8th month | 1,117,084.577 | 120,598.419 | – | |
| 9th month | 616,343.970 | 84,162.292 | – | |
| 10th month | 430,957.398 | 85,228.470 | – | |
| 11th month | 2,145,009.785 | 84,860.512 | – | |
| 12th month | 1,184,693.157 | 274,181.832 | – | |
| *30th year (1765)* | *9,355,040* | *1,315,791* | – | |
| 1st month | 240,681.157 | 13.500 | – | |
| 2nd month | 834,022.758 | 127,279.988 | – | |
| Leap month | 642,944.258 | 89,919.514 | – | |
| 3rd month | 808,143.672 | 86,649.546 | – | |
| 4th month | 515,197.636 | 85,177.231 | – | |
| 5th month | 519,661.258 | 85,748.522 | – | |
| 6th month | 556,999.644 | 86,510.313 | – | |
| 7th month | 528,612.088 | 86,786.308 | – | |
| 8th month | 767,154.038 | 126,263.090 | – | |
| 9th month | 492,229.521 | 84,782.923 | – | |
| 10th month | 648,827.282 | 91,242.972 | – | |
| 11th month | 1,733,830.698 | 86,464.527 | – | |
| 12th month | 1,066,735.996 | 278,952.974 | – | |
| *31st year (1766)* | *11,516,935* | *1,223,258* | – | |
| 1st month | 221,620.700 | – | – | |
| 2nd month | 1,231,617.152 | 122,846.714 | – | |
| 3rd month | 672,655.726 | 84,460.600 | – | |
| 4th month | 405,675.854 | 96,126.922 | – | |
| 5th month | 530,610.933 | 85,560.888 | – | |

TABLE A.8 *Aggregate expenditures of the Silver Treasury during* Qianlong, *1736–1795* (cont.)

| Year | Silver (taels) | Copper coins (strings) | Others | Remarks |
|---|---|---|---|---|
| 6th month | 631,398.029 | 86,440.803 | – | |
| 7th month | 505,387.748 | 87,233.236 | – | |
| 8th month | 3,774,952.159 | 121,204.798 | – | |
| 9th month | 446,788.376 | 85,549.527 | – | |
| 10th month | 389,711.969 | 85,680.861 | – | |
| 11th month | 1,698,260.591 | 96,396.059 | – | |
| 12th month | 1,008,255.906 | 271,757.712 | – | |
| *32nd year (1767)* | *12,456,158* | *1,296,439* | – | *The figure of copper coins of the 1st month is incomplete in the original register* |
| 1st month | 292,930.542 | 1.200 | – | |
| 2nd month | 868,983.675 | 122,039.160 | – | |
| 3rd month | 588,741.419 | 84,180.034 | – | |
| 4th month | 520,787.894 | 90,744.703 | – | |
| 5th month | 638,206.735 | 85,623.666 | – | |
| 6th month | 682,884.468 | 85,164.795 | – | |
| 7th month | 3,600,801.433 | 87,723.965 | – | |
| Leap month | 643,511.053 | 85,645.059 | – | |
| 8th month | 804,187.045 | 124,764.292 | – | |
| 9th month | 531,187.220 | 84,735.107 | – | |
| 10th month | 387,949.158 | 86,003.570 | – | |
| 11th month | 1,952,350.739 | 85,516.718 | – | |
| 12th month | 943,636.460 | 274,296.585 | – | |
| *35th year (1770)* | *7,381,979* | *1,012,815* | – | *The figure of copper coins of the 12th month is incomplete in the original register* |
| 1st month | 234,635.356 | 4.800 | – | |
| 2nd month | 1,011,849.275 | 126,881.052 | – | |
| 3rd month | 484,348.564 | 84,203.209 | – | |
| 4th month | 442,904.257 | 84,537.172 | – | |
| 5th month | 451,504.698 | 83,850.720 | – | |
| Leap month | 502,799.285 | 83,634.517 | – | |
| 6th month | 435,587.684 | 83,660.226 | – | |

| Year | Silver (taels) | Copper coins (strings) | Others | Remarks |
|---|---|---|---|---|
| 7th month | 566,644.353 | 85,297.327 | – | |
| 8th month | 1,544,745.951 | 123,133.124 | – | |
| 9th month | 388,195.625 | 86,046.115 | – | |
| 10th month | 471,012.700 | 85,354.762 | – | |
| 11th month | 842,696.997 | 86,212.410 | – | |
| 12th month | 5,054.100 | 0.019 | – | |
| *36th year (1771)* | *9,450,043* | *1,177,516* | – | |
| 1st month | 303,344.695 | – | – | |
| 2nd month | 1,137,227.157 | 120,721.051 | – | |
| 3rd month | 495,052.697 | 83,819.367 | – | |
| 4th month | 445,775.784 | 83,235.568 | – | |
| 5th month | 468,020.752 | 84,792.323 | – | |
| 6th month | 564,671.042 | 84,869.563 | – | |
| 7th month | 522,718.800 | 85,903.328 | – | |
| 8th month | 1,257,482.238 | 115,875.723 | – | |
| 9th month | 424,126.398 | 81,814.240 | – | |
| 10th month | 497,041.217 | 83,580.077 | – | |
| 11th month | 513,688.577 | 81,949.951 | – | |
| 12th month | 2,820,893.786 | 270,955.280 | – | |
| *37th year (1772)* | *12,071,582* | *1,448,303* | – | |
| 1st month | 420,533.587 | 120,547.825 | – | |
| 2nd month | 1,054,956.264 | 84,041.812 | – | |
| 3rd month | 1,717,340.158 | 84,514.382 | – | |
| 4th month | 520,916.749 | 84,569.129 | – | |
| 5th month | 619,134.497 | 83,989.597 | – | |
| 6th month | 440,195.019 | 85,150.616 | – | |
| 7th month | 1,783,534.824 | 118,766.200 | – | |
| 8th month | 852,810.928 | 82,423.541 | – | |
| 9th month | 404,571.399 | 83,418.746 | – | |
| 10th month | 597,363.040 | 83,013.099 | – | |
| 11th month | 2,739,253.960 | 268,933.786 | – | |
| 12th month | 920,971.940 | 268,933.786 | – | |
| *38th year (1773)* | *19,029,498* | *1,377,817*<br>*1,277,817** | – | |

TABLE A.8 *Aggregate expenditures of the Silver Treasury during* Qianlong, *1736–1795* (cont.)

| Year | Silver (taels) | Copper coins (strings) | Others | Remarks |
|---|---|---|---|---|
| 1st month | 76,219.452 | 4.050 | – | |
| 2nd month | 6,197,097.433 | 121,789.692 | – | |
| 3rd month | 536,069.765 | 84,072.849 | – | |
| Leap month | 500,532.315 | 85,140.391 | – | |
| 4th month | 486,775.168 | 84,944.341 | – | |
| 5th month | 497,050.344 | 84,669.414 | – | |
| 6th month | 5,472,212.776 | 84,765.641 | – | |
| 7th month | 600,333.177 | 84,238.024 | – | |
| 8th month | 831,827.015 | 120,972.522 | – | |
| 9th month | 699,373.072 | 84,859.989 | – | |
| 10th month | 455,271.561 | 84,599.209 | – | |
| 11th month | 1,729,135.399 | 84,384.732 | – | |
| 12th month | 947,600.808 | 373,376.152 | – | |
| *40th year (1775)* | *23,083,250* | *1,254,448* | – | |
| 1st month | 213,839.055 | 5,000.000 | – | |
| 2nd month | 5,921,173.473 | 118,243.986 | – | |
| 3rd month | 532,379.350 | 81,914.424 | – | |
| 4th month | 470,111.383 | 82,494.149 | – | |
| 5th month | 513,407.718 | 81,930.984 | – | |
| 6th month | 5,464,030.627 | 81,960.843 | – | |
| 7th month | 550,916.946 | 83,097.276 | – | |
| 8th month | 934,898.771 | 117,932.176 | – | |
| 9th month | 533,424.225 | 81,704.286 | – | |
| 10th month | 1,708,529.539 | 82,721.740 | – | |
| Leap month | 474,370.026 | 82,224.163 | – | |
| 11th month | 1,757,753.196 | 82,812.776 | – | |
| 12th month | 4,008,415.544 | 272,411.538 | – | |
| *41st year (1776)* | *9,005,900** | *1,295,309** | – | |
| *42nd year (1777)* | *10,956,360** | *1,203,768** | – | |
| *43rd year (1778)* | *9,893,661* | *1,284,113* | – | |

| Year | Silver (taels) | Copper coins (strings) | Others | Remarks |
|---|---|---|---|---|
| 1st month | 111,731.294 | 3.000 | – | |
| 2nd month | 1,282,902.753 | 123,465.482 | – | |
| 3rd month | 571,636.901 | 84,564.571 | – | |
| 4th month | 462,185.360 | 84,486.499 | – | |
| 5th month | 454,337.035 | 84,950.304 | – | |
| 6th month | 477,434.338 | 81,923.717 | – | |
| Leap month | 682,218.332 | 88,956.513 | – | |
| 7th month | 649,054.156 | 81,867.965 | – | |
| 8th month | 866,922.292 | 124,779.179 | – | |
| 9th month | 488,048.794 | 84,545.338 | – | |
| 10th month | 459,509.593 | 84,905.914 | – | |
| 11th month | 1,265,045.267 | 86,079.580 | – | |
| 12th month | 2,122,635.316 | 273,585.281 | – | |
| *45th year (1780)* | *8,030,444*<br>*10,134,444** | *923,883*<br>*1,193,884** | – | *The figure of copper coins of the 12th month is incomplete* |
| 1st month | 168,400.168 | – | – | |
| 2nd month | 1,031,857.765 | 122,712.899 | – | |
| 3rd month | 523,260.289 | 83,661.726 | – | |
| 4th month | 505,841.621 | 85,212.739 | – | |
| 5th month | 520,294.358 | 83,619.367 | – | |
| 6th month | 415,102.320 | 85,144.037 | – | |
| 7th month | 574,586.303 | 84,267.480 | – | |
| 8th month | 925,793.996 | 119,716.049 | – | |
| 9th month | 486,212.898 | 83,354.507 | – | |
| 10th month | 846,221.973 | 86,908.577 | – | |
| 11th month | 233,217.159 | 85,521.308 | – | |
| 12th month | 1,799,655.000 | 3,764.801 | – | |
| *46th year (1781)* | *12,529,821* | *1,285,811* | – | |
| 1st month | 398,068.257 | – | – | |
| 2nd month | 1,202,071.236 | 121,866.329 | – | |
| 3rd month | 515,596.902 | 84,674.476 | – | |
| 4th month | 587,488.953 | 85,493.895 | – | |
| 5th month | 574,585.993 | 85,541.659 | – | |
| Leap month | 521,703.484 | 85,456.643 | – | |

TABLE A.8 *Aggregate expenditures of the Silver Treasury during* Qianlong, *1736–1795* (cont.)

| Year | Silver (taels) | Copper coins (strings) | Others | Remarks |
|---|---|---|---|---|
| 6th month | 531,024.774 | 84,571.386 | – | |
| 7th month | 541,738.291 | 84,317.558 | – | |
| 8th month | 941,937.587 | 122,940.997 | – | |
| 9th month | 462,590.381 | 84,614.891 | – | |
| 10th month | 477,608.860 | 85,307.103 | – | |
| 11th month | 3,863,380.633 | 86,419.386 | – | |
| 12th month | 1,912,025.361 | 274,607.117 | – | |
| *47th year (1782)* | *14,356,482* | *1,145,431* | – | |
| 1st month | 202,579.967 | 6.000 | – | |
| 2nd month | 1,300,620.117 | 122,976.256 | – | |
| 3rd month | 1,525,669.804 | 85,801.587 | – | |
| 4th month | 1,569,523.231 | 85,438.068 | – | |
| 5th month | 1,548,604.617 | 86,780.168 | – | |
| 6th month | 511,841.282 | 24,705.845 | – | |
| 7th month | 563,993.864 | 86,045.942 | – | |
| 8th month | 1,064,212.149 | 121,916.265 | – | |
| 9th month | 540,331.663 | 84,203.338 | – | |
| 10th month | 477,068.817 | 86,550.720 | | |
| 11th month | 3,695,287.705 | 88,256.269 | – | |
| 12th month | 1,356,748.964 | 272,750.415 | – | |
| *49th year (1784)* | *9,557,035* | *1,381,702* | – | |
| 1st month | 160,818.533 | 4.000 | – | |
| 2nd month | 1,085,694.241 | 119,651.945 | – | |
| 3rd month | 572,415.822 | 82,481.495 | – | |
| Leap month | 477,270.376 | 83,106.478 | – | |
| 4th month | 562,932.834 | 87,934.567 | – | |
| 5th month | 546,879.731 | 83,073.129 | – | |
| 6th month | 656,723.637 | 84,036.555 | – | |
| 7th month | 556,511.764 | 90,021.083 | – | |
| 8th month | 858,750.283 | 125,061.259 | – | |
| 9th month | 514,293.389 | 86,216.416 | – | |
| 10th month | 443,811.827 | 122,838.583 | – | |

| Year | Silver (taels) | Copper coins (strings) | Others | Remarks |
|---|---|---|---|---|
| 11th month | 1,763,461.672 | 131,408.733 | – | |
| 12th month | 1,357,470.402 | 285,867.998 | – | |
| *50th year (1785)* | *10,634,978* | *1,230,511* | – | *The figure of copper coins of the 12th month is incomplete.* |
| 1st month | 307,653.125 | 2.250 | – | |
| 2nd month | 1,503,406.360 | 134,219.017 | – | |
| 3rd month | 575,007.819 | 90,978.971 | – | |
| 4th month | 579,158.893 | 85,614.451 | – | |
| 5th month | 598,713.115 | 86,208.978 | – | |
| 6th month | 506,896.154 | 90,247.812 | – | |
| 7th month | 551,883.536 | 84,739.522 | – | |
| 8th month | 1,826,604.603 | 120,042.186 | – | |
| 9th month | 580,726.277 | 86,959.356 | – | |
| 10th month | 496,321.064 | 84,385.239 | – | |
| 11th month | 1,708,244.876 | 84,226.019 | – | |
| 12th month | 1,400,362.586 | 282,886.7xx | – | xx means the digits are missing |
| *51st year (1786)* | *9,339,440* | *1,302,528* | – | |
| 1st month | 347,454.686 | – | – | |
| 2nd month | 1,043,765.510 | 121,166.501 | – | |
| 3rd month | 569,409.622 | 84,422.166 | – | |
| 4th month | 493,367.349 | 84,907.245 | – | |
| 5th month | 735,712.279 | 89,592.826 | – | |
| 6th month | 517,281.099 | 84,337.988 | – | |
| 7th month | 524,680.210 | 85,090.875 | – | |
| Leap month | 528,973.395 | 89,780.494 | – | |
| 8th month | 927,192.941 | 122,245.462 | – | |
| 9th month | 490,206.289 | 85,158.454 | – | |
| 10th month | 470,223.459 | 82,794.189 | – | |
| 11th month | 1,329,467.590 | 88,555.008 | – | |
| 12th month | 1,361,705.186 | 284,476.492 | – | |
| *53rd year (1788)* | *10,664,253* | *1,394,924* | – | |
| 1st month | 153,614.780 | – | – | |

TABLE A.8 *Aggregate expenditures of the Silver Treasury during* Qianlong, *1736–1795* (cont.)

| Year | Silver (taels) | Copper coins (strings) | Others | Remarks |
|---|---|---|---|---|
| 2nd month | 1,232,027.167 | 130,074.091 | – | |
| 3rd month | 684,120.907 | 83,986.780 | – | |
| 4th month | 540,022.886 | 92,382.388 | – | |
| 5th month | 649,821.862 | 85,467.178 | – | |
| 6th month | 557,606.138 | 159,225.004 | – | |
| 7th month | 1,502,546.126 | 161,549.311 | – | |
| 8th month | 889,321.606 | 122,394.506 | – | |
| 9th month | 528,649.987 | 105,099.806 | – | |
| 10th month | 569,603.820 | 91,318.790 | – | |
| 11th month | 1,970,533.662 | 85,948.112 | – | |
| 12th month | 1,386,383.766 | 277,477.771 | – | |
| *54th year (1789)* | *10,286,842* | *1,298,591* | – | |
| 1st month | 174,181.379 | – | – | |
| 2nd month | 1,206,601.709 | 124,025.236 | – | |
| 3rd month | 648,063.132 | 85,046.788 | – | |
| 4th month | 608,447.708 | 90,123.004 | – | |
| 5th month | 570,116.741 | 85,578.231 | – | |
| Leap month | 520,753.510 | 85,834.676 | – | |
| 6th month | 532,522.310 | 86,073.065 | – | |
| 7th month | 537,964.610 | 85,054.284 | – | |
| 8th month | 1,020,202.127 | 122,748.390 | – | |
| 9th month | 539,460.148 | 84,867.095 | – | |
| 10th month | 746,891.567 | 86,339.157 | – | |
| 11th month | 1,859,858.689 | 85,695.279 | – | |
| 12th month | 1,321,778.276 | 277,205.738 | – | |
| *55th year (1790)* | *11,485,435* | *1,215,704* | – | |
| 1st month | 286,951.025 | – | – | |
| 2nd month | 1,258,437.904 | 122,271.011 | – | |
| 3rd month | 642,123.816 | 85,068.633 | – | |
| 4th month | 736,328.160 | 84,972.020 | – | |
| 5th month | 583,354.865 | 83,903.247 | – | |
| 6th month | 1,111,228.772 | 84,156.819 | – | |

| Year | Silver (taels) | Copper coins (strings) | Others | Remarks |
|---|---|---|---|---|
| 7th month | 558,206.605 | 89,173.085 | – | |
| 8th month | 1,848,251.494 | 120,793.420 | – | |
| 9th month | 607,027.124 | 86,048.232 | – | |
| 10th month | 628,282.606 | 85,262.096 | – | |
| 11th month | 1,880,222.822 | 90,942.519 | – | |
| 12th month | 1,345,020.129 | 283,112.819 | – | |
| *56th year (1791)* | *10,486,587* | *1,228,972* | – | |
| 1st month | 165,664.554 | 109.112 | – | |
| 2nd month | 1,184,292.659 | 124,906.065 | – | |
| 3rd month | 725,409.546 | 87,582.572 | – | |
| 4th month | 564,027.046 | 83,410.223 | – | |
| 5th month | 566,261.403 | 86,257.887 | – | |
| 6th month | 546,989.004 | 85,225.530 | – | |
| 7th month | 574,322.202 | 86,482.744 | – | |
| 8th month | 974,885.645 | 128,058.004 | – | |
| 9th month | 645,286.632 | 84,943.794 | – | |
| 10th month | 472,253.308 | 92,573.086 | – | |
| 11th month | 2,719,890.931 | 86,362.634 | – | |
| 12th month | 1,347,304.538 | 283,060.046 | – | |
| *58th year (1793)* | *9,718,023* | *1,212,712* | – | |
| 1st month | 350,989.801 | 4.050 | – | |
| 2nd month | 1,025,378.679 | 123,322.721 | – | |
| 3rd month | 618,883.691 | 85,317.658 | – | |
| 4th month | 1,048,340.343 | 86,604.737 | – | |
| 5th month | 580,522.271 | 86,274.008 | – | |
| 6th month | 516,364.753 | 85,439.845 | – | |
| 7th month | 540,445.707 | 85,615.722 | – | |
| 8th month | 918,221.542 | 123,272.182 | – | |
| 9th month | 565,654.640 | 85,683.293 | – | |
| 10th month | 485,447.209 | 86,114.699 | – | |
| 11th month | 1,698,803.071 | 87,064.912 | – | |
| 12th month | 1,368,971.786 | 277,998.504 | – | |

TABLE A.8 *Aggregate expenditures of the Silver Treasury during* Qianlong, *1736–1795* (cont.)

| Year | Silver (taels) | Copper coins (strings) | Others | Remarks |
|---|---|---|---|---|
| *59th year (1794)* | *12,672,250* | *393,870* | – | *The silver figure of the 12th month is incomplete.* |
| 1st month | 339,420.938 | – | – | |
| 2nd month | 1,052,165.118 | 122,738.438 | – | |
| 3rd month | 612,799.897 | 86,416.021 | – | |
| 4th month | 612,363.719 | 85,779.046 | – | |
| 5th month | 529,949.510 | 96,373.717 | – | |
| 6th month | 523,335.657 | 85,461.278 | – | |
| 7th month | 690,764.875 | 623.536 | – | |
| 8th month | 1,447,621.159 | 540.000 | – | |
| 9th month | 876,471..215 | – | – | |
| 10th month | 599,214.462 | 7,230.672 | – | |
| 11th month | 1,914,609.362 | 11,778.019 | – | |
| 12th month | 4,35x,xx5.483 | 19,668.000 | – | xx means the digits are missing |
| *60th year (1795)* | *10,747,620** | *142,688** | – | |
| *Average of* Qianlong | *10,913,497* | *1,138,334* | – | |

*Source*: figures marked with * are from four-column registers of each of the years; others are based on aggregate expenditure registers of Qianlong, The Yellow Registers (The Silver Treasury of the Ministry of Revenue), Volumes 14–22. In calculating the averages, the figure of copper coins of the 22nd year is based on the record of the aggregate expenditure register; the figure of copper coins of the 38th year and the silver and copper coin figures of the 45th year are based on the four-column registers.

TABLE A.9 *Payment surpluses/deficits of the Silver Treasury during* Qianlong, *1736–1795* (1)

| Year | Aggregate revenue | | Aggregate expenditure | | Surplus/Deficit (+/–) | |
|---|---|---|---|---|---|---|
| | Silver (taels) | Copper coins (strings) | Silver (taels) | Copper coins (strings) | Silver (taels) | Copper coins (strings) |
| 1st year (1736) | 14,789,281 | 645,172 | 15,400,142 | 1,120,449 | –610,861 | –475,277 |
| 3rd year (1738) | 10,427,790 | 653,604 | 9,954,450 | 675,705 | +473,340 | –22,101 |

| Year | Aggregate revenue | | Aggregate expenditure | | Surplus/Deficit (+/–) | |
|---|---|---|---|---|---|---|
| | Silver (taels) | Copper coins (strings) | Silver (taels) | Copper coins (strings) | Silver (taels) | Copper coins (strings) |
| 5th year (1740) | 8,240,136 | 1,006,283 | 10,337,236 | 993,209 | –2,097,100 | +13,074 |
| 13th year (1748) | 8,187,984* | 1,017,312* | 13,087,744* | 1,013,387* | –4,899,760 | +3,925 |
| 18th year (1753) | 11,619,370 | 1,077,567 | 10,379,263 | 1,075,730 | +1,240,107 | +1,837 |
| 20thyear (1755) | 15,639,475 | 1,086,862 | 10,247,839* | 1,086,942* | +5,391,636 | –80 |
| 22nd year (1757) | 9,318,433* | 1,203,957* | 12,388,209 | 1,214,285 | –3,069,776 | –10,328 |
| 25th year (1760) | 10,336,272 | 1,560,585 | 11,572,236 | 1,750,059 | –1,235,964 | –189,474 |
| 26th year (1761) | 11,442,266 | 1,197,764 | 10,300,595 | 1,235,693 | +1,141,671 | –37,929 |
| 28th year (1763) | 14,669,589 | 1,137,386 | 9,533,903* | 1,138,024* | +5,135,686 | –638 |
| 29th year (1764) | 16,868,335 | 1,245,961 | 9,658,131 | 1,244,955 | +7,210,204 | +1,006 |
| 30th year (1765) | 15,417,601 | 1,315,785 | 9,355,040 | 1,315,791 | +606,2561 | –6 |
| 37th year (1772) | 11,871,843 | 1,178,843 | 12,071,582 | 1,448,303 | –199,739 | –269,460 |
| 38th year (1773) | 8,966,307* | 1,277,811* | 19,029,498 | 1,277,817* | –1,006,3191 | –6 |
| 40th year (1775) | 14,134,913* | 1,254,947* | 23,083,250 | 1,254,448 | –8,948,337 | +499 |
| 41st year (1776) | 18,711,298 | 1,294,815* | 9,005,900* | 1,295,309* | +9,705,398 | –494 |
| 42nd year (1777) | 18,117,732* | 1,203,459* | 10,956,360* | 1,203,768* | +7,161,372 | –309 |
| 43rd year (1778) | 11,477,632 | 1,284,266 | 9,893,661 | 1,284,113 | +1,583,971 | +153 |
| 45th year (1780) | 10,567,108* | 1,193,808* | 10,134,444* | 1,193,884* | +432,664 | –76 |
| 46th year (1781) | 13,930,618 | 1,285,728 | 12,529,821 | 1,285,811 | +1,400,797 | –83 |

TABLE A.9 *Payment surpluses/deficits of the Silver Treasury during* Qianlong, (cont.)

| Year | Aggregate revenue | | Aggregate expenditure | | Surplus/Deficit (+/–) | |
|---|---|---|---|---|---|---|
| | Silver (taels) | Copper coins (strings) | Silver (taels) | Copper coins (strings) | Silver (taels) | Copper coins (strings) |
| 47th year (1782) | 13,657,359 | 1,206,487 | 14,356,482 | 1,145,431 | –699,123 | +61,056 |
| 49th year (1784) | 12,407,397 | 1,382,518 | 9,557,035 | 1,381,702 | +2,850,362 | +816 |
| 51st year (1786) | 7,461,334 | 1,301,573 | 9,339,440 | 1,302,528 | –1,878,106 | –955 |
| 55th year (1790) | 16,230,598 | 1,219,814 | 11,485,435 | 1,215,704 | +4,745,163 | +4,410 |
| 58th year (1793) | 10,111,935 | 1,213,081 | 9,718,023 | 1,212,712 | +393,912 | +369 |
| 59th year (1794) | 9,179,009 | 517,268 | 12,672,250 | 393,870 | –3,493,241 | +123,398 |
| 60th year (1795) | 8,665,152 | 142,656 | 10,747,620* | 142,688* | –2,082,468 | –32 |
| *Average of* Qianlong | *12,312,843* | *1,115,012* | *11,733,170* | *1,144,530* | *+579,673* | *–29,518* |

*Source*: based on Tables A.7 and A.8.

TABLE A.10 *Payment surpluses/deficits of the Silver Treasury during* Qianlong, *1736–1795* (2)

| Year | Aggregate revenue (million taels) | Aggregate expenditure (million taels) | Surplus/Deficit (million taels) | Year-end inventories on 1775 list (million taels) |
|---|---|---|---|---|
| 1st year (1736) | 14.79 | 15.40 | –0.61 | 33.96 |
| 2nd year (1737) | 14.73 | (14.30) | +0.43 | 34.39 |
| 3rd year (1738) | 10.43 | 9.95 | +0.47 | 34.86 |
| 4th year (1739) | – | – | –2.28 | 32.58 |

| Year | Aggregate revenue (million taels) | Aggregate expenditure (million taels) | Surplus/Deficit (million taels) | Year–end inventories on 1775 list (million taels) |
|---|---|---|---|---|
| 5th year (1740) | 8.24 | 10.34 | −2.10 | 30.49 |
| 6th year (1741) | – | – | +0.97 | 31.46 |
| 7th year (1742) | – | – | +1.29 | 32.75 |
| 8th year (1743) | (8.01) | 11.64 | −3.63 | 29.12 |
| 9th year (1744) | 13.46 | (11.58)[a] | +1.88 | 31.90[d] |
| 10th year (1745) | – | – | +1.27 | 33.17 |
| 11th year (1746) | 10.62 | (9.16) | +1.46 | 34.63 |
| 12th year (1747) | – | – | −2.27 | 32.36 |
| 13th year (1748) | 8.19* | 13.09* | −4.90 | 27.46 |
| 14th year (1749) | 10.10 | (9.49)[b] | +0.61 | 28.07 |
| 15th year (1750) | – | – | +2.73 | 30.80[e] |
| 16th year (1751) | – | – | +1.69 | 32.49 |
| 17th year (1752) | – | – | +6.14 | 38.63 |
| 18th ear (1753) | 11.62 | 10.38 | +1.24 | 39.87 |
| 19th year (1754) | 14.25 | (16.51) | −2.26 | 37.61 |
| 20th year (1755) | 15.64 | 10.25* | +5.39 | 43.00 |
| 21st year (1756) | – | – | +0.22 | 43.22 |
| 22nd year (1757) | 9.32* | 12.39 | −3.07 | 40.15 |
| 23rd year (1758) | – | – | −3.77 | 36.38 |

TABLE A.10 *Payment surpluses/deficits of the Silver Treasury during* Qianlong. (cont.)

| Year | Aggregate revenue (million taels) | Aggregate expenditure (million taels) | Surplus/Deficit (million taels) | Year–end inventories on 1775 list (million taels) |
|---|---|---|---|---|
| 24th year (1759) | – | – | +0.35 | 36.73 |
| 25th year (1760) | 10.34 | 11.57 | −1.23 | 35.50 |
| 26th year (1761) | 11.44 | 10.30 | +1.14 | 36.64 |
| 27th year (1762) | (15.66) | 10.37 | +5.29 | 41.93 |
| 28th year (1763) | 14.67 | 9.53* | +5.14 | 47.06 |
| 29th year (1764) | 16.87 | 9.66 | +7.21 | 54.27 |
| 30th year (1765) | 15.42 | 9.36 | +6..06 | 60.34 |
| 31st year (1766) | (17.79) | 11.52 | +6.27 | 66.61 |
| 32nd year (1767) | (12.35) | 12.46 | −0.11 | 66.50 |
| 33rd year (1768) | – | – | +5.32 | 71.82 |
| 34th year (1769) | – | – | +4.40 | 76.22 |
| 35th year (1770) | 10.98 | (9.90)[c] | +1.08 | 77.30 |
| 36th year (1771) | (11.09) | 9.45 | +1.64 | 78.94 |
| 37th year (1772) | 11.87 | 12.07 | −0.20 | 78.74 |
| 38th year (1773) | 8.97* | 19.03 | −10.06 | 69.68 (68.68)[f] |
| 39th year (1774) | 17.59 | (13.36) | +4.23 | 73.91 |
| 40th year (1775) | 14.13* | 23.08 | −8.95 | – |
| 41st year (1776) | 18.71 | 9.01* | +9.71 | – |

| Year | Aggregate revenue (million taels) | Aggregate expenditure (million taels) | Surplus/Deficit (million taels) | Year–end inventories on 1775 list (million taels) |
|---|---|---|---|---|
| 42nd year (1777) | 18.12* | 10.96* | +7.16 | – |
| 43rd year (1778) | 11.48 | 9.89 | +1.58 | – |
| 45th year (1780) | 10.57* | 10.13* | +0.43 | – |
| 46th year (1781) | 13.93 | 12.53 | +1.40 | – |
| 47th year (1782) | 13.66 | 14.36 | –0.70 | – |
| 49th year (1784) | 12.41 | 9.56 | +2.85 | – |
| 51st year (1786) | 7.46 | 9.34 | –1.88 | – |
| 55th year (1790) | 16.23 | 11.49 | +4.74 | – |
| 58th year (1793) | 10.11 | 9.72 | +0.39 | – |
| 59th year (1794) | 9.18 | 12.67 | –3.49 | – |
| 60th year (1795) | 8.67 | 10.75* | –2.08 | – |
| *Average of* Qianlong | *12.54* | *11.64* | *+0.99*[g] *+0.90*[h] | – |

*Source*: based on Tables A.7, A.8 and B.43, also see the explanation of the Table A.6.
[a] Recalculating this figure is because that the records of the aggregate expenditure register of this year are imcomplete; [b] Ibid.; [c] Ibid.; [d] According to the surplus of the year, the year-end inventory ought to be 31 million taels; [e] According to the surplus of the year, the year-end inventory ought to be 30.77 million taels; [f] This is the figure recorded by the four-column register of the year; [g] The figure is obtain by calculating on the basis of all the surplus/deficit figures listed in the column; [h] The figure is obtain by calculating the difference between the average revenue and expenditure figures.

TABLE A.11 *Aggregate revenues of the Silver Treasury during* Jiaqing, *1796–1819*

| Year | Silver (taels) | Copper coins (strings) | Remarks |
|---|---|---|---|
| *1st year (1796)* | *5,734,496* | *770,978*<br>*591,663** | |
| 1st month | 35,567.737 | – | |
| 2nd month | 19,907.380 | 10,343.937 | |
| 3rd month | 580,676.248 | 101,301.100 | |
| 4th month | 403,758.427 | 9,400.737 | |
| 5th month | 131,312.332 | 10,308.558 | |
| 6th month | 102,637.008 | 9,601.847 | |
| 7th month | 243,502.688 | 11,140.676 | |
| 8th month | 170,102.227 | 9,910.587 | |
| 9th month | 98,542.917 | 8,210.034 | |
| 10th month | 2,077,438.584 | 97,937.738 | |
| 11th month | 772,285.462 | 12,988.384 | |
| 12th month | 1,098,765.000 | 489,834.559 | |
| *3rd year (1798)* | *1,641,3926* | *529,854* | |
| 1st month | 20,929.790 | – | |
| 2nd month | 12,110.008 | 7,700.904 | |
| 3rd month | 166,184.160 | 9,017.354 | |
| 4th month | 32,496.348 | 8,642.253 | |
| 5th month | 92,613.729 | 9,064.981 | |
| 6th month | 257,046.761 | 8,563.133 | |
| 7th month | 1,720,922.571 | 9,486.039 | |
| 8th month | 140,515.837 | 9,323.477 | |
| 9th month | 4,635,710.160 | 9,730.345 | |
| 10th month | 2,798,562.066 | 9,835.504 | |
| 11th month | 120,024.121 | 17,163.902 | |
| 12th month | 6,416,810.628 | 431,326.304 | |
| *6th year (1801)* | *9,301,963* | *1,166,731* | |
| 1st month | 60,102.784 | 420.000 | |
| 2nd month | 151,888.293 | 134,214.484 | |
| 3rd month | 99,742.434 | 13,358.803 | |
| 4th month | 208,117.689 | 13,223.238 | |

| Year | Silver (taels) | Copper coins (strings) | Remarks |
|---|---|---|---|
| 5th month | 94,057.051 | 51,876.098 | |
| 6th month | 87,171.628 | 123,659.083 | |
| 7th month | 2,355,834.955 | 230,346.017 | |
| 8th month | 233,674.833 | 140,067.763 | |
| 9th month | 910,437.709 | 53,598.805 | |
| 10th month | 489,407.283 | 52,111.211 | |
| 11th month | 743,662.087 | 61,796.563 | |
| 12th month | 3,867,866.402 | 292,058.630 | |
| *7th year (1802)* | *11,496,754* | *1,534,981* | |
| 1st month | 394,694.715 | 1,578.615 | |
| 2nd month | 359,829.415 | 171,168.031 | |
| 3rd month | 34,537.446 | 52,208.990 | |
| 4th month | 409,277.995 | 90,870.142 | |
| 5th month | 371,800.677 | 96,105.438 | |
| 6th month | 187,626.356 | 74,792.724 | |
| 7th month | 60,820.090 | 197,183.457 | |
| 8th month | 101,588.238 | 194,689.206 | |
| 9th month | 5,680,921.733 | 92,167.185 | |
| 10th month | 234,752.495 | 90,061.068 | |
| 11th month | 360,022.463 | 89,582.643 | |
| 12th month | 3,300,882.002 | 384,573.972 | |
| *9th year (1804)* | *13,771,203* | *1,242,982* | |
| 1st month | 98,485.322 | 1,055.226 | |
| 2nd month | 51,164.632 | 65,462.288 | |
| 3rd month | 252,275.126 | 161,265.684 | |
| 4th month | 420,088.428 | 93,164.446 | |
| 5th month | 109,051.698 | 88,947.289 | |
| 6th month | 281,467.628 | 93,351.541 | |
| 7th month | 230,173.797 | 89,178.765 | |
| 8th month | 28,038.957 | 90,107.464 | |
| 9th month | 4,165,598.834 | 91,622.482 | |
| 10th month | 163,187.722 | 89,983.820 | |
| 11th month | 116,158.516 | 90,887.563 | |
| 12th month | 7,855,512.249 | 287,955.263 | |

TABLE A.11 *Aggregate revenues of the Silver Treasury during* Jiaqing, *1796–1819* (cont.)

| Year | Silver (taels) | Copper coins (strings) | Remarks |
|---|---|---|---|
| *10th year (1805)* | *13,933,953* | *1,041,508*<br>*1,327,850** | |
| 1st month | 894,095.601 | – | |
| 2nd month | 464,153.514 | 98,776.481 | |
| 3rd month | 128,420.164 | 88,893.203 | |
| 4th month | 411,582.315 | 95,958.470 | |
| 5th month | 241,612.850 | 92,195.051 | |
| 6th month | 215,991.852 | 92,210.646 | |
| Leap month | 559,059.873 | 100,361.205 | |
| 7th month | 91,777.540 | 93,958.301 | |
| 8th month | 4,740,523.535 | 93,758.323 | |
| 9th month | 547,565.774 | 93,927.988 | |
| 10th month | 1,134,291.370 | 97,097.032 | |
| 11th month | 127,323.043 | 94,371.421 | |
| 12th month | 4,377,555.465 | 286,341.514 | |
| *12th year (1807)* | *6,938,704* | *1,438,237* | |
| 1st month | 299,403.203 | 3.633 | |
| 2nd month | 1,248,233.708 | 109,809.696 | |
| 3rd month | 790,056.856 | 143,904.084 | |
| 4th month | 375,335.429 | 72,261.834 | |
| 5th month | 438,689.693 | 97,420.961 | |
| 6th month | 207,308.428 | 120,906.337 | |
| 7th month | 4,595.017 | 120,979.121 | |
| 8th month | 356,817.465 | 159,852.824 | |
| 9th month | 113,973.660 | 125,009.934 | |
| 10th month | 102,658.879 | 103,604.352 | |
| 11th month | 69,656.020 | 103,360.281 | |
| 12th month | 2,931,975.308 | 281,123.644 | |
| *13th year (1808)* | *9,736,061* | *1,248,030* | |
| 1st month | 518,104.674 | – | |
| 2nd month | 587,448.297 | 85,871.879 | |
| 3rd month | 382,109.476 | 93,460.568 | |

| Year | Silver (taels) | Copper coins (strings) | Remarks |
|---|---|---|---|
| 4th month | 440,681.623 | 103,194.917 | |
| 5th month | 1,469,624.100 | 85,039.384 | |
| Leap month | 599,146.945 | 85,039.348 | |
| 6th month | 819,850.810 | 96,837.229 | |
| 7th month | 22,266.667 | 96,701.374 | |
| 8th month | 444,989.846 | 89,138.261 | |
| 9th month | 511,176.230 | 95,029.756 | |
| 10th month | 247,960.651 | 105,814.336 | |
| 11th month | 374,228.038 | 103,031.390 | |
| 12th month | 3,318,473.818 | 208,871.543 | |
| *14th year (1809)* | *9,579,282* | *1,280,432* | *The totals of the 12th month are obtained by adding up the detailed figures, because the original monly totals are missing.* |
| 1st month | 628,191.929 | 654.640 | |
| 2nd month | 494,193.868 | 91,877.921 | |
| 3rd month | 177,936.021 | 114,563.771 | |
| 4th month | 470,344.666 | 93,226.970 | |
| 5th month | 271,814.696 | 97,737.550 | |
| 6th month | 162,964.163 | 131,498.184 | |
| 7th month | 199,778.195 | 89,393.645 | |
| 8th month | 230,611.166 | 129,005.289 | |
| 9th month | 165,573.630 | 103,204.397 | |
| 10th month | 221,174.134 | 118,294.855 | |
| 11th month | 1,031,626.791 | 99,542.805 | |
| 12th month | (5,525,072.876) | (211,432.040) | The totals of the 12th month are obtained by adding up the detailed figures, because the original monly totals are missing. |
| *16th year (1811)* | *9,448,666** | *1,366,085** | |
| *17th year (1812)* | *7,712,803* | *1,151,100* | |
| 1st month | 23,338.702 | – | |
| 2nd month | 534,302.145 | 88,767.740 | |

TABLE A.11 *Aggregate revenues of the Silver Treasury during* Jiaqing, *1796–1819* (cont.)

| Year | Silver (taels) | Copper coins (strings) | Remarks |
|---|---|---|---|
| 3rd month | 1,045,390.618 | 103,842.740 | |
| 4th month | 435,226.191 | 95,989.532 | |
| 5th month | 716,436.115 | 97,085.644 | |
| 6th month | 324,814.305 | 95,235.240 | |
| 7th month | 120,046.905 | 72,954.301 | |
| 8th month | 169,341.355 | 60,552.318 | |
| 9th month | 319,015.852 | 55,845.627 | |
| 10th month | 220,028.244 | 80,398.869 | |
| 11th month | 313,176.846 | 145,884.137 | |
| 12th month | 3,491,685.464 | 254,544.028 | |
| *19th year (1814)* | *12,100,661* | *1,312,241* | |
| 1st month | 500,425.355 | 500.429 | |
| 2nd month | 910,519.684 | 83,783.200 | |
| Leap month | 494,752.282 | 80,929.240 | |
| 3rd month | 1,135,752.673 | 89,054.522 | |
| 4th month | 611,246.139 | 80,907.282 | |
| 5th month | 126,496.480 | 88,220.332 | |
| 6th month | 589,706.198 | 73,719.662 | |
| 7th month | 560,605.549 | 95,912.000 | |
| 8th month | 281,391.592 | 142,269.119 | |
| 9th month | 277,861.621 | 156,637.886 | |
| 10th month | 364,258.049 | 89,738.381 | |
| 11th month | 233,133.391 | 118,813.360 | |
| 12th month | 6,014,511.823 | 211,755.087 | |
| *20th year (1815)* | *12,435,695* | *1,142,974* | |
| 1st month | 411,633.893 | – | |
| 2nd month | 624,828.166 | 88,829.240 | |
| 3rd month | 391,108.280 | 88,746.240 | |
| 4th month | 447,112.199 | 91,633.446 | |
| 5th month | 4,875,342.899 | 99,411.093 | |
| 6th month | 267,385.795 | 95,343.592 | |
| 7th month | 180,370.550 | 97,659.261 | |

| Year | Silver (taels) | Copper coins (strings) | Remarks |
|---|---|---|---|
| 8th month | 80,706.232 | 96,921.096 | |
| 9th month | 669,480.775 | 94,414.022 | |
| 10th month | 306,800.047 | 90,004.000 | |
| 11th month | 500,296.141 | 91,251.340 | |
| 12th month | 3,680,629.657 | 208,760.747 | |
| *21st year (1816)* | *9,451,035** | *1,496,370** | |
| *22nd year (1817)* | *10,637,957* | *1,168,451* | |
| 1st month | 307,651.444 | – | |
| 2nd month | 1,177,455.442 | 97,868.373 | |
| 3rd month | 912,703.003 | 92,726.000 | |
| 4th month | 751,304.853 | 95,329.640 | |
| 5th month | 310,292.786 | 102,881.531 | |
| 6th month | 419,397.599 | 99,526.709 | |
| 7th month | 415,399.440 | 95,473.030 | |
| 8th month | 434,148.249 | 97,253.536 | |
| 9th month | 664,460.650 | 97,002.167 | |
| 10th month | 1,147,029.542 | 99,008.305 | |
| 11th month | 444,901.663 | 99,496.140 | |
| 12th month | 3,653,212.554 | 191,886.000 | |
| *23rd year (1818)* | *13,990,810** | *1,195,427** | |
| *24th year (1819)* | *15,217,960* | *1,257,461* | |
| 1st month | 814,519.382 | 6.000 | |
| 2nd month | 1,794,329.944 | 30,056.467 | |
| 3rd month | 1,410,486.687 | 165,198.590 | |
| 4th month | 1,338,982.350 | 92,508.618 | |
| Leap month | 1,058,073.193 | 93,304.530 | |
| 5th month | 1,185,852.210 | 86,321.220 | |
| 6th month | 553,370.725 | 96,521.347 | |
| 7th month | 819,628.968 | 100,248.177 | |
| 8th month | 325,470.706 | 87,796.918 | |

TABLE A.11 *Aggregate revenues of the Silver Treasury during* Jiaqing, *1796–1819* (cont.)

| Year | Silver (taels) | Copper coins (strings) | Remarks |
|---|---|---|---|
| 9th month | 967,379.390 | 97,583.660 | |
| 10th month | 1,172,406.165 | 89,645.938 | |
| 11th month | 483,596.130 | 92,765.131 | |
| 12th month | 3,293,864.067 | 225,504.056 | |
| *Average of* Jiaqing | *11,053,055* | *1,202,992* | |

*Source*: figures marked with * are from four-column registers of each of the years; others are based on aggregate revenue registers of Jiaqing, The Yellow Registers · The Silver Treasury of the Ministry of Revenue, Volumes 8–10. In calculating the averages, the figures of copper coins of the 1st year and the 10th year are based on the four-column registers.

TABLE A.12 *Aggregate expenditures of the Silver Treasury during* Jiaqing, *1796–1820*

| Year | Silver (taels) | Copper coins (strings) | Remarks |
|---|---|---|---|
| *1st year (1796)* | *18,541,762* | *591,624* | |
| 1st month | 2,10,082.899 | – | |
| 2nd month | 1,247,380.622 | 10,338.596 | |
| 3rd month | 1,058,542.774 | 10,099.085 | |
| 4th month | 1,411,379.980 | 9,123.021 | |
| 5th month | 648,869.002 | 10,380.345 | |
| 6th month | 632,565.621 | 9,840.168 | |
| 7th month | 594,945.193 | 9,795.052 | |
| 8th month | 2,990,993.503 | 9,027.961 | |
| 9th month | 653,407.450 | 10,457.354 | |
| 10th month | 2,528,263.178 | 9,469.169 | |
| 11th month | 3,988,467.458 | 10,973.318 | |
| 12th month | 2,576,864.547 | 492,120.216 | |
| *2nd year (1797)* | *35,168,049* | *587,088* | |
| 1st month | 160,539.521 | 726.700 | |
| 2nd month | 1,308,271.772 | 9,751.755 | |
| 3rd month | 4,618,336.931 | 10,092.812 | |

| Year | Silver (taels) | Copper coins (strings) | Remarks |
|---|---|---|---|
| 4th month | 990,466.545 | 9,470.161 | |
| 5th month | 662,726.900 | 10,577.624 | |
| 6th month | 4,576,905.937 | 9,319.354 | |
| Leap month | 6,555,199.410 | 10,029.154 | |
| 7th month | 555,261.620 | 10,086.832 | |
| 8th month | 4,977,504.826 | 10,754.401 | |
| 9th month | 1,030,885.536 | 9,813.666 | |
| 10th month | 2,535,771.326 | 11,149.360 | |
| 11th month | 5,957,401.789 | 10,024.984 | |
| 12th month | 1,238,777.321 | 475,291.427 | |
| *3rd year (1798)* | *25,147,965** | *529,739** | |
| *4th year (1799)* | *17,949,180* | *1,382,302* | *Silver figure of the 12th month is incomplete in the original register.* |
| 1st month | 89,644.058 | – | |
| 2nd month | 1,413,628.323 | 10 147.573 | |
| 3rd month | 3,249,706.757 | 9 579.082 | |
| 4th month | 661,580.746 | 11 530.963 | |
| 5th month | 2,140,226.815 | 13 848.642 | |
| 6th month | 695,137.315 | 17 641.119 | |
| 7th month | 1,082,612.375 | 397 144.652 | |
| 8th month | 3,754,704.979 | 16 294.032 | |
| 9th month | 571,188.541 | 32 678.849 | |
| 10th month | 795,599.209 | 39 132.114 | |
| 11th month | 585,020.523 | 50 924.008 | |
| 12th month | 2,910,13x.566 | 783,380.690 | x means the digit is missing. |
| *5th year (1800)* | *13,117,179* | *1,337,367* | |
| 1st month | 956,169.126 | 1,369.876 | |
| 2nd month | 2,725,597.081 | 109,916.847 | |
| 3rd month | 642,948.597 | 109,222.248 | |
| 4th month | 1,046,062.111 | 109,901.445 | |
| Leap month | 1,366,686.794 | 54,069.754 | |
| 5th month | 1,006,911.120 | 51,915.626 | |

TABLE A.12 *Aggregate expenditures of the Silver Treasury during* Jiaqing, *1796–1820* (cont.)

| Year | Silver (taels) | Copper coins (strings) | Remarks |
|---|---|---|---|
| 6th month | 538,980.011 | 56,845.703 | |
| 7th month | 558,063.291 | 55,265.942 | |
| 8th month | 1,019,602.643 | 171,574.812 | |
| 9th month | 629,750.042 | 51,300.241 | |
| 10th month | 803,221.051 | 59,223.168 | |
| 11th month | 571,397.356 | 53,085.659 | |
| 12th month | 1,251,789.326 | 453,675.967 | |
| *7th year (1802)* | *8,972,546* | *1,534,843* | |
| 1st month | 373,044.671 | 173.598 | |
| 2nd month | 1,264,390.913 | 172,184.011 | |
| 3rd month | 755,688.826 | 52,468.304 | |
| 4th month | 594,365.278 | 86,549.127 | |
| 5th month | 657,337.274 | 87,483.526 | |
| 6th month | 551,119.771 | 87,061.393 | |
| 7th month | 541,678.253 | 198,019.779 | |
| 8th month | 1,000,697.489 | 194,354.921 | |
| 9th month | 515,330.608 | 92,063.730 | |
| 10th month | 547,028.902 | 88,442.391 | |
| 11th month | 618,105.692 | 90,103.303 | |
| 12th month | 1,553,758.648 | 385,939.331 | |
| *8th year (1893)* | *9,720,027* | *1,355,672* | *Silver figure of the 12th month is incomplete in the original register.* |
| 1st month | 546,588.630 | 1,342.613 | |
| 2nd month | 1,384,266.385 | 89,180.280 | |
| Leap month | 585,307.889 | 88,168.037 | |
| 3rd month | 574,303.653 | 91,961.611 | |
| 4th month | 669,286.266 | 91,214.281 | |
| 5th month | 492,872.273 | 89,621.502 | |
| 6th month | 642,055.267 | 89,127.170 | |
| 7th month | 682,490.280 | 90,098.252 | |
| 8th month | 1,178,729.557 | 91,877.136 | |
| 9th month | 511,427.764 | 91,881.915 | |

| Year | Silver (taels) | Copper coins (strings) | Remarks |
|---|---|---|---|
| 10th month | 601,063.517 | 97,001.198 | |
| 11th month | 556,374.959 | 92,507.709 | |
| 12th month | 1,295,26x.777 | 351,690.223 | Silver figure of the 12th month is incomplete in the original register. |
| *9th year (1804)* | *9,228,114* | *1,340,321* | |
| 1st month | 227,122.109 | 1,055.226 | |
| 2nd month | 1,305,156.431 | 165,527.617 | |
| 3rd month | 539,107.562 | 160,939.221 | |
| 4th month | 625,276.201 | 93,423.379 | |
| 5th month | 488,340.522 | 89,012.031 | |
| 6th month | 509,176.250 | 93,347.862 | |
| 7th month | 688,521.246 | 89,208.738 | |
| 8th month | 955,806.969 | 90,264.004 | |
| 9th month | 536,775.810 | 91,561.427 | |
| 10th month | 607,849.073 | 89,986.450 | |
| 11th month | 1,302,805.091 | 90,993.039 | |
| 12th month | 1,442,176.927 | 285,001.854 | |
| *10th year (1805)* | *10,117,518*<br>*11,027,518** | *1,330,552* | |
| 1st month | 409,558.937 | 0.500 | |
| 2nd month | 1,185,763.559 | 94,900.171 | |
| 3rd month | 607,151.547 | 94,977.086 | |
| 4th month | 612,614.634 | 96,631.968 | |
| 5th month | 1,997,161.905 | 91,772.849 | |
| 6th month | 551,212.786 | 92,591.660 | |
| Leap month | 669,194.981 | 100,324.255 | |
| 7th month | 735,290.198 | 93,729.496 | |
| 8th month | 101,341.708 | 93,878.974 | |
| 9th month | 503,794.202 | 94,052.664 | |
| 10th month | 519,098.516 | 97,036.500 | |
| 11th month | 642,716.924 | 94,371.172 | |
| 12th month | 1,582,618.378 | 286,284.636 | |
| *12th year (1807)* | *9,871,636* | *1,486,325*<br>*1,446,607** | |

TABLE A.12 *Aggregate expenditures of the Silver Treasury during* Jiaqing, *1796–1820* (cont.)

| Year | Silver (taels) | Copper coins (strings) | Remarks |
|---|---|---|---|
| 1st month | 394,293.347 | 1,808.801 | |
| 2nd month | 1,157,584.234 | 94,318.034 | |
| 3rd month | 766,308.110 | 171,897.807 | |
| 4th month | 579,149.927 | 95,132.109 | |
| 5th month | 536,070.043 | 94,160.660 | |
| 6th month | 678,398.002 | 101,748.652 | |
| 7th month | 625,336.587 | 136,141.910 | |
| 8th month | 1,071,047.269 | 131,498.732 | |
| 9th month | 508,119.509 | 135,961.143 | |
| 10th month | 535,573.787 | 135,961.143 | |
| 11th month | 1,515,307.044 | 100,783.038 | |
| 12th month | 1,504,448.170 | 286,913.133 | |
| *13th year (1808)* | *9,350,104* | *1,159,101* | |
| 1st month | 206,294.429 | – | |
| 2nd month | 142,2761.035 | 96,083.977 | |
| 3rd month | 775,080.431 | 94,377.984 | |
| 4th month | 588,522.551 | 96,886.199 | |
| 5th month | 515,585.781 | 100,602.231 | |
| 6th month | 595,345.888 | 95,934.032 | |
| 7th month | 767,802.651 | 93,927.528 | |
| 8th month | 1,011,997.218 | 91,139.050 | |
| 9th month | 552,744.796 | 92,878.332 | |
| 10th month | 526,508.708 | 92,404.747 | |
| 11th month | 862,180.191 | 96,837.220 | |
| 12th month | 1,525,280.744 | 208,029.611 | |
| *14th year (1809)* | *8,830,739* | *1,294,884* | *Figures of the 12th month are incomplete in the original register.* |
| 1st month | 388,950.946 | 1,234.994 | |
| 2nd month | 1,162,905.722 | 92,426.933 | |
| 3rd month | 652,662.241 | 95,674.072 | |
| 4th month | 505,061.419 | 95,055.999 | |
| 5th month | 564,763.471 | 97,853.102 | |

| Year | Silver (taels) | Copper coins (strings) | Remarks |
|---|---|---|---|
| 6th month | 445,263.845 | 129,901.314 | |
| 7th month | 860,825.239 | 131,900.922 | |
| 8th month | 1,004,347.351 | 130,023.867 | |
| 9th month | 527,566.762 | 91,309.927 | |
| 10th month | 690,027.158 | 136,254.667 | |
| 11th month | 496,562.400 | 90,024.440 | |
| 12th month | 1,531,8x2.554 | 203,224.xxx | Figures of the 12th month are incomplete in the original register. |
| *16th year (1811)* | *11,572,992* | *1,365,986* | |
| 1st month | 423,533.727 | – | |
| 2nd month | 1,172,670.325 | 90,404.798 | |
| 3rd month | 730,169.690 | 100,313.388 | |
| Leap month | 535,512.209 | 94,517.327 | |
| 4th month | 778,482.171 | 95,398.191 | |
| 5th month | 743,715.161 | 93,104.539 | |
| 6th month | 559,722.762 | 94,714.062 | |
| 7th month | 696,706.255 | 101,185.515 | |
| 8th month | 1,123,027.261 | 96,249.163 | |
| 9th month | 610,821.572 | 95,689.956 | |
| 10th month | 664,440.147 | 92,370.459 | |
| 11th month | 1,972,436.531 | 146,327.301 | |
| 12th month | 1,561,754.310 | 265,711.565 | |
| *17th year (1812)* | *9,769,631* | *1,150,003* | |
| 1st month | 369,703.528 | – | |
| 2nd month | 1,225,984.561 | 89,130.690 | |
| 3rd month | 635,123.684 | 102,775.362 | |
| 4th month | 713,257.686 | 99,416.093 | |
| 5th month | 571,083.727 | 93,044.602 | |
| 6th month | 536,781.312 | 95,754.238 | |
| 7th month | 841,428.929 | 95,041.327 | |
| 8th month | 1,024,795.985 | 93,336.248 | |
| 9th month | 536,489.055 | 94,956.246 | |
| 10th month | 637,201.534 | 93,886.857 | |

TABLE A.12 *Aggregate expenditures of the Silver Treasury during* Jiaqing, *1796–1820* (cont.)

| Year | Silver (taels) | Copper coins (strings) | Remarks |
|---|---|---|---|
| 11th month | 1,098,934.624 | 91,258.610 | |
| 12th month | 1,578,845.939 | 201,402.955 | |
| *18th year (1813)* | *9,093,867* | *1,158,252* | |
| 1st month | 336,309.718 | 727.050 | |
| 2nd month | 1,121,850.034 | 93,415.534 | |
| 3rd month | 623,609.103 | 93,601.338 | |
| 4th month | 760,694.134 | 91,297.296 | |
| 5th month | 770,495.869 | 94,127.463 | |
| 6th month | 606,101.267 | 93,762.152 | |
| 7th month | 646,084.998 | 100,702.792 | |
| 8th month | 1,079,231.397 | 94,132.970 | |
| 9th month | 513,142.413 | 92,966.391 | |
| 10th month | 537,422.577 | 96,709.272 | |
| 11th month | 534,100.918 | 95,888.385 | |
| 12th month | 1,564,824.222 | 210,921.634 | |
| *19th year (1814)* | *9,679,662* | *1,300,769* | |
| 1st month | 135,979.105 | 595.283 | |
| 2nd month | 1,341,168.513 | 90,792.917 | |
| Leap month | 599,199.483 | 95,306.497 | |
| 3rd month | 573,044.802 | 98,972.644 | |
| 4th month | 497,670.122 | 101,324.906 | |
| 5th month | 549,824.107 | 93,856.342 | |
| 6th month | 518,366.510 | 94,623.904 | |
| 7th month | 573,335.555 | 121,235.544 | |
| 8th month | 1,092,742.261 | 99,595.138 | |
| 9th month | 545,170.063 | 101,244.906 | |
| 10th month | 507,594.962 | 94,048.882 | |
| 11th month | 546,538.185 | 99,711.273 | |
| 12th month | 2,199,028.033 | 209,461.189 | |
| *20th year (1815)* | *9,686,981* | *1,184,843* | |

| Year | Silver (taels) | Copper coins (strings) | Remarks |
|---|---|---|---|
| 1st month | 373,130.208 | 1,884.655 | |
| 2nd month | 1,136,900.843 | 96,418.493 | |
| 3rd month | 598,668.989 | 99,980.763 | |
| 4th month | 569,729.258 | 98,259.613 | |
| 5th month | 664,921.952 | 100,058.186 | |
| 6th month | 518,208.702 | 99,777.830 | |
| 7th month | 667,760.174 | 93,422.011 | |
| 8th month | 1,012,029.310 | 96,401.755 | |
| 9th month | 486,861.634 | 94,177.310 | |
| 10th month | 557,750.966 | 97,561.878 | |
| 11th month | 1,552,634.929 | 99,076.365 | |
| 12th month | 1,548,384.506 | 207,824.410 | |
| *21st year (1816)* | *8,778,984*<br>*10,379,921** | *1,222,295*<br>*1,429,077** | *Data of the 12th month are missing.* |
| 1st month | 226,835.169 | 3,789.943 | |
| 2nd month | 1,288,814.462 | 94,684.581 | |
| 3rd month | 687,166.225 | 99,225.377 | |
| 4th month | 495,418.723 | 102,074.169 | |
| 5th month | 566,293.070 | 93,366.485 | |
| 6th month | 507,729.337 | 240,591.500 | |
| Leap month | 557,637.477 | 99,320.485 | |
| 7th month | 783,915.053 | 104,346.530 | |
| 8th month | 1,008,958.174 | 94,793.222 | |
| 9th month | 549,788.779 | 98,035.228 | |
| 10th month | 495,068.975 | 96,112.788 | |
| 11th month | 1,611,358.202 | 95,954.468 | |
| *22nd year (1817)* | *10,487,742* | *1,247,637* | |
| 1st month | 388,972.228 | 1,405.075 | |
| 2nd month | 1,240,618.290 | 103,624.802 | |
| 3rd month | 772,818.194 | 114,258.000 | |
| 4th month | 607,064.385 | 93,921.268 | |
| 5th month | 505,584.810 | 111,979.049 | |
| 6th month | 657,123.817 | 114,782.104 | |
| 7th month | 633,092.912 | 103,049.403 | |
| 8th month | 1,105,242.119 | 100,291.933 | |

TABLE A.12 *Aggregate expenditures of the Silver Treasury during* Jiaqing, *1796–1820* (cont.)

| Year | Silver (taels) | Copper coins (strings) | Remarks |
|---|---|---|---|
| 9th month | 579,408.240 | 99,533.393 | |
| 10th month | 537,570.571 | 96,892.268 | |
| 11th month | 674,081.205 | 97,993.791 | |
| 12th month | 2,786,165.626 | 209,905.429 | |
| *23rd year (1818)* | *9,951,357* | *1,151,300* | |
| 1st month | 398,750.099 | – | |
| 2nd month | 1,043,974.650 | 93,361.422 | |
| 3rd month | 729,656.862 | 96,942.529 | |
| 4th month | 585,554.188 | 88,001.886 | |
| 5th month | 571,184.701 | 92,097.038 | |
| 6th month | 566,475.754 | 94,044.184 | |
| 7th month | 905,238.943 | 95,916.566 | |
| 8th month | 932,356.271 | 89,709.089 | |
| 9th month | 609,310.766 | 96,688.497 | |
| 10th month | 561,037.163 | 99,687.178 | |
| 11th month | 601,712.131 | 97,114.324 | |
| 12th month | 2,446,105.423 | 207,737.089 | |
| *24th year (1819)* | *10,933,233* | *1,245,253* | |
| 1st month | 341,302.478 | 2,507.718 | |
| 2nd month | 1,406,687.204 | 90,909.875 | |
| 3rd month | 659,444.280 | 95,422.413 | |
| 4th month | 577,666.324 | 92,869.184 | |
| Leap month | 564,959.105 | 95,259.123 | |
| 5th month | 490,097.682 | 95,974.391 | |
| 6th month | 743,788.796 | 104,117.743 | |
| 7th month | 586,394.500 | 92,592.337 | |
| 8th month | 1,032,306.361 | 96,194.752 | |
| 9th month | 554,861.045 | 90,603.897 | |
| 10th month | 743,134.592 | 91,208.274 | |
| 11th month | 1,616,642.418 | 92,705.069 | |
| 12th month | 1,615,948.692 | 204,887.971 | |

| Year | Silver (taels) | Copper coins (strings) | Remarks |
|---|---|---|---|
| *25th year (1820)* | *11,007,664* | *1,261,375* | |
| 1st month | 147,570.621 | 1,226.769 | |
| 2nd month | 1,287,624.543 | 86,115.656 | |
| 3rd month | 736,977.666 | 92,706.328 | |
| 4th month | 581,474.727 | 93,211.819 | |
| 5th month | 463,647.924 | 89,546.705 | |
| 6th month | 505,457.867 | 92,403.234 | |
| 7th month | 682,342.203 | 215,841.705 | |
| 8th month | 1,005,402.814 | 90,938.718 | |
| 9th month | 723,703.404 | 98,456.367 | |
| 10th month | 987,853.934 | 92,748.389 | |
| 11th month | 644,434.964 | 98,435.220 | |
| 12th month | 3,241,173.393 | 209,744.298 | |
| *Average of* Jiaqing | *12,703,994* | *1,199,300* | |

*Source*: figures marked with * are from four-column registers of each of the years; data of the 13rd year are from the aggregate expenditure register of the same year kept by FHAC; others are based on aggregate expenditure registers of Jiaqing, The Yellow Registers · The Silver Treasury of the Ministry of Revenue, Volumes 23–27. In calculating the averages, the silver figure of the 10th year, coin figure of the 12th year and silver and coin figures of the 21st year are based on the four-column registers.

TABLE A.13 *Payment surpluses/deficits of the Silver Treasury during* Jiaqing*, 1796–1819*

| Year | Aggregate revenue | | Aggregate expenditure | | Surplus/Deficit (+/–) | |
|---|---|---|---|---|---|---|
| | Silver (taels) | Copper coins (strings) | Silver (taels) | Copper coins (strings) | Silver (taels) | Copper soins (strings) |
| 1st year (1796) | 5,734,496 | 591,663* | 18,541,762 | 591,624 | –12,807,266 | +39 |
| 3rd year (1798) | 16,413,926 | 529,854 | 25,147,965* | 529,739* | –8,734,039 | +115 |
| 7th year (1802) | 11,496,754 | 1,534,981 | 8,972,546 | 1,534,843 | +2,524,208 | +138 |

TABLE A.13 *Payment surpluses/deficits of the Silver Treasury during* Jiaqing, *1796–1819* (cont.)

| Year | Aggregate revenue | | Aggregate expenditure | | Surplus/Deficit (+/–) | |
|---|---|---|---|---|---|---|
| | Silver (taels) | Copper coins (strings) | Silver (taels) | Copper coins (strings) | Silver (taels) | Copper soins (strings) |
| 9th year (1804) | 13,771,203 | 1,242,982 | 9,228,114 | 1,340,321 | +4,543,089 | –97,339 |
| 10th year (1805) | 13,933,953 | 1,327,850* | 11,027,518* | 1,330,552 | +2,906,435 | –2,702 |
| 12th year (1807) | 6,938,704 | 1,438,237 | 9,871,636 | 1,446,607* | –2,932,932 | –8,370 |
| 13th year (1808) | 9,736,061 | 1,248,030 | 9,350,104 | 1,159,101 | +385,957 | +88,929 |
| 14th year (1809) | 9,579,282 | 1,280,432 | 8,830,739 | 1,294,884 | +748,543 | –14,452 |
| 16th year (1811) | 9,448,666* | 1,366,085* | 11,572,992 | 1,365,986 | –2,124,326 | +99 |
| 17th year (1812) | 7,712,803 | 1,151,100 | 9,769,631 | 1,150,003 | –2,056,828 | +1,097 |
| 19th year (1814) | 12,100,661 | 1,312,241 | 9,679,662 | 1,300,769 | +2,420,999 | +11,472 |
| 20th year (1815) | 12,435,695 | 1,142,974 | 9,686,981 | 1,184,843 | +2,748,714 | –41,869 |
| 21st year (1816) | 9,451,035* | 1,496,370* | 10,379,921* | 1,429,077* | –928,886 | +67,293 |
| 22nd year (1817) | 10,637,957 | 1,168,451 | 10,487,742 | 1,247,637 | +150,215 | –79,186 |
| 23rd year (1818) | 13,990,810* | 1,195,427* | 9,951,357 | 1,151,300 | +4,039,453 | +44,127 |
| 24th year (1819) | 15,217,960 | 1,257,461 | 10,933,233 | 1,245,253 | +4,284,727 | +12,208 |
| *Average of* Jiaqing | *11,162,498* | *1,205,259* | *11,464,494* | *1,206,409* | *–301,996* | *–1,150* |

*Source*: based on Tables A.11 and A.12.

TABLE A.14 *Aggregate revenues of the Silver Treasury during* Daoguang, *1821–1850*

| Year | Silver (taels) | Copper coins (strings) | Remarks |
|---|---|---|---|
| *1st year (1821)* | *7,630,389* | *1,102,200* *1,202,200** | |
| 1st month | 422,106.530 | – | |
| 2nd month | 159,454.383 | 94,891.928 | |
| 3rd month | 385,615.222 | 52,881.585 | |
| 4th month | 217,332.534 | 45,191.866 | |
| 5th month | 320,465.522 | 94,549.053 | |
| 6th month | 831,167.304 | 103,926.163 | |
| 7th month | 151,014.535 | 91,340.000 | |
| 8th month | 58,059.275 | 102,762.398 | |
| 9th month | 670,691.589 | 102,017.125 | |
| 10th month | 491,875.164 | 94,969.640 | |
| 11th month | 388,290.366 | 94,739.451 | |
| 12th month | 3,534,316.532 | 224,930.458 | |
| *2nd year (1822)* | *7,060,251* | *1,189,489* | |
| 1st month | 718.506.287 | – | |
| 2nd month | 181.055.919 | 68,425.712 | |
| 3rd month | 261.643.130 | 91,695.723 | |
| Leap month | 222.016.789 | 93,802.306 | |
| 4th month | 80.802.377 | 84,846.630 | |
| 5th month | 238.268.355 | 95,801.366 | |
| 6th month | 311.665.935 | 98,652.778 | |
| 7th month | 164.637.318 | 94,402.640 | |
| 8th month | 799.33.214 | 96,977.664 | |
| 9th month | 91.420.503 | 93,511.640 | |
| 10th month | 148.166.410 | 59,025.640 | |
| 11th month | 1.222.092.610 | 115,189.726 | |
| 12th month | 3.340.042.482 | 197,157.286 | |
| *3rd year (1823)* | *8,183,826* | *1,121,547* | |
| 1st month | 689,255.721 | – | |
| 2nd month | 785,257.648 | 98,219.755 | |
| 3rd month | 803,324.439 | 60,429.524 | |

TABLE A.14 *Aggregate revenues of the Silver Treasury during* Daoguang, *1821–1850* (cont.)

| Year | Silver (taels) | Copper coins (strings) | Remarks |
|---|---|---|---|
| 4th month | 864,305.690 | 57,661.166 | |
| 5th month | 589,577.429 | 59,611.490 | |
| 6th month | 346,529.798 | 99,275.600 | |
| 7th month | 299,517.680 | 93,485.500 | |
| 8th month | 152,503.852 | 91,131.040 | |
| 9th month | 223,730.677 | 95,664.000 | |
| 10th month | 138,420.732 | 100,549.087 | |
| 11th month | 277,943.395 | 90,520.739 | |
| 12th month | 3,013,459.104 | 274,999.587 | |
| *4th year (1824)* | *6,979,498* | *1,248,822* | |
| 1st month | 161,276.607 | – | |
| 2nd month | 388,050.207 | 97,092.469 | |
| 3rd month | 247,173.472 | 111,946.614 | |
| 4th month | 261,350.987 | 89,588.323 | |
| 5th month | 296,402.638 | 96,752.774 | |
| 6th month | 24,757.422 | 102,086.084 | |
| 7th month | 233,519.339 | 92,488.214 | |
| Leap month | 443,358.298 | 95,858.658 | |
| 8th month | 266,488.252 | 94,351.030 | |
| 9th month | 293,549.168 | 96,550.155 | |
| 10th month | 958,702.140 | 98,037.413 | |
| 11th month | 171,667.798 | 14,827.911 | |
| 12th month | 3,233,201.972 | 259,242.772 | |
| *5th year (1825)* | *8,507,036* | *1183440* | |
| 1st month | 332,301.159 | – | |
| 2nd month | 462,383.719 | 90,875.000 | |
| 3rd month | 168,525.904 | 94,617.669 | |
| 4th month | 391,206.457 | 95,264.408 | |
| 5th month | 342,403.391 | 90,358.523 | |
| 6th month | 359,713.450 | 95,495.382 | |
| 7th month | 1,054,946.854 | 70,094.096 | |
| 8th month | 724,307.273 | 86,054.666 | |

| Year | Silver (taels) | Copper coins (strings) | Remarks |
|---|---|---|---|
| 9th month | 539,894.969 | 45,003.000 | |
| 10th month | 404,340.823 | 135,540.736 | |
| 11th month | 545,632.747 | 92,427.617 | |
| 12th month | 3,181,378.802 | 287,708.996 | |
| *7th year (1827)* | *23,802,617* | *1,232,145* | |
| 1st month | 520,208.820 | – | |
| 2nd month | 771,402.903 | 90,200.000 | |
| 3rd month | 1,163,824.720 | 96,986.400 | |
| 4th month | 1,375,595.088 | 94,916.859 | |
| 5th month | 637,380.831 | 98,739.856 | |
| Leap month | 485,214.782 | 93,444.268 | |
| 6th month | 656,305.246 | 83,522.925 | |
| 7th month | 1094,964.367 | 96,921.000 | |
| 8th month | 800,430.330 | 95,866.031 | |
| 9th month | 293,246.587 | 101,355.573 | |
| 10th month | 656,488.146 | 93,725.133 | |
| 11th month | 1,012,176.160 | 97,235.500 | |
| 12th month | 14,335,379.239 | 189,231.106 | |
| *8th year (1828)* | *14,422,806* | *1,166,798* | |
| 1st month | 290,795.347 | – | |
| 2nd month | 1,591,436.974 | 94,085.000 | |
| 3rd month | 2,914,259.313 | 94,897.836 | |
| 4th month | 696,170.090 | 96,546.833 | |
| 5th month | 532,505.636 | 97,566.620 | |
| 6th month | 282,639.827 | 93,346.400 | |
| 7th month | 389,287.292 | 95,459.814 | |
| 8th month | 396,941.653 | 96,187.767 | |
| 9th month | 1,175,044.290 | 101,050.616 | |
| 10th month | 994,113.297 | 95,602.582 | |
| 11th month | 1,055,030.711 | 94,551.400 | |
| 12th month | 4,104,581.911 | 207,502.751 | |
| *9th year (1829)* | *11,557,959* | *1,119,826* | |

TABLE A.14 *Aggregate revenues of the Silver Treasury during* Daoguang, *1821–1850* (cont.)

| Year | Silver (taels) | Copper coins (strings) | Remarks |
|---|---|---|---|
| 1st month | 7,282.506 | – | |
| 2nd month | 883,328.881 | 96,846.400 | |
| 3rd month | 816,413.153 | 95,632.500 | |
| 4th month | 846,671.817 | 58,096.400 | |
| 5th month | 1,165,955.276 | 57,058.115 | |
| 6th month | 507,528.460 | 58,076.000 | |
| 7th month | 1,156,244.368 | 95,149.838 | |
| 8th month | 244,676.943 | 95,018.693 | |
| 9th month | 1,260,225.088 | 98,164.997 | |
| 10th month | 483,221.299 | 97,978.548 | |
| 11th month | 1,317,235.200 | 97,546.400 | |
| 12th month | 2,869,175.784 | 270,258.442 | |
| *10th year (1830)* | *11,289,651* | *1,172,528* | |
| 1st month | 350,283.095 | – | |
| 2nd month | 1,073,480.713 | 94,860.000 | |
| 3rd month | 1,246,290.457 | 94,754.400 | |
| 4th month | 842,317.011 | 92,556.400 | |
| Leap month | 882,412.623 | 100,572.256 | |
| 5th month | 313,753.322 | 79,050.400 | |
| 6th month | 621,281.536 | 96,846.400 | |
| 7th month | 267,916.146 | 86,500.000 | |
| 8th month | 553,818.493 | 75,317.497 | |
| 9th month | 1,110,246.711 | 75,249.600 | |
| 10th month | 837,775.857 | 89,337.400 | |
| 11th month | 244,772.384 | 75,351.244 | |
| 12th month | 2,945,302.695 | 212,132.113 | |
| *12th year (1832)* | *8,019,701* | *1,212,995* | |
| 1st month | 99,273.948 | – | |
| 2nd month | 372,331.811 | 98,052.250 | |
| 3rd month | 830,038.932 | 88,538.932 | |
| 4th month | 997,975.642 | 91,416.689 | |
| 5th month | 1,150,735.175 | 79,231.580 | |

| Year | Silver (taels) | Copper coins (strings) | Remarks |
|---|---|---|---|
| 6th month | 414,761.422 | 93,546.800 | |
| 7th month | 275,533.779 | 101,003.891 | |
| 8th month | 90,895.282 | 77,400.000 | |
| 9th month | 406,162.184 | 117,519.211 | |
| Leap month | 346,155.182 | 97,979.000 | |
| 10th month | 191,824.895 | 92,573.796 | |
| 11th month | 94,210.302 | 88,290.641 | |
| 12th month | 2,749,802.020 | 187,442.573 | |
| *13th year (1833)* | *7,160,869* | *1,152,766* | |
| 1st month | 224,164.282 | – | |
| 2nd month | 254,795.164 | 86,182.400 | |
| 3rd month | 1,506,952.511 | 94,036.927 | |
| 4th month | 596,014.978 | 96,295.149 | |
| 5th month | 234,004.520 | 87,626.545 | |
| 6th month | 436,383.596 | 99,481.008 | |
| 7th month | 343,958.349 | 92,749.031 | |
| 8th month | 15,509.315 | 96,916.843 | |
| 9th month | 299,547.671 | 99,695.285 | |
| 10th month | 687,522.206 | 97,302.115 | |
| 11th month | 98,299.352 | 94,499.573 | |
| 12th month | 2,463,716.784 | 207,981.059 | |
| *14th year (1834)* | *15,522,250* | *1,183,232* | *The figure of copper coins of the 11th month does not match with the sum of the detailed amounts. There are errors in the detailed amounts.* |
| 1st month | 200,283.496 | – | |
| 2nd month | 356,421.662 | 95,025.672 | |
| 3rd month | 426,898.013 | 95,096.136 | |
| 4th month | 280,687.932 | 95,141.773 | |
| 5th month | 521,282.964 | 100,815.261 | |
| 6th month | 291,688.083 | 96,386.095 | |
| 7th month | 465,146.941 | 91,489.042 | |
| 8th month | 440,468.964 | 94,141.376 | |
| 9th month | 678,221.798 | 98,522.739 | |
| 10th month | 57,374.778 | 93,724.642 | |

TABLE A.14 *Aggregate revenues of the Silver Treasury during* Daoguang, *1821–1850* (cont.)

| Year | Silver (taels) | Copper coins (strings) | Remarks |
|---|---|---|---|
| 11th month | 627,845.827 | 96,400.569 | The figure of copper coins of the 11th month does not match with the sum of the detailed amounts. There are errors in the detailed amounts. |
| 12th month | 11,175,929.346 | 226,488.679 | |
| *16th year (1836)* | *9,551,051* | *1,148,372* | |
| 1st month | 400,116.451 | – | |
| 2nd month | 491,007.072 | 90,863.400 | |
| 3rd month | 1,174,381.012 | 95,943.393 | |
| 4th month | 1,015,092.361 | 96,224.167 | |
| 5th month | 829,462.991 | 92,701.655 | |
| 6th month | 480,721.308 | 95,288.237 | |
| 7th month | 378,676.882 | 94,645.278 | |
| 8th month | 280,446.349 | 92,946.740 | |
| 9th month | 592,038.501 | 95,093.345 | |
| 10th month | 435,908.661 | 97,197.353 | |
| 11th month | 780,960.563 | 94,437.391 | |
| 12th month | 2,692,239.319 | 203,031.452 | |
| *19th year (1839)* | *8,691,741* | *1,143,851* | |
| 1st month | 643,712.464 | – | |
| 2nd month | 1,020,240.070 | 96,468.255 | |
| 3rd month | 301,374.877 | 93,316.656 | |
| 4th month | 630,745.268 | 91,543.861 | |
| 5th month | 786,536.711 | 92,042.236 | |
| 6th month | 717,250.039 | 94,566.372 | |
| 7th month | 100,885.777 | 94,837.743 | |
| 8th month | 598,008.430 | 93,333.389 | |
| 9th month | 469,624.436 | 92,975.375 | |
| 10th month | 325,199.452 | 95,415.289 | |
| 11th month | 548,839.601 | 93,327.352 | |
| 12th month | 2,549,323.801 | 206,024.040 | |

| Year | Silver (taels) | Copper coins (strings) | Remarks |
|---|---|---|---|
| *20th year (1840)* | *10,349,975* | *1,137,631* | *The totals of the 3rd and the 12th months do not match with the sums of the detailed amounts.* |
| 1st month | – | – | |
| 2nd month | 2,532,343.951 | 90,849.874 | |
| 3rd month | 311,098.948 | 92,923.904 | The totals are different from the sums of the detailed amounts. |
| 4th month | 592,661.132 | 102,331.732 | |
| 5th month | 837,295.959 | 86,043.236 | |
| 6th month | 859,340.333 | 95,692.972 | |
| 7th month | 388,362.711 | 90,659.833 | |
| 8th month | 196,099.136 | 94,947.301 | |
| 9th month | 758,248.378 | 92,608.013 | |
| 10th month | 486,070.264 | 95,266.675 | |
| 11th month | 978,994.441 | 92,037.968 | |
| 12th month | 2,409,459.954 | 204,269.402 | The totals are different from the sums of the detailed amounts. |
| *21st year (1841)* | *6,796,038* | *1,233,614* | |
| 1st month | 790,755.792 | – | |
| 2nd month | 621,875.102 | 101,450.232 | |
| 3rd month | 634,056.134 | 132,139.359 | |
| Leap month | 220,368.375 | 49,610.029 | |
| 4th month | 608,758.011 | 191,884.535 | |
| 5th month | 481,516.345 | 91,575.331 | |
| 6th month | 128,276.633 | 88,926.100 | |
| 7th month | 251,318.792 | 9,361.457 | |
| 8th month | 157,627.257 | 10,4031.109 | |
| 9th month | 119,963.137 | 60,468.270 | |
| 10th month | 268,593.051 | 54,203.182 | |
| 11th month | 348,087.586 | 158,320.251 | |
| 12th month | 2,164,841.718 | 191,644.388 | |
| *22nd year (1842)* | *10,914,111* | *1,144,433* | |
| 1st month | 475,998.686 | – | |
| 2nd month | 330,572.588 | 175,527.293 | |

TABLE A.14 *Aggregate revenues of the Silver Treasury during* Daoguang, *1821–1850* (cont.)

| Year | Silver (taels) | Copper coins (strings) | Remarks |
|---|---|---|---|
| 3rd month | 198,743.842 | 93,144.014 | |
| 4th month | 34,165.837 | 97,174.047 | |
| 5th month | 77,268.513 | 89,614.565 | |
| 6th month | 114,200.401 | 94,291.051 | |
| 7th month | 308,786.032 | 18,445.063 | |
| 8th month | 165,712.279 | 166,244.726 | |
| 9th month | 82,038.102 | 97,112.311 | |
| 10th month | 227,278.212 | 94,377.639 | |
| 11th month | 310,264.438 | 101,507.966 | |
| 12th month | 8,589,081.672 | 116,994.148 | |
| *23rd year (1843)* | *7,919,693* | *1,222,831* | |
| 1st month | 227,955.472 | – | |
| 2nd month | 43,860.306 | 170,663.661 | |
| 3rd month | 935,423.594 | 90,914.540 | |
| 4th month | 31,781.878 | 93,288.571 | |
| 5th month | 437,111.643 | 91,211.566 | |
| 6th month | 183,915.041 | 93,330.543 | |
| 7th month | 414,428.496 | 93,312.588 | |
| Leap month | 137,439.691 | 15,786.888 | |
| 8th month | 172,811.901 | 168,196.015 | |
| 9th month | 344,713.887 | 92,791.864 | |
| 10th month | 1,890,457.477 | 94,339.764 | |
| 11th month | 134,311.227 | 98,385.762 | |
| 12th month | 2,965,482.032 | 120,609.669 | |
| *25th year (1845)* | *9,069,654* | *1,160,832* | |
| 1st month | 131,602.842 | – | |
| 2nd month | 1,077,193.107 | 97,022.200 | |
| 3rd month | 1,206,446.535 | 96,960.200 | |
| 4th month | 456,961.761 | 96,545.679 | |
| 5th month | 562,692.529 | 97,016.403 | |
| 6th month | 748,176.714 | 96,920.200 | |
| 7th month | 763,379.300 | 97,685.099 | |

| Year | Silver (taels) | Copper coins (strings) | Remarks |
|---|---|---|---|
| 8th month | 501,250.242 | 96,997.568 | |
| 9th month | 300,124.865 | 96,938.864 | |
| 10th month | 1,123,807.918 | 96,967.500 | |
| 11th month | 477,137.254 | 97,112.168 | |
| 12th month | 1,720,880.756 | 190,666.089 | |
| *26th year (1846)* | *9,044,024* | *1,209,094* | |
| 1st month | 948,142.290 | – | |
| 2nd month | 620,221.621 | 97,035.200 | |
| 3rd month | 301,669.974 | 97,030.200 | |
| 4th month | 545,507.824 | 95,386.990 | |
| 5th month | 609,384.736 | 98,691.660 | |
| Leap month | 846,788.182 | 96,940.200 | |
| 6th month | 583,838.289 | 73,504.000 | |
| 7th month | 324,512.377 | 97,895.994 | |
| 8th month | 380,748.359 | 95,157.193 | |
| 9th month | 461,805.045 | 90,178.316 | |
| 10th month | 627,816.808 | 88,415.309 | |
| 11th month | 1,259,396.755 | 88,501.308 | |
| 12th month | 1,534,191.946 | 190,357.852 | |
| *28th year (1848)* | *8,872,940* | *1,165,946* | |
| 1st month | 220,040.678 | – | |
| 2nd month | 708,583.596 | 97,409.427 | |
| 3rd month | 1,050,502.213 | 92,496.989 | |
| 4th month | 674,479.145 | 91,145.051 | |
| 5th month | 1,010,705.963 | 100,263.558 | |
| 6th month | 435,513.821 | 100,440.412 | |
| 7th month | 682,494.255 | 103,476.414 | |
| 8th month | 507,032.949 | 97,431.120 | |
| 9th month | 720,590.034 | 97,333.120 | |
| 10th month | 255,629.921 | 97,333.120 | |
| 11th month | 273,155.315 | 97,444.439 | |
| 12th month | 2,334,211.745 | 191,172.397 | |
| *29th year (1849)* | *8,507,408* | *1,238,528* | |

TABLE A.14 *Aggregate revenues of the Silver Treasury during* Daoguang, *1821–1850* (cont.)

| Year | Silver (taels) | Copper coins (strings) | Remarks |
|---|---|---|---|
| 1st month | 737,928.259 | – | |
| 2nd month | 874,168.705 | 97,333.120 | |
| 3rd month | 738,083.369 | 97,383.120 | |
| 4th month | 288,618.234 | 96,925.770 | |
| Leap month | 1,046,670.696 | 97,333.120 | |
| 5th month | 273,969.676 | 75,323.659 | |
| 6th month | 124,944.355 | 95,549.966 | |
| 7th month | 963,305.148 | 97,963.019 | |
| 8th month | 95,493.078 | 97,333.120 | |
| 9th month | 462,376.847 | 97,354.258 | |
| 10th month | 500,153.575 | 97,342.738 | |
| 11th month | 1,234,358.644 | 97,408.225 | |
| 12th month | 1,441,307.392 | 191,277.739 | |
| *30th year (1850)* | *7.748.585* | *1,076,127* | *Data of the 12th month are incomplete in the original register.* |
| 1st month | 599.431.572 | – | |
| 2nd month | 332.881.142 | 97,333.120 | |
| 3rd month | 578.614.782 | 97,333.120 | |
| 4th month | 528.806.603 | 96,881.064 | |
| 5th month | 477.775.819 | 97,333.120 | |
| 6th month | 1.103.676.583 | 97,333.120 | |
| 7th month | 221.504.416 | 97,998.014 | |
| 8th month | 787.746.471 | 97,333.120 | |
| 9th month | 934.060.932 | 93,864.132 | |
| 10th month | 823.699.315 | 100,806.018 | |
| 11th month | 767.787.833 | 94,123.951 | |
| 12th month | 592.599.529 | 105,788.544 | Data of the 12th month are incomplete. |
| *Average of* Daoguang | *9.895.742* | *1,176,828* | |

*Source*: based on aggregate revenue registers of Daoguang, The Yellow Registers (The Silver Treasury of the Ministry of Revenue), Volumes 10–11 (the coin figure of annual total of the 1st year marked with * is from the four-column register of the year). In calculating the averages, the coin figure of the 1st year is based on the record of the four-column register.

TABLE A.15 *Aggregate expenditures of the Silver Treasury during* Daoguang, *1821–1850*

| Year | Silver (taels) | Copper coins (strings) | Remarks |
|---|---|---|---|
| *1st year* (*1821*) | *11,351,701* | *1,203,759*<br>*1,203,756** | |
| 1st month | 254,724.448 | 7,298.253 | |
| 2nd month | 1,569,563.499 | 93,470.385 | |
| 3rd month | 751,146.078 | 98,817.300 | |
| 4th month | 631,476.168 | 102,054.830 | |
| 5th month | 578,519.546 | 96,682.598 | |
| 6th month | 591,623.700 | 102,664.413 | |
| 7th month | 517,516.820 | 91,266.175 | |
| 8th month | 1,208,115.683 | 102,738.895 | |
| 9th month | 734,434.031 | 102,292.452 | |
| 10th month | 609,516.635 | 96,536.727 | |
| 11th month | 507,291.271 | 92,441.359 | |
| 12th month | 3,397,773.241 | 217,495.729 | |
| *2nd year* (*1822*) | *8,448,826*<br>*11,210,691** | *986,526*<br>*1,199,720** | *Data of the 12th month are missing.* |
| 1st month | 139,292.688 | 3,393.148 | |
| 2nd month | 1,548,753.309 | 92,908.063 | |
| 3rd month | 650,175.570 | 99,073.865 | |
| Leap month | 560,295.169 | 93,565.583 | |
| 4th month | 674,386.685 | 99,887.084 | |
| 5th month | 579,860.201 | 95,649.309 | |
| 6th month | 527,527.663 | 99,833.543 | |
| 7th month | 615,536.358 | 94,602.233 | |
| 8th month | 1,229,145.158 | 95,744.948 | |
| 9th month | 681,428.277 | 94,427.007 | |
| 10th month | 665,039.947 | 59,156.375 | |
| 11th month | 577,384.577 | 58,284.961 | |
| *3rd year* (*1823*) | *9,948,689* | *1,094,563* | |
| 1st month | 130,482.030 | 1,739.218 | |
| 2nd month | 1,504,358.997 | 95,733.084 | |
| 3rd month | 815,085.308 | 59,909.869 | |
| 4th month | 609,468.508 | 60,454.250 | |

TABLE A.15 *Aggregate expenditures of the Silver Treasury during* Daoguang, *1821–1850* (cont.)

| Year | Silver (taels) | Copper coins (strings) | Remarks |
|---|---|---|---|
| 5th month | 567,152.362 | 96,508.584 | |
| 6th month | 516,137.016 | 97,808.142 | |
| 7th month | 621,731.251 | 91,147.333 | |
| 8th month | 1,886,377.333 | 93,657.878 | |
| 9th month | 677,686.456 | 101,613.487 | |
| 10th month | 599,281.068 | 92,214.536 | |
| 11th month | 556,700.443 | 91,094.631 | |
| 12th month | 1,464,228.339 | 212,682.142 | |
| *5th year (1825)* | *9,218,328* | *1,151,721* | |
| 1st month | 135,695.306 | 713.712 | |
| 2nd month | 1,511,894.065 | 89,826.308 | |
| 3rd month | 613,398.795 | 94,968.379 | |
| 4th month | 574,947.973 | 93,798.052 | |
| 5th month | 803,830.379 | 94,083.247 | |
| 6th month | 526,025.125 | 90,906.201 | |
| 7th month | 551,896.228 | 94,612.920 | |
| 8th month | 1,117,062.210 | 95,953.493 | |
| 9th month | 582,514.123 | 93,323.712 | |
| 10th month | 567,175.549 | 97,760.534 | |
| 11th month | 551,473.032 | 93,872.321 | |
| 12th month | 1,682,414.985 | 211,902.523 | |
| *6th year (1826)* | *10,935,445* | *1,154,420* | |
| 1st month | 147,700.959 | 264.364 | |
| 2nd month | 1,449,965.988 | 89,540.890 | |
| 3rd month | 874,805.015 | 93,784.072 | |
| 4th month | 578,758.192 | 96,513.373 | |
| 5th month | 535,172.510 | 93,715.998 | |
| 6th month | 528,178.453 | 96,204.979 | |
| 7th month | 506,190.341 | 96,918.959 | |
| 8th month | 1,096,075.101 | 98,376.682 | |
| 9th month | 507,468.131 | 91,730.384 | |
| 10th month | 2,560,809.908 | 92,530.645 | |

| Year | Silver (taels) | Copper coins (strings) | Remarks |
|---|---|---|---|
| 11th month | 596,308.937 | 95,697.572 | |
| 12th month | 1,554,011.320 | 209,142.393 | |
| *7th year (1827)* | *11,373,705* | *1,252,178* | |
| 1st month | 121,294.364 | – | |
| 2nd month | 1,452,239.210 | 90,242.559 | |
| 3rd month | 613,795.226 | 95,062.377 | |
| 4th month | 527,673.934 | 97,137.812 | |
| 5th month | 537,690.115 | 94,124.162 | |
| Leap month | 493,526.694 | 92,217.873 | |
| 6th month | 509,054.245 | 95,410.124 | |
| 7th month | 478,887.613 | 96,086.479 | |
| 8th month | 2,045,116.312 | 98,812.430 | |
| 9th month | 675,664.998 | 97,166.498 | |
| 10th month | 584,751.085 | 89,858.893 | |
| 11th month | 502,249.237 | 97,451.524 | |
| 12th month | 2,831,762.017 | 208,607.513 | |
| *8th year (1828)* | *10,951,956* | *1,158,856* | |
| 1st month | 134,704.355 | 2,048.757 | |
| 2nd month | 1420,172.933 | 90,689.772 | |
| 3rd month | 609,093.182 | 94,236.247 | |
| 4th month | 609,939.361 | 97,912.541 | |
| 5th month | 463,215.974 | 92,380.638 | |
| 6th month | 753,601.217 | 95,764.941 | |
| 7th month | 539,511.519 | 91,209.102 | |
| 8th month | 1,116,347.971 | 98,339.234 | |
| 9th month | 574,953.555 | 96,720.616 | |
| 10th month | 534,124.714 | 94,953.257 | |
| 11th month | 675,224.434 | 97,660.757 | |
| 12th month | 3,521,066.979 | 206,940.554 | |
| *9th year (1829)* | *11,713,017* | *1,047,489* | |
| 1st month | 125,042.046 | – | |
| 2nd month | 1,829,209.021 | 96,700.913 | |

TABLE A.15 *Aggregate expenditures of the Silver Treasury during* Daoguang, *1821–1850* (cont.)

| Year | Silver (taels) | Copper coins (strings) | Remarks |
|---|---|---|---|
| 3rd month | 702,639.340 | 95,040.831 | |
| 4th month | 621,144.561 | 57,937.012 | |
| 5th month | 570,790.288 | 55,179.925 | |
| 6th month | 565,387.956 | 57,665.319 | |
| 7th month | 684,424.330 | 93,668.987 | |
| 8th month | 1,380,087.128 | 96,444.558 | |
| 9th month | 477,035.563 | 94,607.042 | |
| 10th month | 610,349.080 | 97,605.560 | |
| 11th month | 570,508.495 | 98,096.303 | |
| 12th month | 3,576,398.974 | 204,542.259 | |
| *10th year (1830)* | *12,575,834* | *1,245,338*<br>*1,244,338** | |
| 1st month | 137,323.214 | – | |
| 2nd month | 1,442,660.549 | 95,784.330 | |
| 3rd month | 673,066.215 | 94,212.881 | |
| 4th month | 546,275.836 | 92,010.535 | |
| Leap month | 617,937.838 | 99,230.344 | |
| 5th month | 573,954.828 | 96,689.623 | |
| 6th month | 500,926.410 | 93,702.443 | |
| 7th month | 500,859.910 | 89,743.447 | |
| 8th month | 1,082,857.529 | 95,093.699 | |
| 9th month | 691,353.189 | 97,260.532 | |
| 10th month | 1,514,717.543 | 92,516.453 | |
| 11th month | 1,521,614.466 | 93,084.511 | |
| 12th month | 2,772,286.734 | 206,009.009 | |
| *11th year (1831)* | *10,392,799* | *1,136,417* | |
| 1st month | 180,665.917 | – | |
| 2nd month | 1,330,447.603 | 93,057.078 | |
| 3rd month | 617,637.894 | 94,044.599 | |
| 4th month | 523,519.575 | 94,314.255 | |
| 5th month | 574,374.393 | 92,000.245 | |
| 6th month | 517,937.147 | 93,925.915 | |
| 7th month | 1,024,109.336 | 93,125.005 | |

| Year | Silver (taels) | Copper coins (strings) | Remarks |
|---|---|---|---|
| 8th month | 1,059,679.105 | 89,424.657 | |
| 9th month | 605,310.827 | 92,866.686 | |
| 10th month | 520,872.939 | 97,468.879 | |
| 11th month | 518,350.654 | 90,462.063 | |
| 12th month | 2,919,893.911 | 205,727.208 | |
| *12th year (1832)* | *10,987,586* | *1,226,884* | |
| 1st month | 129,328.533 | 1,556.890 | |
| 2nd month | 1,638,535.795 | 86,813.849 | |
| 3rd month | 668,593.170 | 98,104.850 | |
| 4th month | 510,202.890 | 91,367.366 | |
| 5th month | 659,062.567 | 93,851.277 | |
| 6th month | 518,052.923 | 91,925.256 | |
| 7th month | 573,016.041 | 96,078.820 | |
| 8th month | 1,113,815.825 | 92,212.079 | |
| 9th month | 534,668.870 | 91,234.541 | |
| Leap month | 551,739.554 | 99,498.009 | |
| 10th month | 745,504.594 | 92,417.189 | |
| 11th month | 574,904.681 | 89,714.929 | |
| 12th month | 2,770,160.803 | 202,108.762 | |
| *13th year (1833)* | *10,886,616* | *1,151,531* | |
| 1st month | 133,859.237 | – | |
| 2nd month | 1,599,706.064 | 86,181.056 | |
| 3rd month | 643,280.770 | 94,028.255 | |
| 4th month | 712,786.457 | 96,410.598 | |
| 5th month | 736,359.640 | 90,892.470 | |
| 6th month | 503,516.268 | 95,393.360 | |
| 7th month | 522,530.378 | 92,156.756 | |
| 8th month | 1,503,535.235 | 93,448.149 | |
| 9th month | 550,751.290 | 100,582.515 | |
| 10th month | 588,104.786 | 102,457.370 | |
| 11th month | 642,292.906 | 93,189.902 | |
| 12th month | 2,749,892.730 | 206,790.464 | |

TABLE A.15 *Aggregate expenditures of the Silver Treasury during* Daoguang, *1821–1850* (cont.)

| Year | Silver (taels) | Copper coins (strings) | Remarks |
|---|---|---|---|
| *14th year (1834)* | *10,773,739* | *1,160,590* | |
| 1st month | 131,370.496 | 5,189.923 | |
| 2nd month | 1,430,026.269 | 89,441.634 | |
| 3rd month | 662,251.214 | 98,050.935 | |
| 4th month | 726,425.930 | 96,953.614 | |
| 5th month | 572,704.924 | 96,199.996 | |
| 6th month | 502,202.241 | 93,511.944 | |
| 7th month | 788,447.561 | 93,991.443 | |
| 8th month | 1,167,065.476 | 96,283.061 | |
| 9th month | 542,477.791 | 95,581.424 | |
| 10th month | 581,456.287 | 93,719.942 | |
| 11th month | 541,645.374 | 97,269.512 | |
| 12th month | 3,127,665.106 | 204,396.911 | |
| *17th year (1837)* | *9,627,521* | *1,153,751* | |
| 1st month | 128,241.461 | – | |
| 2nd month | 1,349,473.860 | 93,431.838 | |
| 3rd month | 754,137.066 | 94,954.184 | |
| 4th month | 644,527.068 | 92,367.912 | |
| 5th month | 601,444.904 | 93,448.482 | |
| 6th month | 595,349.523 | 96,881.616 | |
| 7th month | 510,701.222 | 91,933.396 | |
| 8th month | 1,101,863.215 | 95,295.610 | |
| 9th month | 482,833.559 | 95,325.715 | |
| 10th month | 535,379.774 | 97,098.936 | |
| 11th month | 625,906.335 | 95,541.805 | |
| 12th month | 2,297,662.766 | 207,471.558 | |
| *18th year (1838)* | *8,109,147* | *770,252* | *Data of the 12th month are missing.* |
| 1st month | 130,809.030 | – | |
| 2nd month | 1,448,914.051 | 53,266.455 | |
| 3rd month | 666,615.445 | 19,142.635 | |
| 4th month | 701,934.803 | 55,517.234 | |

| Year | Silver (taels) | Copper coins (strings) | Remarks |
|---|---|---|---|
| Leap month | 604,085.443 | 75,793.575 | |
| 5th month | 509,329.739 | 74,640.693 | |
| 6th month | 551,510.610 | 76,438.960 | |
| 7th month | 577,247.886 | 73,664.776 | |
| 8th month | 1,144,399.948 | 76,448.129 | |
| 9th month | 633,776.930 | 75,545.838 | |
| 10th month | 508,595.758 | 92,987.268 | |
| 11th month | 631,926.859 | 96,806.222 | |
| *19th year (1839)* | *10,127,680* | *1,143,703* | |
| 1st month | 162,493.491 | 837.550 | |
| 2nd month | 1,485,461.003 | 95,703.555 | |
| 3rd month | 634,843.365 | 93,206.046 | |
| 4th month | 652,606.785 | 91,578.431 | |
| 5th month | 570,718.542 | 92,033.195 | |
| 6th month | 588,724.104 | 94,528.504 | |
| 7th month | 589,954.511 | 94,855.043 | |
| 8th month | 1,049,455.925 | 93,315.270 | |
| 9th month | 527,715.911 | 92,980.460 | |
| 10th month | 551,826.985 | 95,365.589 | |
| 11th month | 587,653.716 | 93,301.252 | |
| 12th month | 2,726,225.454 | 205,997.613 | |
| *20th year (1840)* | *10,312,241* | *1,139,506* | |
| 1st month | 163,085.754 | – | |
| 2nd month | 1,324,944.722 | 95,253.904 | |
| 3rd month | 769,505.161 | 92,526.371 | |
| 4th month | 661,963.238 | 93,525.219 | |
| 5th month | 593,560.303 | 94,929.258 | |
| 6th month | 603,212.334 | 92,935.732 | |
| 7th month | 561,786.983 | 93,311.891 | |
| 8th month | 1,079,540.900 | 91,956.316 | |
| 9th month | 527,525.934 | 93,751.381 | |
| 10th month | 668,670.410 | 95,801.765 | |
| 11th month | 552,707.167 | 92,506.846 | |

TABLE A.15 *Aggregate expenditures of the Silver Treasury during* Daoguang, *1821–1850* (cont.)

| Year | Silver (taels) | Copper coins (strings) | Remarks |
|---|---|---|---|
| 12th month | 2,805,737.976 | 203,007.633 | |
| *21st year (1841)* | *15,733,178* | *1,233,598* | |
| 1st month | 184,153.032 | – | |
| 2nd month | 2,413,326.351 | 96703.039 | |
| 3rd month | 598,248.032 | 92,102.729 | |
| Leap month | 1,186,865.467 | 91,026.652 | |
| 4th month | 580,897.143 | 91,447.276 | |
| 5th month | 615,086.446 | 94,247.113 | |
| 6th month | 583,178.864 | 92,270.280 | |
| 7th month | 490,938.411 | 94,051.414 | |
| 8th month | 1,084,805.914 | 95,658.980 | |
| 9th month | 3,511,974.635 | 96,150.482 | |
| 10th month | 556,018.903 | 92,258.784 | |
| 11th month | 1,484,340.118 | 93,557.306 | |
| 12th month | 2,443,344.761 | 204,124.252 | |
| *22nd year (1842)* | *13,519,847* | *1,140,848* | |
| 1st month | 1,151,872.414 | – | |
| 2nd month | 2,353,477.650 | 93,287.819 | |
| 3rd month | 670,584.104 | 92,536.133 | |
| 4th month | 616,060.960 | 103,786.148 | |
| 5th month | 1,043,463.413 | 90,581.901 | |
| 6th month | 1,132,507.512 | 92,402.333 | |
| 7th month | 529,673.311 | 94,640.437 | |
| 8th month | 1,081,721.143 | 90,806.584 | |
| 9th month | 557,171.961 | 96,802.863 | |
| 10th month | 571,373.448 | 93,966.178 | |
| 11th month | 666,180.179 | 91,295.401 | |
| 12th month | 3,145,760.538 | 200,742.554 | |
| *23rd year (1843)* | *10,989,389* <br> *10,992,455** | *1,270,073* | |
| 1st month | 194,746.983 | – | |

| Year | Silver (taels) | Copper coins (strings) | Remarks |
| --- | --- | --- | --- |
| 2nd month | 1,449,476.139 | 94,499.100 | |
| 3rd month | 675,143.349 | 92,108.634 | |
| 4th month | 672,355.133 | 93,186.325 | |
| 5th month | 587,940.901 | 91,708.700 | |
| 6th month | 523,128.446 | 92,504.797 | |
| 7th month | 517,434.165 | 92,229.516 | |
| Leap month | 475,141.050 | 92,271.285 | |
| 8th month | 1,063,789.052 | 91,898.725 | |
| 9th month | 492,363.072 | 94,459.642 | |
| 10th month | 2,000,197.677 | 94,356.582 | |
| 11th month | 547,923.132 | 91,249.881 | |
| 12th month | 1,789,749.872 | 249,599.813 | |
| *24th year (1844)* | *9,018,625* | *1,266,883* | |
| 1st month | 135,501.058 | – | |
| 2nd month | 1,272,180.462 | 114,250.534 | |
| 3rd month | 490,019.686 | 111,814.661 | |
| 4th month | 609,650.176 | 111,606.605 | |
| 5th month | 512,117.580 | 121,433.885 | |
| 6th month | 472,430.271 | 112,936.289 | |
| 7th month | 451,081.546 | 108,481.816 | |
| 8th month | 1,099,215.233 | 111,847.752 | |
| 9th month | 1,565,157.847 | 117,739.808 | |
| 10th month | 439,196.284 | 112,699.572 | |
| 11th month | 485,565.308 | 112,045.322 | |
| 12th month | 1,486,509.214 | 246,277.072 | |
| *25th year (1845)* | *8,737,519* | *1,014,232* | |
| 1st month | 118,762.500 | – | |
| 2nd month | 1,352,444.276 | 75,566.934 | |
| 3rd month | 608,593.639 | 73,765.974 | |
| 4th month | 535,418.106 | 77,426.144 | |
| 5th month | 516,642.224 | 72,365.404 | |
| 6th month | 600,263.089 | 76,184.168 | |
| 7th month | 503,758.174 | 71,468.109 | |
| 8th month | 1,045,237.843 | 73,296.061 | |

TABLE A.15 *Aggregate expenditures of the Silver Treasury during* Daoguang, *1821–1850* (cont.)

| Year | Silver (taels) | Copper coins (strings) | Remarks |
|---|---|---|---|
| 9th month | 521,987.086 | 77,150.783 | |
| 10th month | 561,212.101 | 95,197.830 | |
| 11th month | 517,303.275 | 96,585.072 | |
| 12th month | 1,855,896.561 | 225,225.733 | |
| *27th year (1847)* | *8,479,905* | *1,158,391* | |
| 1st month | 143,654.641 | – | |
| 2nd month | 1,420,248.285 | 98,005.390 | |
| 3rd month | 523,073.634 | 90,090.412 | |
| 4th month | 629,182.276 | 92,850.817 | |
| 5th month | 552,059.716 | 95,068.883 | |
| 6th month | 489,083.281 | 92,834.130 | |
| 7th month | 472,170.176 | 90,828.401 | |
| 8th month | 1,141,483.026 | 117,768.692 | |
| 9th month | 480,658.927 | 97,495.797 | |
| 10th month | 601,551.716 | 90,150.484 | |
| 11th month | 519,838.344 | 94,366.240 | |
| 12th month | 1,506,901.414 | 198,931.857 | |
| *29th year (1849)* | *9,340,395* | *1,219,044* | |
| 1st month | 161,266.871 | – | |
| 2nd month | 1,364,097.034 | 94,119.042 | |
| 3rd month | 750,691.183 | 89,290.649 | |
| 4th month | 551,383.767 | 97,686.832 | |
| Leap month | 586,430.451 | 88,288.292 | |
| 5th month | 525,347.217 | 95,539.978 | |
| 6th month | 573,486.443 | 91,164.874 | |
| 7th month | 515,125.051 | 90,801.871 | |
| 8th month | 1,106,711.024 | 96,300.063 | |
| 9th month | 520,653.181 | 97,430.319 | |
| 10th month | 576,395.527 | 89,927.420 | |
| 11th month | 540,292.246 | 92,397.539 | |
| 12th month | 1,568,514.589 | 196,096.944 | |

| Year | Silver (taels) | Copper coins (strings) | Remarks |
|---|---|---|---|
| *30th year (1850)* | *9,531,910* | *1,177,265* | |
| 1st month | 160,962.943 | – | |
| 2nd month | 1,359,309.507 | 91,576.668 | |
| 3rd month | 1,065,948.171 | 95,769.625 | |
| 4th month | 623,997.678 | 92,807.997 | |
| 5th month | 584,331.445 | 96,767.617 | |
| 6th month | 533,848.767 | 92,279.090 | |
| 7th month | 555,273.303 | 93,155.414 | |
| 8th month | 1,198,881.019 | 112,999.939 | |
| 9th month | 674,856.901 | 93,864.132 | |
| 10th month | 634,592.896 | 109,099.148 | |
| 11th month | 551,137.036 | 94,123.951 | |
| 12th month | 1,588,770.553 | 204,821.747 | |
| *Average of* Daoguang | *10,633,899* | *1,154,840* | |

*Source*: figures marked with * from four-column registers of each of the years; others are based on aggregate expenditure registers of Daoguang, The Yellow Registers (The Silver Treasury of the Ministry of Revenue), Volumes 28–32. In calculating the averages, the coin figure of the 1st year and the silver and coin figures of the 2nd year are based on the four-column registers, and the coin figure of the 10th year and the silver figure of the 23rd year are based on the aggregate expenditure registers.

TABLE A.16 *Payment surpluses/deficits of the Silver Treasury during* Daoguang, *1821–1850*

| Year | Aggregate revenue | | Aggregate expenditure | | Surplus/Deficit (+/–) | |
|---|---|---|---|---|---|---|
| | Silver (taels) | Copper coins (strings) | Silver (taels) | Copper coins (strings) | Silver (taels) | Copper coins (strings) |
| 1st year (1821) | 7,630,389 | 1,202,200* | 11,351,701 | 1,203,756* | –3,721,312 | –1,556 |
| 2nd year (1822) | 7,060,251 | 1,189,489 | 11,210,691* | 1,199,720* | –4,150,440 | –10,231 |
| 3rd year (1823) | 8,183,826 | 1,121,547 | 9,948,689 | 1,094,563 | –1,764,863 | +26,984 |
| 5th year (1825) | 8,507,036 | 1,183,440 | 9,218,328 | 1,151,721 | –711,292 | +31,719 |

TABLE A.16 *Payment surpluses/deficits of the Silver Treasury during* Daoguang, *1821–1850* (cont.)

| Year | Aggregate revenue | | Aggregate expenditure | | Surplus/Deficit (+/–) | |
|---|---|---|---|---|---|---|
| | Silver (taels) | Copper coins (strings) | Silver (taels) | Copper coins (strings) | Silver (taels) | Copper coins (strings) |
| 7th year (1827) | 23,802,617 | 1,232,145 | 11,373,705 | 1,252,178 | +12,428,912 | –20,033 |
| 8th year (1828) | 14,422,806 | 1,166,798 | 10,951,956 | 1,158,856 | +3,470,850 | +7,942 |
| 9th year (1829) | 11,557,959 | 1,119,826 | 11,713,017 | 1,047,489 | –155,058 | +72,337 |
| 10th year (1830) | 11,289,651 | 1,172,528 | 12,575,834 | 1,245,338 | –1,286,183 | –72,810 |
| 12th year (1832) | 8,019,701 | 1,212,995 | 10,987,586 | 1,226,884 | –2,967,885 | –13,889 |
| 13th year (1833) | 7,160,869 | 1,152,766 | 10,886,616 | 1,151,531 | –3,725,747 | +1,235 |
| 14th year (1834) | 15,522,250 | 1,183,232 | 10,773,739 | 1,160,590 | +4,748,511 | +22,642 |
| 19th year (1839) | 8,691,741 | 1,143,851 | 10,127,680 | 1,143,703 | –1,435,939 | +148 |
| 20th year (1840) | 10,349,975 | 1,137,631 | 10,312,241 | 1,139,506 | +37,734 | –1,875 |
| 21st year (1841) | 6,796,038 | 1,233,614 | 15,733,178 | 1,233,598 | –8,937,140 | +16 |
| 22nd year (1842) | 10,914,111 | 1,144,433 | 13,519,847 | 1,140,848 | –2,605,736 | +3,585 |
| 23rd year (1843) | 7,919,693 | 1,222,831 | 10,989,389 | 1,270,073 | –3,069,696 | –47,242 |
| 25th year (1845) | 9,069,654 | 1,160,832 | 8,737,519 | 1,014,232 | +332,135 | +146,600 |
| 29th year (1849) | 8,507,408 | 1,238,528 | 9,340,395 | 1,219,044 | –832,987 | +19,484 |
| 30th year (1850) | 7,748,585 | 1,076,127 | 9,531,910 | 1,177,265 | –1,783,325 | –101,138 |
| *Average of* Daoguang | *10,166,029* | *1,173,411* | *11,014,948* | *1,170,047* | *–848,919* | *+3,364* |

*Source*: based on Tables A.14 and A.15.

TABLE A.17 *Aggregate revenues of the Silver Treasury during* Xianfeng, *1851–1853*

| Year | Silver (taels) | Copper coins (strings) | Remarks |
|---|---|---|---|
| *1st year (1851)* | *7,635,529* | *1,245,930* | |
| 1st month | 1,525,569.079 | – | |
| 2nd month | 1,329,839.478 | 97,204.534 | |
| 3rd month | 1,002,092.995 | 97,461.706 | |
| 4th month | 338,559.449 | 96,573.290 | |
| 5th month | 886,681.396 | 97,150.762 | |
| 6th month | 356,532.827 | 97,820.006 | |
| 7th month | 87,966.292 | 97,997.952 | |
| 8th month | 479,941.837 | 99,173.805 | |
| Leap month | 85,406.547 | 92,308.903 | |
| 9th month | 96,121.281 | 76,687.532 | |
| 10th month | 172,691.393 | 97,418.668 | |
| 11th month | 326,480.205 | 96,256.000 | |
| 12th month | 947,645.780 | 199,877.150 | |
| *2nd year (1852)* | *8,361,837* | *1,434,110* | |
| 1st month | 535,084.550 | – | |
| 2nd month | 208,381.694 | 85,406.928 | |
| 3rd month | 633,799.721 | 74,336.600 | |
| 4th month | 1,546,111.648 | 74,076.937 | |
| 5th month | 694,168.519 | 73,749.530 | |
| 6th month | 456,287.187 | 66,062.567 | |
| 7th month | 483,952.692 | 66,726.172 | |
| 8th month | 228,801.770 | 665,285.481 | |
| 9th month | 1,223,874.115 | 66,202.000 | |
| 10th month | 829,191.265 | 65,992.000 | |
| 11th month | 534,030.097 | 66,069.574 | |
| 12th month | 988,153.425 | 130,201.955 | |
| *3rd year (1853)* | *4,443,174* | *1,195,207* | *The original monthly totals of the 12th month are missing. Figures in parentheses are the sum of the existing detailed amounts.* |
| 1st month | 853,073.657 | – | |

TABLE A.17 *Aggregate revenues of the Silver Treasury during* Xianfeng, *1851–1853* (cont.)

| Year | Silver (taels) | Copper coins (strings) | Remarks |
|---|---|---|---|
| 2nd month | 334,128.268 | 54,574.789 | |
| 3rd month | 603,901.850 | 66,113.646 | |
| 4th month | 230,745.976 | 59,992.000 | |
| 5th month | 210,329.841 | 65,892.000 | |
| 6th month | 430,286.913 | 105,663.824 | |
| 7th month | 317,162.843 | 104,091.360 | |
| 8th month | 519,855.142 | 121,332.099 | |
| 9th month | 281,702.261 | 92,716.385 | |
| 10th month | 145,612.595 | 170,671.162 | |
| 11th month | 337,139.877 | 171,979.207 | |
| 12th month | (179,235.126) | (182,180.289) | Figures in parentheses are the sum of the existing detailed amounts. |

*Source*: based on the aggregate revenue registers, The Yellow Registers (The Silver Treasury of the Ministry of Revenue), Volume 12.

TABLE A.18 *Aggregate revenues of the Silver Treasury during* Xianfeng, *1854–1861*

| Year | Silver (taels) | Coins (strings) | Jing Piao (strings) | Baochao (strings) | Weiling Duitiao Qian (strings) | Remarks |
|---|---|---|---|---|---|---|
| *4th year (1854)* | *4,996,127** | *3,045,824** | *7,846,072** | – | – | |
| *5th year (1855)* | *3,067,774* | *1,598,807 (1,898,807)* | *7,791,060* | *4,087,693 (4,088,318)* | – | *Figures in parentheses are the yearly totals based on the corrected monthly totals.* |
| 1st month | 268,417.999 | – | 15,193.560 | 35,027.500 | – | |
| 2nd month | 130,114.122 | 214,899.570 | 1,178,476.773 | 42,678.000 | – | |
| 3rd month | 325,749.457 | 216,001.822 | 563,140.015 | 104,612.500 | – | |
| 4th month | 146,171.881 | 216,003.121 | 522,737.487 | 327,013.500 | – | |

| Year | Silver (taels) | Coins (strings) | Jing Piao (strings) | Baochao (strings) | Weiling Duitiao Qian (strings) | Remarks |
|---|---|---|---|---|---|---|
| 5th month | 284,714.948 | 213,268.508 | 666,695.610 | 374,038.500 | – | |
| 6th month | 401,577.768 | 213,718.713 | 550,742.526 | 364,033.000 | – | |
| 7th month | 178,070.378 | 217,521.629 | 612,100.822 | 350,000.626 | – | The monthly total of Baochao of the 7th month ought to be 350,626.000. |
| 8th month | 194,605.849 | 12,438.698 | 648,390.313 | 894,334.500 | – | |
| 9th month | 298,974.562 | 9,248.995 | 589,671.918 | 281,941.500 | – | |
| 10th month | 184,315.433 | 150,892.972 | 555,539.218 | 326,168.500 | – | |
| 11th month | 226,554.889 | 6,886.845 | 613,002.813 | 273,892.500 | – | |
| 12th month | 428,507.050 | 127,925.753 | 1,275,369.442 | 713,952.000 | – | The monthly total of coins of the 12th month ought to be 427,925.753. |
| *6th year (1856)* | *2,669,663* | *811,063* | *7884489* | *7,282,490* *4,405,082** | *154* | |
| 1st month | 208,340.084 | – | 32,927.214 | – | – | |
| 2nd month | 326,670.200 | 51,874.100 | 611,441.160 | 1,004,719.000 | – | |
| 3rd month | 254,484.952 | 77,896.365 | 619,552.554 | 282,937.000 | – | |
| 4th month | 17,405.694 | 48,598.033 | 610,118.721 | 295,526.500 | – | |
| 5th month | 221,918.352 | 113,122.205 | 951,293.584 | 275,948.500 | – | |
| 6th month | 182,267.155 | 34,694.036 | 577,884.037 | 266,438.500 | – | |
| 7th month | 250,390.737 | 32,674.621 | 577,620.034 | 277,729.000 | – | |
| 8th month | 318,917.580 | 32,842.154 | 652,164.421 | 288,715.500 | – | |
| 9th month | 141,100.046 | 33,073.167 | 498,661.658 | 307,772.000 | 24.467 | |
| 10th month | 114,863.801 | 26,538.012 | 513,473.775 | 3,197,120.000 | 31.196 | |
| 11th month | 126,436.166 | 304,406.385 | 574,118.282 | 310,817.000 | 45.658 | |
| 12th month | 506,867.915 | 55,344.376 | 1,665,233.394 | 774,767.000 | 52.787 | |
| *9th year (1859)* | *4,463,478* | *968,530* | *19,131,590* | *2,133,825* | *409* | *The silver total of the 7th month and the Jing Piao total of the 12th month do not match with the sum of their detailed numbers.* |
| 1st month | 146,281.320 | – | 1,145.276 | – | – | |

TABLE A.18 *Aggregate revenues of the Silver Treasury during* Xianfeng, *1854–1861* (cont.)

| Year | Silver (taels) | Coins (strings) | Jing Piao (strings) | Baochao (strings) | Weiling Duitiao Qian (strings) | Remarks |
|---|---|---|---|---|---|---|
| 2nd month | 160,208.605 | – | 1,205,310.939 | 100,437.000 | 20.209 | |
| 3rd month | 86,556.078 | – | 3,206,216.712 | 173,326.000 | 22.625 | |
| 4th month | 376,648.218 | 406,708.000 | 2,065,419.607 | 129,616.500 | 26.064 | |
| 5th month | 284,957.020 | 1,035.070 | 1,690,462.428 | 87,488.000 | 21.170 | |
| 6th month | 428,376.238 | – | 1,760,871.451 | 147,727.000 | 26.131 | |
| 7th month | 585,543.175 | 8,110.000 | 1,475,606.609 | 106,727.500 | 27.940 | The figure of the silver total of the 7th month is more than the sum of the detailed numbers. |
| 8th month | 313,992.151 | 450,000.000 | 1,782,874.311 | 101,379.500 | 25.242 | |
| 9th month | 374,409.120 | 62,178.000 | 1,337,509.941 | 99,708.500 | 22.148 | |
| 10th month | 276,569.705 | 50.000 | 1,013,888.369 | 233,873.000 | 74.399 | |
| 11th month | 418,786.205 | 23,473.449 | 1,321,208.725 | 437,079.500 | 65.883 | |
| 12th month | 1,011,150.121 | 16,975.601 | 2,271,075.781 | 516,462.500 | 77.041 | The Jing Piao total of the 12th month is 4 strings less than the sum of the detailed numbers. |
| *10th year (1860)* | *5,429,091* | *366,762* | *4,315,242* | *3,321,595* | *616* | *Some of the monthly totals of the year do not match with the sum of their detailed figures.* |
| 1st month | 616,217.894 | 60.750 | 6,118.562 | 289,501.000 | 16.130 | |
| 2nd month | 144,605.262 | 11,108.000 | 1,024,922.777 | 598,859.000 | 72.068 | |
| 3rd month | 226,223.773 | 106.000 | 1,059,360.497 | 173,872.500 | 26.500 | |
| Leap month | 414,750.014 | – | 466,631.642 | 195,303.000 | 44.666 | |
| 4th month | 268,846.338 | – | 240,896.008 | 122,956.500 | 50.377 | |
| 5th month | 564,826.070 | 11,650.300 | 176,256.635 | 136,829.500 | 42.140 | |
| 6th month | 448,352.779 | – | 317,442.790 | 215,635.500 | 34.747 | |
| 7th month | 620,654.719 | – | 276,826.467 | 436,518.000 | 68.068 | |
| 8th month | 216,347.919 | – | 53,673.500 | 418,838.000 | 8.030 | |
| 9th month | 68,904.380 | 67,483.350 | 159,816.544 | 95,543.000 | 25.388 | |
| 10th month | 451,253.358 | 67,511.430 | 73,138.447 | 120,520.000 | 59.658 | |

| Year | Silver (taels) | Coins (strings) | Jing Piao (strings) | Baochao (strings) | Weiling Duitiao Qian (strings) | Remarks |
|---|---|---|---|---|---|---|
| 11th month | 391,115.302 | 67,511.420 | 40,302.000 | 383,151.500 | 134.739 | |
| 12th month | 996,992.969 | 141,330.740 | 419,855.714 | 134,067.500 | 33.581 | |
| *11th year (1861)* | *6,678,614** | *295,355** | *408,881** | *155,518** | *185** | |

*Source*: figures with marked with * are from four-column registers of each of the years; others are based on aggregate revenue registers of Xianfeng, The Yellow Registers (The Silver Treasury of the Ministry of Revenue), Volume 12.

TABLE A.19 *Aggregate expenditures of the Silver Treasury during* Xianfeng, *1852–1853*

| Year | Silver (taels) | Copper coins (strings) | Remarks |
|---|---|---|---|
| *2nd year (1852)* | *10,268,561* | *835,110* | *The totals of the 12th month are missing. Figures in parentheses are the sum of the detailed amounts.* |
| 1st month | 107,932.500 | – | |
| 2nd month | 1,425,500.377 | 77,279.753 | |
| 3rd month | 563,054.981 | 74,336.600 | |
| 4th month | 595,805.150 | 74,076.937 | |
| 5th month | 739,820.784 | 74,416.623 | |
| 6th month | 595,657.107 | 73,426.469 | |
| 7th month | 553,502.850 | 63,446.086 | |
| 8th month | 1,148,999.737 | 63,453.097 | |
| 9th month | 599,770.124 | 63,576.096 | |
| 10th month | 619,000.829 | 63,484.590 | |
| 11th month | 763,895.326 | 63,487.407 | |
| 12th month | (2,555,621.005) | (144,126.059) | Figures in parentheses are the sum of the detailed amounts. |
| *3rd year (1853)* | *8,471,746* | *1,368,406* | |
| 1st month | 176,169.231 | – | |
| 2nd month | 1,051,220.048 | 52,245.879 | |

TABLE A.19 *Aggregate expenditures of the Silver Treasury during* Xianfeng, *1852–1853* (cont.)

| Year | Silver (taels) | Copper coins (strings) | Remarks |
|---|---|---|---|
| 3rd month | 878,771.776 | 63,577.922 | |
| 4th month | 1,245,602.410 | 63,318.974 | |
| 5th month | 681,893.024 | 63,443.091 | |
| 6th month | 559,309.201 | 96,845.054 | |
| 7th month | 536,965.716 | 93,760.597 | |
| 8th month | 806,369.761 | 79,136.126 | |
| 9th month | 688,601.448 | 92,716.385 | |
| 10th month | 529,218.577 | 195,015.820 | |
| 11th month | 625,254.250 | 176,922.897 | |
| 12th month | 692,370.143 | 391,423.518 | |

*Source*: based on the aggregate expenditure registers of Xianfeng, The Yellow Registers (The Silver Treasury of the Ministry of Revenue), Volume 33.

TABLE A.20 *Aggregate expenditures of the Silver Treasury during* Xianfeng, *1854–1861*

| Year | Silver (taels) | Coins (strings) | Jing Piao (strings) | Baochao (strings) | Weiling Duitiao Qian (strings) | Remarks |
|---|---|---|---|---|---|---|
| *4th year (1854)* | *5,031,019** | *3,040,550** | *7,834,543** | – | – | |
| *6th year (1856)* | *2,704,989** | *517,736** | *7,950,869** | *4,405,082** | *154** | |
| *8th year (1858)* | *3,061,904* | *629,857* | *11,360,116* | *1,510,663* | *267* | *Data of the 1st month aremissing in the original register.* |
| 2nd month | 227,190.660 | 109,612.680 | 1,386,351.803 | 132,758.500 | 14.413 | |
| 3rd month | 208,403.349 | 40,000.000 | 888,241.989 | 200,393.500 | 19.449 | |
| 4th month | 199,839.858 | – | 767,661.461 | 118,573.000 | 21.034 | |

| Year | Silver (taels) | Coins (strings) | Jing Piao (strings) | Baochao (strings) | Weiling Duitiao Qian (strings) | Remarks |
|---|---|---|---|---|---|---|
| 5th month | 380,221.888 | 71.918 | 1,039,556.136 | 109,069.500 | 17.594 | |
| 6th month | 174,538.713 | – | 1,055,884.269 | 95,432.000 | 23.616 | |
| 7th month | 144,520.434 | 12,144.829 | 738,134.771 | 183,745.000 | 27.907 | |
| 8th month | 395,449.512 | 13,732.586 | 1,101,750.655 | 187,821.000 | 17.893 | |
| 9th month | 310,168.315 | 212,168.083 | 722,128.721 | 87,378.500 | 17.941 | |
| 10th month | 273,382.743 | 240,264.656 | 1,010,046.641 | 57,234.000 | 20.007 | |
| 11th month | 216,878.513 | – | 646,408.457 | 112,383.500 | 39.857 | |
| 12th month | 531,310.334 | 1,862.680 | 2,003,950.623 | 225,874.000 | 47.305 | |
| *9th year (1859)* | *3,808,417* | *703,324*<br>*903,324** | *13,976,064*<br>*16,046,203** | *2,124,455*<br>*2,133,825** | *43*<br>*409** | |
| 1st month | 257,611.139 | – | – | – | – | |
| 2nd month | 266,348.057 | – | 1,214,860.948 | 100,437.000 | 20.209 | |
| 3rd month | 225,508.868 | – | 1,905,632.499 | 173,326.000 | 22.625 | |
| 4th month | 287,744.221 | 400,000.000 | 1,565,702.419 | 129,616.500 | – | |
| 5th month | 293,105.617 | 71.918 | 988,572.068 | 87,488.000 | – | |
| 6th month | 242,736.167 | – | 1,984,221.644 | 147,727.000 | – | |
| 7th month | 205,712.354 | 1,603.620 | 826,273.893 | 106,727.500 | – | |
| 8th month | 336,666.823 | 250,000.000 | 2,457,871.146 | 98,175.500 | – | |
| 9th month | 327,362.876 | 50,000.000 | 734,287.272 | 98,788.500 | – | |
| 10th month | 388,885.455 | – | 1,182,333.830 | 228,627.000 | – | |
| 11th month | 348,010.061 | – | 1,116,307.929 | 437,079.500 | – | |
| 12th month | 628,725.786 | 1,648.702 | – | 516,462.500 | – | |
| *11th year (1861)* | *6,331,926** | *169,540** | *174,287** | *155,431** | *182** | |

*Source*: figures marked with * are from the four-column registers of each of the years; others are based on the aggregate expenditure registers of Xianfeng, The Yellow Registers (The Silver Treasury of the Ministry of Revenue), Volume 33.

TABLE A.21 *Payment surpluses/deficits of the Silver Treasury during* Xianfeng, *1852–1861*

| Year | Aggregate revenue | | Aggregate expenditure | | Surplus/Deficit (+/–) | |
|---|---|---|---|---|---|---|
| | Silver (taels) | Coins (strings) | Silver (taels) | Coins (strings) | Silver (taels) | Coins (strings) |
| 2nd year (1852) | 8,361,837 | 1,434,110 | 10,268,561 | 835,110 | –1,906,724 | +599,000 |
| 3rd year (1853) | 4,443,174 | 1,195,207 | 8,471,746 | 1,368,406 | –4,028,572 | –173,199 |
| 4th year (1854) | 4,996,127* | 10,891,896* | 5,031,019* | 10,875,093* | –34,892 | +16,803 |
| 5th year (1855) | 3,067,744 | 13,778,185 | (3,233,178) | (13,692,023) | –165,434 | +86,162 |
| 6th year (1856) | 2,669,663 | 13,100,788* | 2,704,989* | 12,873,841* | –35,326 | +226,947 |
| 9th year (1859) | 4,463,478 | 22,234,354 | 3,808,417 | 16,803,886 | +655,061 | +5,430,468 |
| 10th year (1860) | 5,429,091 | 8,004,216 | (7,279,488) | (11,099,596) | –1,850,397 | –3,095,380 |
| 11th year (1861) | 6,678,614* | 859,939* | 6,331,926* | 499,440* | +346,688 | +360,499 |
| *Average of* Xianfeng | *5,013,716* | *8,937,337* | *5,891,166* | *8,505,924* | *–877,450* | *+431,413* |

*Source*: based on Tables A.17–A.20. The revenue/expenditure figures of coins are the sums of coins, Jing Piao, Baochao and Weiling Duitiao Qian (尾零对条钱) in the table. The aggregate expenditures of the 5th and 10th years in parentheses have been calculated on the basis of the aggregate revenue of each of the years and the inventories of the previous years and the years concerned (see Table B.46).

TABLE A.22 *Aggregate revenues of the Silver Treasury during* Tongzhi, *1865–1867*

| Year | Silver (taels) | Coins (strings) | Remarks |
|---|---|---|---|
| *4th year (1865)* | *8,495,356* | *186,292* | *The totals of the 12th month in parentheses have been calculated by adding up the detailed amounts.* |
| 1st month | 523,054.189 | – | |

| Year | Silver (taels) | Coins (strings) | Remarks |
|---|---|---|---|
| 2nd month | 547,237.414 | 13,593.266 | |
| 3rd month | 616,697.095 | 12,521.511 | |
| 4th month | 707,314.904 | 13,174.306 | |
| 5th month | 734,370.308 | 14,098.311 | |
| Leap month | 1,043,711.251 | 15,485.044 | |
| 6th month | 956,323.549 | 12,684.929 | |
| 7th month | 612,759.166 | 14,279.260 | |
| 8th month | 464,929.255 | 14,867.134 | |
| 9th month | 469,034.472 | 13,622.531 | |
| 10th month | 376,336.112 | 16,380.548 | |
| 11th month | 349,344.204 | 14,251.842 | |
| 12th month | (1,094,244.126) | (31,333.396) | The monthly totals are missing. |
| *5th year (1866)* | *8,579,764* | *139,299* | *Data of the 12th month are missing.* |
| 1st month | 584,628.209 | – | |
| 2nd month | 621,243.209 | 14,143.989 | |
| 3rd month | 351,524.417 | 12,774.331 | |
| 4th month | 763,628.412 | 12,682.062 | |
| 5th month | 930,910.794 | 14,277.439 | |
| 6th month | 1,140,873.544 | 14,845.420 | |
| 7th month | 785,071.441 | 13,225.441 | |
| 8th month | 661,959.015 | 14,918.305 | |
| 9th month | 626,922.152 | 13,892.430 | |
| 10th month | 956,215.277 | 12,833.394 | |
| 11th month | 1,156,787.524 | 15,705.724 | |
| *6th year (1867)* | *12,348,311* | *148,869* | |
| 1st month | 665,703.885 | 151.067 | |
| 2nd month | 742,264.985 | 14,594.180 | |
| 3rd month | 932,922.366 | 11,294.097 | |
| 4th month | 1,277,988.803 | 11,551.309 | |
| 5th month | 1,193,800.058 | 14,482.573 | |
| 6th month | 1,295,642.882 | 11,641.016 | |
| 7th month | 807,371.389 | 11,939.605 | |
| 8th month | 922,193.177 | 12,614.689 | |
| 9th month | 867,536.766 | 11,452.906 | |

TABLE A.22 *Aggregate revenues of the Silver Treasury during* Tongzhi, *1865–1867* (cont.)

| Year | Silver (taels) | Coins (strings) | Remarks |
|---|---|---|---|
| 10th month | 682,423.544 | 11,663.088 | |
| 11th month | 1,084,358.889 | 13,418.265 | |
| 12th month | 1,876,103.824 | 24,066.666 | |
| Average of Tongzhi | 9,807,810 | 158,153 | |

*Source*: based on the aggregate revenue registers of Tongzhi, The Yellow Registers (The Silver Treasury of the Ministry of Revenue), Volume 12.

TABLE A.23 *Aggregate expenditures of the Silver Treasury during* Tongzhi, *1863–1869*

| Year | Silver (taels) | Coins (strings) | Remarks |
|---|---|---|---|
| *2nd year (1863)* | *7,263,494* | *155,583* | |
| 1st month | 239,775.677 | 2,943.117 | |
| 2nd month | 550,110.307 | 14,899.592 | |
| 3rd month | 472,840.334 | 11,313.946 | |
| 4th month | 511,062.184 | 10,907.843 | |
| 5th month | 564,665.781 | 11,029.746 | |
| 6th month | 516,844.481 | 11,918.915 | |
| 7th month | 533,882.434 | 12,310.623 | |
| 8th month | 756,437.721 | 13,142.317 | |
| 9th month | 534,547.208 | 11,850.854 | |
| 10th month | 731,754.845 | 20,820.285 | |
| 11th month | 860,707.211 | 14,259.622 | |
| 12th month | 990,866.030 | 20,185.694 | |
| *4th year (1865)* | *8,349,347* | *183,750* | *The totals of the 12th month have been calculated by adding up the detailed amounts.* |
| 1st month | 276,196.044 | – | |
| 2nd month | 714,182.634 | 13,593.266 | |
| 3rd month | 483,654.272 | 12,521.511 | |
| 4th month | 747,294.161 | 13,174.306 | |

| Year | Silver (taels) | Coins (strings) | Remarks |
|---|---|---|---|
| 5th month | 724,066.331 | 14,098.311 | |
| Leap month | 574,078.968 | 15,485.044 | |
| 6th month | 491,222.980 | 12,684.929 | |
| 7th month | 540,813.851 | 14,279.260 | |
| 8th month | 789,737.183 | 14,867.134 | |
| 9th month | 855,184.383 | 13,622.531 | |
| 10th month | 616,445.823 | 13,838.598 | |
| 11th month | 564,105.307 | 14,251.842 | |
| 12th month | (972,365.047) | (31333.394) | The totals of the month are missing in the original register. |
| *5th year (1866)* | *8,240,574* | *160,990* | |
| 1st month | 480,392.184 | – | |
| 2nd month | 797,936.960 | 14,143.989 | |
| 3rd month | 662,342.878 | 12,774.331 | |
| 4th month | 810,885.445 | 12,682.062 | |
| 5th month | 573,375.284 | 14,277.439 | |
| 6th month | 521,455.768 | 14,845.420 | |
| 7th month | 518,451.880 | 13,225.441 | |
| 8th month | 805,236.316 | 14,918.305 | |
| 9th month | 512,347.831 | 13,892.430 | |
| 10th month | 824,250.607 | 12,833.394 | |
| 11th month | 581,771.494 | 15,705.724 | |
| 12th month | 1,152,127.844 | 21,691.730 | |
| *6th year (1867)* | *10,293,685* | *148,869* | |
| 1st month | 285,319.168 | 151.067 | |
| 2nd month | 975,274.611 | 14,594.180 | |
| 3rd month | 826,700.028 | 11,294.097 | |
| 4th month | 809,192.520 | 11,551.309 | |
| 5th month | 1,130,410.153 | 14,482.573 | |
| 6th month | 716,436.533 | 11,641.016 | |
| 7th month | 711,181.589 | 11,939.605 | |
| 8th month | 1,125,558.724 | 12,614.689 | |
| 9th month | 631,066.943 | 11,452.906 | |
| 10th month | 779,857.064 | 11,663.088 | |

TABLE A.23 *Aggregate expenditures of the Silver Treasury during* Tongzhi, *1863–1869* (cont.)

| Year | Silver (taels) | Coins (strings) | Remarks |
|---|---|---|---|
| 11th month | 908,440.125 | 13,418.265 | |
| 12th month | 1,394,247.691 | 24,066.666 | |
| *8th year (1869)* | *11,336,640* | *153,776* | *The totals of the 12th month have been calculated by adding up the detailed amounts.* |
| 1st month | 293,667.742 | – | |
| 2nd month | 1,148,578.699 | 12,865.705 | |
| 3rd month | 1,320,093.302 | 11,432.754 | |
| 4th month | 1,108,077.428 | 11,187.881 | |
| 5th month | 882,459.806 | 18,130.246 | |
| 6th month | 777,412.358 | 12,541.339 | |
| 7th month | 715,844.556 | 11,298.551 | |
| 8th month | 925,612.862 | 13,861.112 | |
| 9th month | 679,625.976 | 11,565.061 | |
| 10th month | 680,622.944 | 12,350.040 | |
| 11th month | 673,697.130 | 19,427.404 | |
| 12th month | (2,130,947.267) | (19,116.186) | The totals of the month are missing in the original register. |
| *Average of* Tongzhi | *9,096,748* | *160,594* | |

*Source*: based on the aggregate expenditure registers of Tongzhi, The Yellow Registers (The Silver Treasury of the Ministry of Revenue), Volume 34.

TABLE A.24 *Payment surpluses/deficits of the Silver Treasury during* Tongzhi, *1865–1867*

| Year | Aggregate revenue | | Aggregate expenditure | | Surplus/Deficit (+/-) | |
|---|---|---|---|---|---|---|
| | Silver (taels) | Coins (strings) | Silver (taels) | Coins (strings) | Silver (taels) | Coins (strings) |
| 4th year (1865) | 8,495,356 | 186,292 | 8,349,347 | 183,750 | +146,009 | +2,542 |
| 5th year (1866) | 8,579,764 | 139,299 | 8,240,574 | 160,990 | +339,190 | -21,691 |

| Year | Aggregate revenue | | Aggregate expenditure | | Surplus/Deficit (+/-) | |
|---|---|---|---|---|---|---|
| | Silver (taels) | Coins (strings) | Silver (taels) | Coins (strings) | Silver (taels) | Coins (strings) |
| 6th year (1867) | 12,348,311 | 148,869 | 10,293,685 | 148,869 | +2,054,626 | 0 |
| *Average of* Tongzhi | *9,807,810* | *158,153* | *8,961,202* | *164,536* | *+846,608* | *-6,383* |

*Source*: based on Tables A.22 and A.23.

TABLE A.25 *Aggregate revenues of the Silver Treasury during* Guangxu, *1883–1899*

| Year | Silver (taels) | Coins (strings) | Copper coins (strings) | Remarks |
|---|---|---|---|---|
| *9th year (1883)* | *15,638,588** | *228,309** | – | *The amount of silver is the sum of the revenues of Kuping silver and various special funds.* |
| *17th year (1891)* | *19,265,207** | *1,390,436** | – | *The amount of silver is the sum of the revenues of Kuping silver and various special funds.* |
| *18th year (1892)* | *16,068,086* | *1,578,138* | – | *Besides the amount of revenues of Kuping silver listed, there are another 4,791,195.362 taels of special funds (40% of import duties and funds for the northeast border defence and for preparing soldiers' pay); if add these, the total sum will be 20,859,281 taels.* |
| 1st month | 968,985.347 | 2,470.000 | – | |
| 2nd month | 1,048,161.663 | 110,950.500 | – | |
| 3rd month | 1,230,839.724 | 135,708.500 | – | |
| 4th month | 733,078.393 | 105,794.500 | – | |
| 5th month | 1,596,091.927 | 119,367.073 | – | |
| 6th month | 1,377,789.495 | 116,603.000 | – | |
| Leap month | 934,572.716 | 111,513.000 | – | |
| 7th month | 1,100,889.036 | 135,395.901 | – | |
| 8th month | 1,529,398.703 | 118,835.500 | – | |
| 9th month | 1,306,121.626 | 139,054.000 | – | |

TABLE A.25 *Aggregate revenues of the Silver Treasury during* Guangxu, *1883–1899* (cont.)

| Year | Silver (taels) | Coins (strings) | Copper coins (strings) | Remarks |
|---|---|---|---|---|
| 10th month | 690,484.370 | 119,360.000 | – | |
| 11th month | 1,335,169.664 | 116,302.500 | – | |
| 12th month | 2,216,503.108 | 246,783.916 | – | |
| *22nd year (1896)* | *19,063,325* | *234,467* | *201,866* | *Besides the amount of revenues of Kuping silver listed, there are another3,715,975.175 taels of special funds (40% of import duties and funds for the northeast border defence and for preparing soldiers' pay); if add these, the total sum will be 22,779,300 taels.* |
| 1st month | 1,285,171.889 | 4,431.500 | – | |
| 2nd month | 1,360,400.482 | 42,365.500 | – | |
| 3rd month | 1,970,588.059 | 25,536.500 | – | |
| 4th month | 993,005.792 | 14,556.500 | – | |
| 5th month | 1,651,338.486 | 45,019.500 | – | |
| 6th month | 1,405,672.930 | 25,032.455 | – | |
| 7th month | 1,333,138.282 | 33,651.000 | – | |
| 8th month | 1,476,597.661 | 15,842.000 | – | |
| 9th month | 1,186,145.426 | 8,106.000 | 49,678.430 | |
| 10th month | 1,297,113.407 | 18,018.000 | – | |
| 11th month | 2,257,416.846 | – | 49,992.000 | |
| 12th month | 2,846,735.898 | 1,908.000 | 102,195.966 | |
| *23rd year (1897)* | *19,369,702*<br>*23,283,344** | *94,061* | *246,964* | – *Besides the 19,369,702 taels listed, there are another 102,317.236 taels of 40% of import duties, 1,865,000 taels of fund for the northeast border defence and 1,652,260 taels of fund for preparing soldiers' pay; if added these, the total sum will be 22,989,279 taels.*<br>– *Figure marked with * is the aggregate revenue recorded by the four-column register (revenues of Kuping silver and special funds are all included).*<br>– *According to the four-column register, the aggregate revenue in coins this year is 341,025 strings, which is equal to the sum of figures listed in columns of "coins" and "copper coins".* |

TABLE A.25 *Aggregate revenues of the Silver Treasury during* Guangxu, *1883–1899* (cont.)

| Year | Silver (taels) | Coins (strings) | Copper coins (strings) | Remarks |
|---|---|---|---|---|
| 1st month | 1,380,449.369 | – | – | |
| 2nd month | 1,435,304.675 | 27,937.000 (10–cash) | 51,494.000 | |
| 3rd month | 1,369,227.573 | 1,908.000 (10–cash) | 36,992.700 | |
| 4th month | 1,192,418.863 | 20,426.000 (10–cash) | 33,492.160 | |
| 5th month | 1,326,531.927 | – | 49,997.080 | |
| 6th month | 1,288,350.768 | 1,908.000 (10–cash) | – | |
| 7th month | 1,907,556.922 | 19,803.000 (10–cash) | – | |
| 8th month | 1,807,187.138 | – | – | |
| 9th month | 1,515,867.844 | 1,908.000 (10–cash) | 74,988.000 | |
| 10th month | 2,070,484.479 | 18,263.000 (10–cash) | – | |
| 11th month | 1,702,351.365 | – | – | |
| 12th month | 2,373,971.146 | 1,908.000 (10–cash) | – | |
| *24th year (1898)* | *23,952,689* *28,802,656** | *97,366* | *332,343* | – *Besides the 23,952,689 taels listed, there are another 72,561.579 taels of 40% of import duties, 1,804,000 taels of fund for the northeast border defence and 1,741,333.333 taels of fund for preparing soldiers' pay; if added these, the total sum will be 27,570,584 taels.* – *Figure marked with * is the aggregate revenue recorded by the four–column register (revenues of Kuping silver and special funds are all included).* – *According to the four–column register, the aggregate revenue in coins this year is 439,708 strings. The sum of figures listed in columns of "coins" and "copper coins" is 429,709 strings.* |
| 1st month | 1,454,612.418 | – | – | |
| 2nd month | 1,759,099.202 | 28,355.600 (10–cash) | – | |

TABLE A.25 *Aggregate revenues of the Silver Treasury during* Guangxu, *1883–1899* (cont.)

| Year | Silver (taels) | Coins (strings) | Copper coins (strings) | Remarks |
|---|---|---|---|---|
| 3rd month | 1,002,155.432 | 1,908.000 (10–cash) | – | |
| Leap month | 1,889,972.087 | 19,292.000 (10–cash) | 37,599.483 | |
| 4th month | 1,454,820.994 | – | 37,494.000 | |
| 5th month | 2,404,021.328 | – | 37,495.620 | |
| 6th month | 1,347,755.130 | 2,544.000 (10–cash) | 37,495.620 | |
| 7th month | 1,268,000.534 | 24,934.000 (10–cash) | – | |
| 8th month | 2,801,798.220 | – | – | |
| 9th month | 2,138,044.791 | – | – | |
| 10th month | 1,808,739.130 | 1,908.000 (10–cash) | – | |
| 11th month | 1,358,964.725 | 18,424.000 (10–cash) | 37,494.000 | |
| 12th month | 3,264,704.856 | – | 144,764.119 | |
| *25th year (1899)* | *18,869,369* *24,447,335** | *327,333* | *265,111* | – *Besides the 18,869,369 taels listed, there are another 365,001.381 taels of 40% of import duties, 2,488,031.771 taels of fund for the northeast border defence and 1,746,614.668 taels of fund for preparing soldiers' pay; if added these, the total sum will be 23,469,017 taels.* – *Figure marked with * is the aggregate revenue recorded by the four–column register (revenues of Kuping silver and special funds are all included).* – *According to the four–column register, the aggregate revenue in coins this year is 371,167 strings. The sum of figures listed in columns of "coins" and "copper coins" is 592,444 strings.* |
| 1st month | 686,660.827 | – | 1,430.500 | |
| 2nd month | 1,799,785.551 | 31,000.000 (10–cash) | 3,032.700 | |
| 3rd month | 1,502,987.068 | – | 4,220.300 | |
| 4th month | 1,158,613.925 | 1,908.000 (10–cash) | 5,036.400 | |

| Year | Silver (taels) | Coins (strings) | Copper coins (strings) | Remarks |
|---|---|---|---|---|
| 5th month | 1,453,760.768 | 19,215.000 (10–cash) | 5,035.700 | |
| 6th month | 834,779.693 | – | 4,984.200 | |
| 7th month | 2,248,340.051 | – | 18,730.200 | |
| 8th month | 1,264,774.430 | 1,908.000 (10–cash) | 15,989.500 | |
| 9th month | 1,671,722.220 | – | 29,368.000 | |
| 10th month | 1,996,058.681 | 21,109.000 (10–cash) | 31,769.700 | |
| 11th month | 1,679,191.386 | – | 31,492.400 | |
| 12th month | 2,572,694.091 | 252,192.920 (10–cash) | 114,021.570 | |
| *Average of* Guangxu | *22,153,673* | *677,326* | | |

*Source*: figures marked with * are from the four-column registers of each of the years; figures of the 23rd, 24th and 25th years are from the aggregate revenue registers kept by FHAC; others are based on the aggregate revenue registers kept by IE, The Yellow Registers (The Silver Treasury of the Ministry of Revenue), Volume 12. In calculating the averages, special funds are included; and whenever there is a difference between the figures of aggregate revenue registers and the four-column registers, we use that of the latter.

TABLE A.26 *Aggregate expenditures of the Silver Treasury during* Guangxu, *1879–1899*

| Year | Silver (taels) | Coins (strings) | Copper coins (strings) | Remarks |
|---|---|---|---|---|
| *5th year (1879)* | *10,877,085* | *164,025* | – | *Data of the 11th month are missing. And the totals of the 12th month have been calculated by adding up the detailed amounts.* |
| 1st month | 325,425.043 | – | – | |
| 2nd month | 1,003,969.449 | 15,663.499 | – | |
| 3rd month | 928,750.705 | 13,447.413 | – | |
| Leap month | 676,428.210 | 14,158.432 | – | |
| 4th month | 983,275.552 | 15,846.834 | – | |
| 5th month | 768,573.297 | 13,766.403 | – | |
| 6th month | 745,291.898 | 16,021.522 | – | |
| 7th month | 775,220.368 | 14,047.985 | – | |
| 8th month | 1,186,602.209 | 14,329.703 | – | |

TABLE A.26 *Aggregate expenditures of the Silver Treasury during* Guangxu, *1879–1899* (cont.)

| Year | Silver (taels) | Coins (strings) | Copper coins (strings) | Remarks |
|---|---|---|---|---|
| 9th month | 812,199.627 | 14,133.633 | – | |
| 10th month | 698,847.086 | 13,886.895 | – | |
| 12th month | (1,972,501.130) | (18,722.472) | – | |
| *9th year (1883)* | *11,623,013* <br> *13,845,311** | *404,120* | – | *Figure marked with * is the record of the four-column register, which is the sum of expenditures of Kuping silver (same as the record of aggregate expenditure register) and those of 40% import duties and the fund for northeast border defence.* |
| 1st month | 305,177.381 | 17,743.391 | – | |
| 2nd month | 1,966,611.609 | 14,421.894 | – | |
| 3rd month | 868,783.995 | 12,939.500 | – | |
| 4th month | 719,876.836 | 23,976.719 | – | |
| 5th month | 921,531.957 | 30,799.815 | – | |
| 6th month | 713,092.516 | 12,427.596 | – | |
| 7th month | 602,492.858 | 25,173.026 | – | |
| 8th month | 1,029,827.390 | 13,192.795 | – | |
| 9th month | 938,415.321 | 111,919.372 | – | |
| 10th month | 725,738.619 | 11,790.037 | – | |
| 11th month | 1,052,110.160 | 12,008.557 | – | |
| 12th month | 1,779,353.875 | 117,727.587 | – | |
| *17th year (1891)* | *13,559,182* <br> *17,115,933** | *348,210* | *1,231,964* | – *Figure marked with * is the record of the four-column register, which is the sum of expenditures of Kuping silver and those of various special funds* <br> – *According to the four-column register, the total sum of coin expenditures this year is 1,586,173 strings. The sum of "coins" and "copper coins" in the table is 1,580,174 strings.* |
| 1st month | 273,994.731 | – | – | |
| 2nd month | 1,698,241.969 | 18,132.930 | 102,759.000 | |
| 3rd month | 848,018.081 | 12,625.038 | 102,840.000 | |
| 4th month | 1,380,894.603 | 117,000.044 | 133,764.000 | |
| 5th month | 774,757.710 | 18,820.549 | 72,152.500 | |

| Year | Silver (taels) | Coins (strings) | Copper coins (strings) | Remarks |
|---|---|---|---|---|
| 6th month | 793,185.311 | 16,843.689 | 103,029.500 | |
| 7th month | 791,043.397 | 12,916.248 | 103,095.000 | |
| 8th month | 1,530,060.044 | 20,317.612 | 103,133.500 | |
| 9th month | 1,287,033.571 | 18,919.131 | 103,199.500 | |
| 10th month | 710,259.263 | 14,105.768 | 103,219.000 | |
| 11th month | 887,620.380 | 35,173.338 | 103,465.500 | |
| 12th month | 2,584,073.111 | 63,355.267 | 201,306.500 | |
| *23rd year (1897)* | *19,321,219*<br>*24,835,690** | *517,131* | – | – *Besides the 19,321,219 taels of Kuping expenditures, other expenses of the year included 280,000 taels of 40% of import duties, 1,792,472.893 taels of fund for the northeast border defence and 2,500,000 taels of fund for preparing soldiers' pay.*<br>– *If added these, the total sum of expenditures of the year would be 23,893,692 taels.*<br>– *The figure marked with * is the record of the four-column register, including both expenditures of Kuping silver and those of various special funds* |
| 1st month | 446,333.883 | – | – | |
| 2nd month | 1,877,957.866 | 75,847.102 | – | |
| 3rd month | 1,507,960.709 | 67,360.806 | – | |
| 4th month | 1,313,010.851 | 68,259.894 | – | |
| 5th month | 1,457,407.492 | 74,815.307 | – | |
| 6th month | 1,330,752.205 | 15,585.534 | – | |
| 7th month | 1,400,688.239 | 13,477.759 | – | |
| 8th month | 1,893,780.532 | 20,030.825 | – | |
| 9th month | 1,550,196.780 | 14,849.694 | – | |
| 10th month | 1,300,123.652 | 13,363.602 | – | |
| 11th month | 2,253,594.583 | 19,578.596 | – | |
| 12th month | 2,989,411.934 | 133,961.702 | – | |

TABLE A.26 *Aggregate expenditures of the Silver Treasury during* Guangxu, *1879–1899* (cont.)

| Year | Silver (taels) | Coins (strings) | Copper coins (strings) | Remarks |
|---|---|---|---|---|
| *24th year (1898)* | *22,136,132*<br>*29,212,916** | *625,381* | – | – *Besides the 22,136,132 taels of Kuping expenditures, other expenses of the year included 12,475.468 taels of 40% of import duties, 2,669,338.55 taels of fund for the northeast border defence and 2,745,831.764 taels of fund for preparing soldiers' pay. If added these, the total sum of expenditures of the year would be 27,563,778 taels.*<br>– *The figure marked with * is the record of the four–column register, including both expenditures of Kuping silver and those of various special funds* |
| 1st month | 307,138.804 | – | – | |
| 2nd month | 2,446,218.313 | 133,405.609 | – | |
| 3rd month | 1,213,662.952 | 13,783.413 | – | |
| Leap month | 1,220,979.035 | 68,051.457 | – | |
| 4th month | 1,373,165.385 | 68,034.716 | – | |
| 5th month | 2,069,170.126 | 76,293.755 | – | |
| 6th month | 1,170,028.028 | 68,150.128 | – | |
| 7th month | 1,669,027.927 | 14,516.096 | – | |
| 8th month | 2,525,247.994 | 14,826.828 | – | |
| 9th month | 1,794,816.402 | 20,033.131 | – | |
| 10th month | 1,228,991.278 | 13,768.163 | – | |
| 11th month | 2,004,340.137 | 13,555.853 | – | |
| 12th month | 3,113,345.803 | 120,961.441 | – | |
| *25th year (1899)* | *19,454,588*<br>*24,533,482** | *250,912* | *306,538* | – *Besides the 19,454,588 taels of Kuping expenditures, other expenses of the year included 595,180 taels of 40% of import duties, 2,461,470.951 taels of fund for the northeast border defence and 1,310,000 taels of fund for preparing soldiers' pay. If added these, the total sum of expenditures of the year would be 23,821,239 taels.*<br>– *The figure marked with * is the record of the four–column register, including both expenditures of Kuping silver and those of various special funds.*<br>– *According to the four–column register, the total sum of coin expenditures this year is 337,510 strings. The sum of "coins" and "copper coins" in the table is 557,450 strings.* |

| Year | Silver (taels) | Coins (strings) | Copper coins (strings) | Remarks |
|---|---|---|---|---|
| 1st month | 315,561.820 | – | – | |
| 2nd month | 2,450,043.320 | 6,116.873 | 3,086.807 | |
| 3rd month | 1,324,720.571 | 267.349 | 2,693.554 | |
| 4th month | 1,744,336.748 | 6,092.050 | 2,749.901 | |
| 5th month | 1,186,050.783 | 1,398.275 | 2,688.864 | |
| 6th month | 1,209,091.398 | 213.895 | 2,678.542 | |
| 7th month | 1,312,105.436 | 45.375 | 2,796.315 | |
| 8th month | 1,713,597.738 | 7,419.694 | 2,818.046 | |
| 9th month | 1,573,335.661 | 226.175 | 57,635.038 | |
| 10th month | 1,539,973.212 | 38.890 | 57,697.267 | |
| 11th month | 1,442,683.865 | 39.400 | 57,656.104 | |
| 12th month | 3,643,086.996 | 229,054.013 | 114,037.608 | |
| *Average of* Guangxu | *20,070,070* | *605,723* | | |

*Source*: figures marked with * are from the four-column registers of each of the years; figures of the 23rd, 24th and 25th years are from the aggregate expenditure registers kept by FHAC; others are based on the aggregate expenditure registers kept by IE, The Yellow Registers (The Silver Treasury of the Ministry of Revenue), Volume 35. In calculating the averages, special funds are included; and whenever there is a difference between the figures of aggregate expenditure registers and the four-column registers, we use that of the latter.

TABLE A.27 *Payment surpluses/deficits of the Silver Treasury during* Guangxu, *1883–1899*

| Year | Aggregate revenue | | Aggregate expenditure | | Surplus/Deficit (+/–) | |
|---|---|---|---|---|---|---|
| | Silver (taels) | Coins (strings) | Silver (taels) | Coins (strings) | Silver (taels) | Coins (strings) |
| 9th year (1883) | 15,638,588* | 228,309* | 13,845,311* | 404,120 | +1,793,277 | –175,811 |
| 17th year (1891) | 19,265,207* | 1,390,436* | 17,115,933* | 1,586,173* | +2,149,274 | –195,737 |
| 23rd year (1897) | 23,283,344* | 341,025 | 24,835,690* | 517,131 | –1,552,346 | –176,106 |
| 24th year (1898) | 28,802,656* | 439,708* | 29,202,916* | 625,381 | –400,260 | –185,673 |

TABLE A.27 *Payment surpluses/deficits of the Silver Treasury during* Guangxu, *1883–1899* (cont.)

| Year | Aggregate revenue | | Aggregate expenditure | | Surplus/Deficit (+/–) | |
|---|---|---|---|---|---|---|
| | Silver (taels) | Coins (strings) | Silver (taels) | Coins (strings) | Silver (taels) | Coins (strings) |
| 25th year (1899) | 24,447,335* | 371,167* | 24,533,482* | 337,510* | –86,147 | +33,657 |
| *Average of* Guangxu | *22,287,426* | *554,129* | *21,908,666* | *694,063* | *+378,760* | *–139,934* |

*Source*: based on Tables A.25 and A.26.

# Appendix B: Inventories of the Silver Treasury under Different Reigns

TABLE B.1 *Inventories of the Silver Treasury from* Kangxi *to* Qianlong, *1667–1774*

| Year/reign | Inventory (Treasury taels) | Year/reign | Inventory (Treasury taels) |
|---|---|---|---|
| 6th year of *Kangxi* (1667) | 2,488,492 | 1styear of *Qianlong* (1736) | 33,959,624 |
| 11th year of *Kangxi* (1672) | 18,096,850 | 2ndyear of *Qianlong* (1737) | 34,385,138 |
| 12th year of *Kangxi* (1673) | 21,358,006 | 3rdyear of *Qianlong* (1738) | 34,858,748 |
| 16th year of *Kangxi* (1677) | 5,307,216 | 4th year of *Qianlong* (1739) | 32,582,976 |
| 17th year of *Kangxi* (1678) | 3,339,920 | 5th year of *Qianlong* (1740) | 30,485,876 |
| 25th year of *Kangxi* (1686) | 26,052,735 | 6th year of *Qianlong* (1741) | 31,463,539 |
| 26th year of *Kangxi* (1687) | 28,964,499 | 7th year of *Qianlong* (1742) | 32,746,752 |
| 30th year of *Kangxi* (1691) | 31,849,719 | 8th year of *Qianlong* (1743) | 29,121,104 |
| 31st year of *Kangxi* (1692) | 34,255,285 | 9th year of *Qianlong* (1744) | 31,902,518 |
| 32nd year of *Kangxi* (1693) | 37,600,663 | 10th year of *Qianlong* (1745) | 33,170,655 |
| 33rdyear of *Kangxi* (1694) | 41,007,790 | 11th year of *Qianlong* (1746) | 34,633,177 |
| 34th year of *Kangxi* (1695) | 42,263,516 | 12th year of *Qianlong* (1747) | 32,363,404 |
| 35th year of *Kangxi* (1696) | 42,628,989 | 13th year of *Qianlong* (1748) | 27,463,645 |
| 36th year of *Kangxi* (1697) | 40,639,920 | 14th year of *Qianlong* (1749) | 28,073,043 |
| 37th year of *Kangxi* (1698) | 40,542,966 | 15th year of *Qianlong* (1750) | 30,796,177 |
| 42ndyear of *Kangxi* (1703) | 38,368,105 | 16th year of *Qianlong* (1751) | 32,493,786 |
| 43rdyear of *Kangxi* (1704) | 39,985,306 | 17th year of *Qianlong* (1752) | 38,630,287 |
| 47th year of *Kangxi* (1708) | 47,184,788 | 18th year of *Qianlong* (1753) | 39,870,394 |
| 48th year of *Kangxi* (1709) | 43,767,094 | 19th year of *Qianlong* (1754) | 37,605,422 |
| 49th year of *Kangxi* (1710) | 45,881,072 | 20th year of *Qianlong* (1755) | 42,997,048 |
| 52ndyear of *Kangxi* (1713) | 43,094,239 | 21styear of *Qianlong* (1756) | 43,222,030 |
| 53rdyear of *Kangxi* (1714) | 40,734,825 | 22ndyear of *Qianlong* (1757) | 40,152,254 |
| 57th year of *Kangxi* (1718) | 44,319,033 | 23rdyear of *Qianlong* (1758) | 36,380,809 |
| 58th year of *Kangxi* (1719) | 47,368,645 | 24th year of *Qianlong* (1759) | 36,732,865 |
| 59th year of *Kangxi* (1720) | 39,317,103 | 25th year of *Qianlong* (1760) | 35,496,902 |
| 60th year of *Kangxi* (1721) | 32,622,421 | 26th year of *Qianlong* (1761) | 36,638,572 |
| 1styear of *Yongzheng* (1723) | 23,711,920 | 27th year of *Qianlong* (1762) | 41,927,924 |
| 2ndyear of *Yongzheng* (1724) | 31,627,608 | 28th year of *Qianlong* (1763) | 47,063,610 |
| 3rdyear of *Yongzheng* (1725) | 40,434,744 | 29th year of *Qianlong* (1764) | 54,273,814 |
| 4th year of *Yongzheng* (1726) | 47,409,780 | 30th year of *Qianlong* (1765) | 60,336,375 |
| 5th year of *Yongzheng* (1727) | 55,252,933 | 31styear of *Qianlong* (1766) | 66,613,127 |
| 6th year of *Yongzheng* (1728) | 58,235,780 | 32ndyear of *Qianlong* (1767) | 66,501,052 |

 | DOI 10.1163/9789004307339_009

TABLE B.1 *Inventories of the Silver Treasury from* Kangxi *to* Qianlong, *1667–1774* (cont.)

| Year/reign | Inventory (Treasury taels) | Year/reign | Inventory (Treasury taels) |
|---|---|---|---|
| 7th year of *Yongzheng* (1729) | 60,248,747 | 33rdyear of *Qianlong* (1768) | 71,823,888 |
| 8th year of *Yongzheng* (1730) | 62,183,349 | 34th year of *Qianlong* (1769) | 76,222,877 |
| 9th year of *Yongzheng* (1731) | 50,375,953 | 35th year of *Qianlong* (1770) | 77,299,736 |
| 10th year of *Yongzheng* (1732) | 44,392,848 | 36th year of *Qianlong* (1771) | 78,940,001 |
| 11th year of *Yongzheng* (1733) | 37,933,743 | 37th year of *Qianlong* (1772) | 78,740,262 |
| 12th year of *Yongzheng* (1734) | 32,503,428 | 38th year of *Qianlong* (1773) | 69,677,071 |
| 13th year of *Yongzheng* (1735) | 34,530,485 | 39th year of *Qianlong* (1774) | 73,905,610 |

*Source*: based on the inventory attached to the memorial by Junji Dachen (军机大臣, Grand Councillor) on the 29th day of the 1st month of the 40th year of Qianlong concerning the inventories of the Silver Treasury during Kangxi, Yongzheng and Qianlong; in Junjichu Shangyu Dang (军机处上谕档, Imperial Edict Documents of the Grand Council), FHAC. See Lishi Dang'an, (4) 1984, pp.19–21.

*Attached*: Memorial to the throne by *Junji Dachen* about the inventories of the Silver Treasury during *Kangxi*, *Yongzheng* and *Qianlong*
(On the 29th day of the 1st month of the 40th year of Qianlong)

In accordance with the order of Your Majesty, we have investigated the actual silver inventories of the Silver Treasury from Kangxi to the 39th year of Qianlong and made a list. Since the archives of Kangxi are mildewed and rotten, it is impossible to list all the annual figures during that period. Our report is as follows.

TABLE B.2 *Four-column totals of gold, silver and copper coins of the 1st year of* Yongzheng, *1723*

| Item[a] | Initial balance | Revenue | Expenditure | Final balance |
|---|---|---|---|---|
| Gold (taels) | 2,554.528 | – | 320.000 another 498.528 are in the red | 1,736.000 |
| Silver (taels) | 27,119,286.750 | – 7,380,701.563<br>– Contributions: 1,981,626<br>– Capital officials' donation for purchasing mules in the 59th year of *Kangxi*: 9,775.5<br>– Compensated silve by Sun chaqi孙查齐 et al. from the 4th day of the 11th month of the 1styear to the 28th day of the 3rd month of the 2nd year of *Yongzheng*: 29,407 | 10,351,722.345 Another 2,592,957.631 are in the red | 23,576,116.837 |

| Item[a] | Initial balance | Revenue | Expenditure | Final balance |
|---|---|---|---|---|
| Impure silver (taels) | 35,801.668 | – | – | 35,801.668 |
| Copper coins (strings) | 138,598.498 | 486,986.700 | – 471,152.176<br>– Another 9,324.820 are in the red | 138,108.202 |

*Source*: based on the four-column register of the 1st year of Yongzheng, The Yellow Registers (The Silver Treasury of the Ministry of Revenue), Volume 35.
[a] There many items in the original register, the four of which listed here being the most important ones.

TABLE B.3 *Four-column totals of gold, silver and copper coins of the 13th year of* Qianlong, *1748*

| Item | Initial balance | Revenue | Expenditure | Final balance | Remarks |
|---|---|---|---|---|---|
| Gold (taels) | 26.326 | – | – | 26.326 | The amounts of impure silver have been included in the figures of silver. |
| Silver (taels) | 32,363,404.840 | 8,187,984.131 | 13,087,743.910 | 27,463,645.061 | |
| Impure silver (taels) | (211,174.673) | (7,916.859) | (13,703.862) | (205,387.670) | |
| Copper coins (strings) | 5,119.815 | 1,017,312.085 | 1,013,387.471 | 9,044.429 | |

*Source*: based on the four-column register of the 13th year of Qianlong, The Yellow Registers (The Silver Treasury of the Ministry of Revenue), Volume 35.

TABLE B.4 *Four-column totals of silver and copper coins of the 18th year of* Qianlong, *1753*

| Item | Initial balance | Revenue | Expenditure | Final balance | Remarks |
|---|---|---|---|---|---|
| Silver (taels) | 38,630,287.559 | 11,619,370.383 | 10,379,263.332 | 39,870,394.610 | The amounts of impure silver have been included in the figures of silver. |
| Impure silver (taels) | (161,497.964) | (83.868) | (7,357.875) | (154,223.957) | |
| Old silver seals (taels) | – | 1,613.350 (43 seals) | 1,613.350 (43 seals) | – | |
| Copper coins (strings) | 5,742.669 | 1,077,567.077 | 1,075,729.822 | 7,579.924 | |

*Source*: based on the four-column register of the 18th year of Qianlong, The Yellow Registers·The Silver Treasury of the Ministry of Revenue, Volume 35.

TABLE B.5 *Four-column totals of silver and copper coins of the 20th year of* Qianlong, *1755*

| Item | Initial balance | Revenue | Expenditure | Final balance | Remarks |
|---|---|---|---|---|---|
| Silver (taels) | 37,605,422.688 | 15,639,464.928 | 10,247,839.051 | 42,997,048.566 | The amounts of impure silver have been included in the figures of silver. |
| Impure silver (taels) | (144,643.537) | – | (8,605.100) | (136,038.437) | |
| Old silver seals | 153.000 taels (2 seals) | – | – | 153.000 taels (2 seals) | |
| Copper coins (strings) | 2,315.824 | 1,086,862.013 | 1,086,942.003 | 2,235.834 | |

*Source*: based on the four-column register of the 20th year of Qianlong, The Yellow Registers (The Silver Treasury of the Ministry of Revenue), Volume 35.

TABLE B.6 *Four-column totals of silver and copper coins of the 22nd year of* Qianlong, *1757*

| Item | Initial balance | Revenue | Expenditure | Final balance | Remarks |
|---|---|---|---|---|---|
| Silver (taels) | 43,222,030.164 | 9,318,432.873 | 12,388,208.860 | 40,152,254.177 | The amounts of impure silver have been included in the figures of silver. |
| Impure silver (taels) | (125,798.871) | | (8,038.140) | (117,760.731) | |
| Old silver seals | 905.780 taels (9 seals) | 434.000 taels (4 seals) | – | 1,339.780 taels (13 seals) | |
| Copper coins (strings) | 10,994.744 | 1,203,956.556 | 1,214,282.625 | 668.675 | |

*Source*: based on the four-column register of the 22nd year of Qianlong, The Yellow Registers (The Silver Treasury of the Ministry of Revenue), Volume 35.

TABLE B.7 *Four-column totals of silver and copper coins of the 28th year of* Qianlong, *1763*

| Item | Initial balance | Revenue | Expenditure | Final balance | Remarks |
|---|---|---|---|---|---|
| Silver (taels) | 41,927,924.821 | 14,669,588.724 | 9,533,903.023 | 47,063,610.522 | The amounts of impure silver have been included in the figures of silver. |
| Impure silver (taels) | (83,228.984) | (231.360) | (6,597.053) | (76,863.291) | |
| Copper coins (strings) | 909.432 | 1,137,385.645 | 1,138,023.804 | 2,710.273 | |

*Source*: based on the four-column register of the 28th year of Qianlong, The Yellow Registers (The Silver Treasury of the Ministry of Revenue), Volume 35.

TABLE B.8 *Four-column totals of silver and copper coins of the 38th year of* Qianlong, *1773*

| Item | Initial balance | Revenue | Expenditure | Final balance |
|---|---|---|---|---|
| Silver (taels) | 78,740,262.373 | 8,966,307.137 | 19,029,498.285 | 68,677,071.225 |
| Copper coins (strings) | 652.431 | 1,277,810.952 | 1,277,817.006 | 646.377 |

*Source*: based on the four-column register of the 38th year of Qianlong, The Yellow Registers (The Silver Treasury of the Ministry of Revenue), Volume 35.

TABLE B.9 *Four-column totals of silver and copper coins of the 40th year of* Qianlong, *1775*

| Item | Initial balance | Revenue | Expenditure | Final balance | Remarks |
|---|---|---|---|---|---|
| Silver (taels) | 73,905,610.545 | 14,134,912.786 | 23,083,249.853 | 64,957,273.478 | The amounts of impure silver have been included in the figures of silver. |
| Impure silver (taels) | (732.010) | – | (732.010) | – | |
| Copper coins (strings) | 1,512.404 | 1,254,946.655 | 1,254,448.341 | 2,010.718 | |

*Source*: based on the four-column register of the 40th year of Qianlong, The Yellow Registers (The Silver Treasury of the Ministry of Revenue), Volume 35.

TABLE B.10 *Four-column totals of silver and copper coins of the 41st year of* Qianlong, *1776*

| Item | Initial balance | Revenue | Expenditure | Final balance |
|---|---|---|---|---|
| Silver (taels) | 64,957,273.478 | 18,711,298.122 | 9,005,900.154 | 74,662,671.446 |
| Copper coins (strings) | 2,010.718 | 1,294,815.208 | 1,295,308.891 | 1,517.035 |

*Source*: based on the four-column register of the 41st year of Qianlong, The Yellow Registers (The Silver Treasury of the Ministry of Revenue), Volume 35.

TABLE B.11 *Four-column totals of silver and copper coins of the 42nd year of* Qianlong, *1777*

| Item | Initial balance | Revenue | Expenditure | Final balance |
|---|---|---|---|---|
| Silver (taels) | 74,662,671.446 | 18,117,731.619 | 10,956,359.955 | 81,824,043.710 |
| Copper coins (strings) | 1,517.035 | 1,203,459.324 | 1,203,768.109 | 1,208.250 |

*Source*: based on the four-column register of the 42nd year of Qianlong, The Yellow Registers (The Silver Treasury of the Ministry of Revenue), Volume 35.

TABLE B.12 *Four-column totals of silver and copper coins of the 45th year of* Qianlong, *1780*

| Item | Initial balance | Revenue | Expenditure | Final balance |
|---|---|---|---|---|
| Silver (taels) | 75,042,230.504 | 10,567,107.722 | 10,134,444.361 | 75,474,893.865 |
| Copper coins (strings) | 1,596.157 | 1,193,808.115 | 1,193,883.517 | 1,520.755 |

*Source*: based on the four-column register of the 45th year of Qianlong, The Yellow Registers (The Silver Treasury of the Ministry of Revenue), Volume 35.

TABLE B.13 *Four-column totals of silver and copper coins of the 60th year of* Qianlong, *1795*

| Item | Initial balance | Revenue | Expenditure | Final balance |
|---|---|---|---|---|
| Silver (taels) | 71,474,457.860 | 8,665,152.147 | 10,747,620.360 | 69,391,989.647 |
| Copper coins (strings) | 69.792 | 142,656.178 | 142,687.660 | 38.310 |

*Source*: based on the four-column register of the 60th year of Qianlong, The Yellow Registers (The Silver Treasury of the Ministry of Revenue), Volume 35.

TABLE B.14 *Four-column totals of silver and copper coins of the 1st year of* Jiaqing, *1796*

| Item | Initial balance | Revenue | Expenditure | Final balance |
|---|---|---|---|---|
| Silver (taels) | 69,391,989.647 | 5,734,496.110 | 18,541,762.227 | 56,584,723.530 |
| Copper coins (strings) | 38.310 | 591,663.159 | 591,624.285 | 77.184 |

*Source*: based on the four-column register of the 1st year of Jiaqing, The Yellow Registers (The Silver Treasury of the Ministry of Revenue), Volume 35.

TABLE B.15 *Four-column totals of silver and copper coins of the 3rd year of* Jiaqing, *1798*

| Item | Initial balance | Revenue | Expenditure | Final balance |
|---|---|---|---|---|
| Silver (taels) | 27,919,630.838 | 16,413,926.179 | 25,147,964.563 | 19,185,592.454 |
| Copper coins (strings) | 16.553 | 529,854.198 | 529,738.660 | 132.091 |

*Source*: based on the four-column register of the 3rd year of Jiaqing, The Yellow Registers (The Silver Treasury of the Ministry of Revenue), Volume 35.

TABLE B.16 *Four-column totals of silver and copper coins of the 7th year of* Jiaqing, *1802*

| Item | Initial balance | Revenue | Expenditure | Final balance |
|---|---|---|---|---|
| Silver (taels) | 16,934,764.947 | 11,496,754.125 | 8,972,546.325 | 19,458,972.747 |
| Copper coins (strings) | 214 · 614 | 1,534,981.471 | 1,534,843.414 | 352.671 |

*Source*: based on the four-column register of the 7th year of Jiaqing, The Yellow Registers (The Silver Treasury of the Ministry of Revenue), Volume 35.

TABLE B.17 *Four-column totals of silver and copper coins of the 10th year of* Jiaqing, *1805*

| Item | Initial balance | Revenue | Expenditure | Final balance |
|---|---|---|---|---|
| Silver (taels) | 21,645,470.832 | 13,933,952.896 | 11,027,518.275 | 24,551,905.453 |
| Copper coins (strings) | 3,023.771 | 1,327,849.635 | 1,330,551.931 | 321.475 |

*Source*: based on the four-column register of the 10th year of Jiaqing, The Yellow Registers (The Silver Treasury of the Ministry of Revenue), Volume 35.

TABLE B.18 *Four-column totals of silver and copper coins of the 12th year of* Jiaqing, *1807*

| Item | Initial balance | Revenue | Expenditure | Final balance |
|---|---|---|---|---|
| Silver (taels) | 22,928,502.326 | 6,938,703.666 | 9,871,636.029 | 19,995,569.963 |
| Copper coins (strings) | 86,201.869 | 1,438,236.701 | 1,446,607.438 | 77,831.132 |

*Source*: based on the four-column register of the 12th year of Jiaqing, The Yellow Registers (The Silver Treasury of the Ministry of Revenue), Volume 35.

TABLE B.19 *Four-column totals of silver and copper coins of the 16th year of* Jiaqing, *1811*

| Item | Initial balance | Revenue | Expenditure | Final balance |
|---|---|---|---|---|
| Silver (taels) | 22,908,791.917 | 9,448,665.643 | 11,572,992.121 | 20,784,465.439 |
| Copper coins (strings) | 106,877.069 | 1,366,084.509 | 1,365,986.264 | 106,975.314 |

*Source*: based on the four-column register of the 16th year of Jiaqing, The Yellow Registers (The Silver Treasury of the Ministry of Revenue), Volume 35.

TABLE B.20 *Four-column totals of silver and copper coins of the 20th year of* Jiaqing, *1815*

| Item | Initial balance | Revenue | Expenditure | Final balance |
|---|---|---|---|---|
| Silver (taels) | 21,659,563.284 | 12,435,694.634 | 9,686,981.471 | 24,408,276.447 |
| Copper coins (strings) | 118,943.009 | 1,142,974.077 | 1,184,843.269 | 77,073.817 |

*Source*: based on the four-column register of the 20th year of Jiaqing, The Yellow Registers (The Silver Treasury of the Ministry of Revenue), Volume 35.

TABLE B.21 *Four-column totals of silver and copper coins of the 21st year of* Jiaqing, *1816*

| Item | Initial balance | Revenue | Expenditure | Final balance |
|---|---|---|---|---|
| Silver (taels) | 24,408,276.447 | 9,451,035.088 | 10,379,921.253 | 23,479,390.282 |
| Copper coins (strings) | 77,073.817 | 1,496,370.043 | 1,429,076.819 | 144,367.041 |

*Source*: based on the four-column register of the 21st year of Jiaqing, The Yellow Registers (The Silver Treasury of the Ministry of Revenue), Volume 35.

TABLE B.22 *Four-column totals of silver and copper coins of the 22nd year of* Jiaqing, *1817*

| Item | Initial balance | Revenue | Expenditure | Final balance |
|---|---|---|---|---|
| Silver (taels) | 23,479,390.282 | 10,637,957.225 | 10,487,742.397 | 23,629,605.110 |
| Copper coins (strings) | 144,367.041 | 1,168,451.439 | 1,247,636.515 | 65,181.965 |

*Source*: based on the four-column register of the 22nd year of Jiaqing, The Yellow Registers (The Silver Treasury of the Ministry of Revenue), Volume 35.

TABLE B.23 *Four-column totals of silver and copper coins of the 23rd year of* Jiaqing, *1818*

| Item | Initial balance | Revenue | Expenditure | Final balance |
|---|---|---|---|---|
| Silver (taels) | 22,629,605.110 | 13,990,810.002 | 9,951,356.951 | 27,669,058.161 |
| Copper coins (strings) | 65,181.965 | 1,195,426.508 | 1,151,299.802 | 109,308.671 |

*Source*: based on the four-column register of the 23rd year of Jiaqing, The Yellow Registers (The Silver Treasury of the Ministry of Revenue), Volume 35.

TABLE B.24 *Four-column totals of silver and copper coins of the 1st year of* Daoguang, *1821*

| Item | Initial balance | Revenue | Expenditure | Final balance |
|---|---|---|---|---|
| Silver (taels) | 31,211,102.267 | 7,630,388.956 | 11,351,701.120 | 27,489,790.103 |
| Copper coins (strings) | 53,411.041 | 1,202,199.667 | 1,203,756.116 | 51,854.592 |

*Source*: based on the four-column register of the 1st year of Daoguang, The Yellow Registers (The Silver Treasury of the Ministry of Revenue), Volume 35.

TABLE B.25 *Four-column totals of silver and copper coins of the 2nd year of* Daoguang, *1822*

| Item | Initial balance | Revenue | Expenditure | Final balance |
|---|---|---|---|---|
| Silver (taels) | 27,489,790.103 | 7,060,251.329 | 11,210,691.122 | 23,339,350.310 |
| Copper coins (strings) | 51,854.592 | 1,189,489.111 | 1,199,720.433 | 41,623.270 |

*Source*: based on the four-column register of the 2nd year of Daoguang, The Yellow Registers (The Silver Treasury of the Ministry of Revenue), Volume 35.

TABLE B.26 *Four-column totals of silver and copper coins of the 7th year of* Daoguang, *1827*

| Item | Initial balance | Revenue | Expenditure | Final balance |
|---|---|---|---|---|
| Silver (taels) | 17,580,793.680 | 23,802,617.219 | 11,373,705.050 | 30,009,705.849 |
| Copper coins (strings) | 65,050.381 | 1,232,144.651 | 1,252,178.244 | 45,016.788 |

*Source*: based on the four-column register of the 7th year of Daoguang, The Yellow Registers (The Silver Treasury of the Ministry of Revenue), Volume 35.

TABLE B.27 *Four-column totals of silver and copper coins of the 8th year of* Daoguang, *1828*

| Item | Initial balance | Revenue | Expenditure | Final balance |
|---|---|---|---|---|
| Silver (taels) | 30,009,705.849 | 14,422,806.341 | 10,951,956.194 | 33,480,555.996 |
| Copper coins (strings) | 45,016.788 | 1,166,797.619 | 1,158,856.416 | 52,957.991 |

*Source*: based on the four-column register of the 8th year of Daoguang, The Yellow Registers (The Silver Treasury of the Ministry of Revenue), Volume 35.

TABLE B.28 *Four-column totals of silver and copper coins of the 10th year of* Daoguang, *1830*

| Item | Initial balance | Revenue | Expenditure | Final balance |
|---|---|---|---|---|
| Silver (taels) | 33,325,497.989 | 11,289,651.043 | 12,575,834.261 | 32,039,314.771 |
| Copper coins (strings) | 124,492.615 | 1,172,528.710 | 1,244,337.807 | 52,683.518 |

*Source*: based on the four-column register of the 10th year of Daoguang, The Yellow Registers (The Silver Treasury of the Ministry of Revenue), Volume 35.

TABLE B.29 *Four-column totals of silver and copper coins of the 13th year of* Daoguang, *1833*

| Item | Initial balance | Revenue | Expenditure | Final balance |
|---|---|---|---|---|
| Silver (taels) | 25,689,153.883 | 7,160,868.728 | 10,886,615.761 | 21,963,406.850 |
| Copper coins (strings) | 47,014.195 | 1,152,765.935 | 1,151,530.895 | 48,249.235 |

*Source*: based on the four-column register of the 13th year of Daoguang, The Yellow Registers (The Silver Treasury of the Ministry of Revenue), Volume 35.

TABLE B.30 *Four-column totals of silver and copper coins of the 14th year of* Daoguang, *1834*

| Item | Initial balance | Revenue | Expenditure | Final balance | Remarks |
|---|---|---|---|---|---|
| Silver (taels) | 21,963,406.850 | 15,522,249.804 | 10,773,738.669 | 26,711,917.985 | The amount of copper coins of the initial balance is not equal to that of the final balance of the 13th year. |
| Copper coins (strings) | 48,244.601 | 1,183,231.984 | 1,160,590.339 | 70,886.246 | |

*Source*: based on the four-column register of the 14th year of Daoguang, The Yellow Registers (The Silver Treasury of the Ministry of Revenue), Volume 35.

TABLE B.31 *Four-column totals of silver and copper coins of the 23rd year of* Daoguang, *1843*

| Item | Initial balance | Revenue | Expenditure | Final balance |
|---|---|---|---|---|
| Silver (taels) | 13,006,552.601 | 7,919,692.645 | 10,992,455.454 | 9,933,789.792 |
| Copper coins (strings) | 49,634.630 | 1,222,831.431 | 1,270,073.000 | 2,393.061 |

*Source*: based on the four-column register of the 23rd year of Daoguang, The Yellow Registers (The Silver Treasury of the Ministry of Revenue), Volume 35.

TABLE B.32 *Four-column totals of silver and coins of the 4th year of* Xianfeng, *1854*

| Item | Initial balance | Revenue | Expenditure | Final balance | Remarks |
|---|---|---|---|---|---|
| Silver (taels) | 1,696,894.984 | 4,996,127.336 | 5,031,018.775 | 1,662,005.545 | The final balance of silver ought to be 1,662,003.545 taels. |
| Coins (strings) | 2,707.720 | 3,045,823.584 | 3,040,549.541 | 7,981.763 | |
| Jing Piao (strings) | 13,183.652 | 7,846,071.882 | 7,834,542.621 | 24,712.913 | |

*Source*: based on the four-column register of the 4th year of Xianfeng, The Yellow Registers (The Silver Treasury of the Ministry of Revenue), Volume 35.

TABLE B.33 *Four-column totals of silver and coins of the 6th year of* Xianfeng, *1856*

| Item | Initial balance | Revenue | Expenditure | Final balance |
|---|---|---|---|---|
| Silver (taels) | 1,496,601.811 | 2,669,662.682 | 2,704,989.316 | 1,461,275.177 |
| Coins (strings) | 52,475.627 | 811,063.454 | 517,736.361 | 345,802.720 |
| Jing Piao (strings) | 66,381.214 | 7,884,488.834 | 7,950,869.448 | 0.600 |
| Baochao (strings) | – | 4,405,082.000 | 4,405,082.000 | – |
| Weiling Duitiao Qian (strings) | – | 154.108 | 154.108 | – |

*Source*: based on the four-column register of the 6th year of Xianfeng, The Yellow Registers (The Silver Treasury of the Ministry of Revenue), Volume 35.

TABLE B.34 *Four-column totals of gold, silver and coins of the 9th year of* Xianfeng, *1859*

| Item | Initial balance | Revenue | Expenditure | Final balance |
|---|---|---|---|---|
| Gold (taels) | 189.929 | – | – | 189.929 |
| Silver (taels) | 2,370,433.947 | 4,463,477.956 | 3,808,417.524 | 3,025,494.379 |
| Coins (strings) | 367,444.249 | 968,530.138 | 903,324.258 | 432,650.129 |

TABLE B.34 *Four-column totals of gold, silver and coins of the 9th year of* Xianfeng, *1859* (cont.)

| Item | Initial balance | Revenue | Expenditure | Final balance |
|---|---|---|---|---|
| Jing Piao (strings) | 31,959.628 | 19,131,590.149 | 16,046,202.670 | 3,117,347.107 |
| Baochao (strings) | – | 2,133,825.000 | 2,133,825.000 | – |
| Weiling Duitiao Qian (strings) | – | 408.852 | 408.852 | – |

*Source*: based on the four-column register of the 9th year of Xianfeng, The Yellow Registers (The Silver Treasury of the Ministry of Revenue), Volume 35.

TABLE B.35 *Four-column totals of gold, silver and coins of the 11th year of* Xianfeng, *1861*

| Item | Initial balance | Revenue | Expenditure | Final balance |
|---|---|---|---|---|
| Gold (taels) | 189.929 | – | – | 189.929 |
| Silver (taels) | 1,175,096.676 | 6,678,613.514 | 6,331,925.933 | 1,521,784.257 |
| Coins (strings) | 379,419.809 | 295,354.819 | 169,540.327 | 505,234.301 |
| Jing Piao (strings) | 75,196.998 | 408,881.064 | 174,287.254 | 309,790.808 |
| Baochao (strings) | – | 155,518.000 | 155,431.000 | 87.000 |
| Weiling Duitiao Qian (strings) | – | 184.903 | 182.203 | 2.700 |

*Source*: based on the four-column register of the 11th year of Xianfeng, The Yellow Registers (The Silver Treasury of the Ministry of Revenue), Volume 35.

TABLE B.36 *The Four-column totals of gold, silver and coins of the 9th year of* Guangxu, *1883*

| Item | Initial balance | Revenue | Expenditure | Final balance |
|---|---|---|---|---|
| Gold (taels) | 189.929 | – | – | 189.929 |
| Zubao silver samples and others (taels) | 31,401.000 | – | – | 31,401.000 |

| Item | Initial balance | Revenue | Expenditure | Final balance |
|---|---|---|---|---|
| Actual silver reserves of the inner treasury (taels) | 1,095,900.000 (According to an audit report in the 5th month of the 8th year of Guangxu, there were 750 taels in the red. So, the real amount of reserves now is: 1,095,150 taels) | – | – | 1,095,900.000 (According to an audit report in the 5th month of the 8th year of Guangxu, there were 750 taels in the red. So, the real amount of reserves now is: 1,095,150 taels) |
| Actual silver reserves of the outer treasury (taels) | 6,239,945.359 | 11,274,429.907 | 11,623,012.517 | 5,891,362.741 |
| 40% of import duties (taels) | 441,987.236 | 2,474,619.860 | 782,298.680 | 2,134,308.416 |
| Fund for the northeast border defence (taels) | 1,373,537.585 | 1,853,537.990 | 1,440,000.000 | 1,787,075.575 |
| Fund for disaster relief (taels) | – | 36,000.000 | – | 36,000.000 |
| Coins (strings) | 306,848.551 | 228,309.082 | 404,120.289 | 131,037.344 |

*Source*: based on the four-column register of the 9th year of Guangxu, The Yellow Registers (The Silver Treasury of the Ministry of Revenue), Volume 35.

TABLE B.37 *Four-column totals of gold, silver and coins of the 17th year of* Guangxu, *1891*

| Item | Initial balance | Revenue | Expenditure | Final balance |
|---|---|---|---|---|
| Gold (taels) | 189.929 | – | – | 189.929 |
| Zubao silver samples and others (taels) | 31,401.000 | – | – | 31,401.000 |

TABLE B.37 *Four-column totals of gold, silver and coins of the 17th year of* Guangxu, *1891* (cont.)

| Item | Initial balance | Revenue | Expenditure | Final balance |
|---|---|---|---|---|
| Actual silver reserves of the inner treasury (taels) | 1,095,900.000 | – | – | 1,095,900.000 |
| Actual silver reserves of the outer treasury (taels) | 899,713.563 | 14,245,371.621 (Kuping) | 13,052,960.471 (Kuping) | 2,092,124.713 |
| New contribution for coastal defence (taels) | 51,628.000 | 283,435.000 | 250,000.000 | 85,063.000 |
| New contribution for coastal defence (the 8th, 9th and 10th months of the 16th year) (taels) | 87,745.000 | – | – | 300,000.000 (the total of the left two columns) |
| Surpluses of the Contribution for disaster relief of the Shuntian Prefecture (taels) | – | 212,255.000 | – | |
| Silver for purchasing copper and lead (taels) | 1,456,096.518 | 742,777.800 | 390,875.901 | 1,807,998.417 |
| 40% of import duties (taels) | 150,350.081 | 241,367.405 | 280,000.000 | 111,717.486 |
| Fund for the northeast border defence (taels) | 5,585,575.172 | 3,540,000.000 | 3,142,096.360 | 5,983,478.812 |
| Coins (strings) | 957,412.265 | 1,390,436.144 | 1,586,172.614 | 761,675.795 |

*Source*: based on the four-column register of the 1th year of Guangxu, The Yellow Registers (The Silver Treasury of the Ministry of Revenue), Volume 35.

TABLE B.38 *Four-column totals of gold, silver and coins of the 23rd year of* Guangxu, *1897*

| Item | Initial balance | Revenue | Expenditure | Final balance |
|---|---|---|---|---|
| Gold (taels) | 189.929 | – | – | 189.929 |
| Zubao silver samples and others (taels) | 31,401.000 | – | – | 31,401.000 |
| Actual silver reserves of the inner treasury (taels) | 1,095,900.000 | – | – | 1,095,900.000 |
| Actual silver reserves of the outer treasury (taels) | 366,499.322 | 15,540,823.594 (Kuping) | 15,142,508.129 (Kuping) | 764,814.787 |
| 40% of import duties (taels) | 430,106.036 | 102,317.236 | 280,000.000 | 252,423.272 |
| Fund for northeast border defence (taels) | 899,084.208 | 1,865,000.000 | 1,792,472.893 | 971,611.315 |
| Fund for preparing soldiers' pay (taels) | 1,870,000.000 | 1,652,260.000 | 2,500,000.000 | 1,022,260.000 |
| New contribution for coastal defence (taels) | 354,654.496 | 944,593.652 | 636,091.201 | 663,156.947 |
| Silver for purchasing copper and lead (taels) | 506,883.132 | 274,109.384 | 362,000.000 | 418,992.516 |
| Income from using two different silver scales (fang er liang ping kouhui liu fen pingyin (放二两平扣回六分平银) (taels) | 434,268.143 | 977,064.384 | 942,000.000 | 462,332.527 |
| New contribution for purchasing firearms (taels) | 40,000.000 | – | 40,000.000 | – |
| Navy fund (taels) | 41,182.564 | 305,511.000 | 316,149.322 | 30,544.242 |
| Provincial taxes and likin levied on Domestic opium (taels) | 50,393.289 | 564,215.915 | 614,000.000 | 609.204 |

TABLE B.38 *Four-column totals of gold, silver and coins of the 23rd year of* Guangxu, *1897* (cont.)

| Item | Initial balance | Revenue | Expenditure | Final balance |
|---|---|---|---|---|
| Fund for coastal defence (taels) | 86,725.035 | 230,000.000 | 292,000.000 | 24,725.035 |
| Fund for disaster relief (taels) | 180,250.000 | 108,372.367 | 152,372.367 | 136,250.000 |
| Silver for purchasing naval warships and weapons (taels) | 556,532.799 | – | 556,532.799 | – |
| Railway fund (taels) | 75,000.000 | 310,000.000 | 375,000.000 | 10,000.000 |
| Fund for the Putuoyu tomb project (taels) | 862,437.286 | – | 406,000.000 | 456,437.286 |
| Fund prepared for soldiers' pay (taels) | 71,928.908 | 209,076.157 | 278,562.908 | 2,442.157 |
| Monthly soldiers' pay of the newly established land army (taels) | – | 200,000.000 | 150,000.000 | 50,000.000 |
| Coins (strings) | 687,602.644 | 341,024.940 | 517,130.821 | 511,496.763 |

*Source*: based on the Guangxu Ershisan Nianfen Jiuguan Xinshou Kaichu Shizai Jin Yin Qian Shumu Huangce (光绪二十三年分旧管新收开除实在金银钱数目黄册, Four-column Yellow Register of Gold, Silver and Coins of the 23rd Year of Guangxu), kept by FHAC.

TABLE B.39 *Four-column totals of gold, silver and coins of the 24th year of* Guangxu, *1898*

| Item | Initial balance | Revenue | Expenditure | Final balance |
|---|---|---|---|---|
| Gold (taels) | 189.929 | – | – | 189.929 |
| Zubao silver samples and others (taels) | 31,401.000 | – | – | 31,401.000 |
| Actual silver reserves of the inner treasury (taels) | 1,095,900.000 | – | – | 1,095,900.000 |

| Item | Initial balance | Revenue | Expenditure | Final balance |
|---|---|---|---|---|
| Actual silver reserves of the outer treasury (taels) | 764,814.787 | 18,359,330.537 (Kuping) | 18,010,663.282 (Kuping) | 1,113,482.042 |
| 40% of import duties (taels) | 252,423.272 | 72,561.579 | 12,475.468 | 312,509.383 |
| Fund for northeast border defence (taels) | 971,611.315 | 1,724,000.000 | 2,589,338.550 | 106,272.765 |
| Fund for preparing soldiers' pay (taels) | 1,022,260.000 | 1,671,333.333 | 2,675,831.764 | 17,761.569 |
| New contribution for coastal defence (taels) | 663,156.947 | 797,272.044 | 1,452,144.000 | 8,284.991 |
| Silver for purchasing copper and lead (taels) | 418,992.516 | 139,528.091 | 509,433.960 | 49,086.647 |
| Income from using two different silver scales (fang er liang ping kouhui liu fen pingyin 放二两平扣回六分平银) (taels) | 462,332.527 | 1,224,253.914 | 1,631,320.000 | 55,266.441 |
| Navy fund (taels) | 30,544.242 | 280,859.859 | 311,404.101 | – |
| Taxes and likin levied on Domestic opium (taels) | 609.204 | 536,465.748 | 537,000.000 | 74.952 |
| Fund for coastal defence (taels) | 24,725.035 | 280,000.000 | 252,325.035 | 52,400.000 |
| Fund for disaster relief (taels) | 136,250.000 | 154,872.366 | 70,000.000 | 221,122.366 |
| Railway fund (taels) | 10,000.000 | 268,600.000 | 255,200.000 | 23,400.000 |
| Fund for the Putuoyu tomb project (taels) | 456,437.286 | – | 164,518.126 | 291,919.160 |
| Fund prepared for soldiers' pay (taels) | 2,442.157 | 125,500.202 | 120,000.000 | 7,942.359 |

TABLE B.39 *Four-column totals of gold, silver and coins of the 24th year of* Guangxu, *1898* (cont.)

| Item | Initial balance | Revenue | Expenditure | Final balance |
|---|---|---|---|---|
| The monthly soldiers' pay of the Tianjin land army (taels) | 50,000.000 | 150,000.000 | 197,383.680 | 2,616.320 |
| Zhaoxin Stock (taels) | – | 2,530,200.000 | | 2,530,200.000 |
| Funds for the Tianjin Customs (Jin Haiguan bafen jingfei yin 津海关八分经费银) (taels) | – | 40,000.000 | 6,000.000 | 34,000.000 |
| Funds of shipyard (taels) | – | 140,000.000 | 100,000.000 | 40,000.000 |
| Silver dollars (zhengxiang yinyuan正项银元) (yuan) | – | 150,000.000 | 150,000.000 | – |
| Fund for border defence in silver dollars (yuan) | – | 80,000.000 | 80,000.000 | – |
| Fund prepared for soldiers' pay in silver dollars (yuan) | – | 70,000.000 | 70,000.000 | – |
| Income from using two different silver scales (fang er liang ping kouhui liu fen ping yinyuan 放二两平扣回六分平银元) (yuan) | – | 7,878.380 | 7,878.380 | – |
| Coins (strings) | 511,496.763 | 439,708.442 | 625,380.590 | 325,824.615 |

*Source*: based on the Guangxu Ershisi Nianfen Jiuguan Xinshou Kaichu Shizai Jin Yin Qian Shumu Huangce (光绪二十四年分旧管新收开除实在金银钱数目黄册, Four-column Yellow Register of Gold, Silver and Coins of the 24th Year of Guangxu), kept by FHAC.

TABLE B.40 *Four-column totals of gold, silver and coins of the 25th year of* Guangxu, *1899*

| Item | Initial balance | Revenue | Expenditure | Final balance |
|---|---|---|---|---|
| Gold (taels) | 189.929 | – | – | 189.929 |
| Zubao silver samples and others (taels) | 31,401.000 | – | – | 31,401.000 |
| Actual silver reserves of the inner treasury (taels) | 1,095,900.000 | – | – | 1,095,900.000 |
| Actual silver reserves of the outer treasury (taels) | 1,113,482.042 | 14,543,209.120 (Kuping) | 15,258,045.763 (Kuping) | 398,645.399 |
| 40% of import duties (taels) | 312,509.383 | 365,001.381 | 595,180.000 | 82,330.764 |
| Fund for the northeast border defence (taels) | 106,272.765 | 2,488,031.771 | 2,461,740.951 | 132,833.585 |
| Fund for preparing soldiers' pay (taels) | 17,761.569 | 1,746,614.668 | 1,310,000.000 | 454,376.237 |
| New contribution for coastal defence (taels) | 8,284.991 | 478,197.416 | 480,362.867 | 6,119.540 |
| Silver for purchasing copper and lead (taels) | 49,086.647 | 531,423.737 | 372,664.960 | 207,845.424 |
| Income from using two different silver scales (fang er liang ping kouhui liu fen pingyin 放二两平扣回六分平银) (taels) | 55,266.441 | 978,318.611 | 711,973.800 | 321,611.252 |
| Taxes and likin levied on Domestic opium (taels) | 74.952 | 590,792.052 | 585,500.000 | 5,367.004 |
| Fund for disaster relief (taels) | 221,122.366 | 57,872.366 | 40,000.000 | 238,994.732 |
| Fund for the Putuoyu tomb project (taels) | 291,919.160 | 500,000.000 | 280,000.000 | 511,919.160 |

TABLE B.40 *Four-column totals of gold, silver and coins of the 25th year of* Guangxu*, 1899* (cont.)

| Item | Initial balance | Revenue | Expenditure | Final balance |
|---|---|---|---|---|
| Fund prepared for the soldiers' pay (taels) | 7,942.359 | – | 6,486.720 | 1,455.639 |
| The monthly soldiers' pay of Tianjin land army (taels) | 2,616.320 | 530,000.000 | 532,552.002 | 64.318 |
| Railway fund (taels) | 23,400.000 | 159,000.000 | 60,000.000 | 122,400.000 |
| Zhaoxin Stock (taels) | 2,530,200.000 | 5,000.000 | 500,000.000 | 2,035,200.000 |
| Funds for the Tianjin Customs (Jin Haiguan bafen jingfei yin (津海关八分经费银) (taels) | 34,000.000 | 60,000.000 | 50,000.000 | 44,000.000 |
| Fund for coastal defence (taels) | 52,400.000 | 300,000.000 | 272,864.000 | 79,536.000 |
| Funds of shipyard (taels) | 40,000.000 | 805,000.000 | 820,000.000 | 25,000.000 |
| Navy fund (taels) | – | 200,000.000 | 196,111.236 | 3,888.764 |
| Recurrent contribution in silver dollars (yuan) | – | 30,255.000 | – | 30,255.000 |
| New contribution for coastal defence in silver dollars (yuan) | – | 21,669.000 | – | 21,699.000 |
| Silver dollars (zhengxiang yinyuan 正项银元) (yuan) | – | 33,950.000 | – | 33,950.000 |
| Railway fund in silver dollars (yuan) | – | 23,000.000 | – | 23,000.000 |
| Coins (strings) | 325,824.615 | 371,167.170 | 337,510.135 | 359,481.650 |

*Source*: based on the Guangxu Ershiwu Nianfen Jiuguan Xinshou Kaichu Shizai Jin Yin Qian Shumu Huangce (光绪二十五年分旧管新收开除实在金银钱数目黄册, Four-column Yellow Register of Gold, Silver and Coins of the 25th Year of Guangxu), kept by FHAC.

TABLE B.41 *Inventories of the Silver Treasury during* Kangxi, *1667–1722*

| Year | Year-end inventory | |
|---|---|---|
| | Silver (taels) | Copper coins (strings) |
| 6th year (1667) | 2,488,492 | – |
| 11th year (1672) | 18,096,850 | – |
| 12th year (1673) | 21,358,006 | – |
| 16th year (1677) | 5,307,216 | – |
| 17th year (1678) | 3,339,920 | – |
| 25th year (1686) | 26,052,735 | – |
| 26th year (1687) | 28,964,499 | – |
| 30th year (1691) | 31,849,719 | – |
| 31st year (1692) | 34,255,285 | – |
| 32nd year (1693) | 37,600,663 | – |
| 33rd year (1694) | 41,007,790 | – |
| 34th year (1695) | 42,263,516 | – |
| 35th year (1696) | 42,628,989 | – |
| 36th year (1697) | 40,639,920 | – |
| 37th year (1698) | 40,542,966 | – |
| 42nd year (1703) | 38,368,105 | – |
| 43rd year (1704) | 39,985,306 | – |
| 47th year (1708) | 47,184,788 | – |
| 48th year (1709) | 43,767,094 | – |
| 49th year (1710) | 45,881,072 | – |
| 52nd year (1713) | 43,094,239 | – |
| 53rd year (1714) | 40,734,825 | – |
| 57th year (1718) | 44,319,033 | – |
| 58th year (1719) | 47,368,645 | – |
| 59th year (1720) | 39,317,103 | – |
| 60th year (1721) | 32,622,421 | – |
| 61st year (1722) | 27,155,088[a] | 138,598 |

*Source*: based on Tables B.1 and B.2.
[a] This figure includes 35,802 taels of impure silver.

TABLE B.42 *Inventories of the Silver Treasury during* Yongzheng, *1723–1735*

| Year | Year-end inventory | |
|---|---|---|
| | Silver (taels) | Copper coins (strings) |
| 1st year (1723) | 23,611,919[a] | 138,108 |
| 2nd year (1724) | 31,627,608 | – |
| 3rd year (1725) | 40,434,744 | – |
| 4th year (1726) | 47,409,780 | – |
| 5th year (1727) | 55,252,933 | – |
| 6th year (1728) | 58,235,780 | – |
| 7th year (1729) | 60,248,747 | – |
| 8th year (1730) | 62,183,349 | – |
| 9th year (1731) | 50,375,953 | – |
| 10th year (1732) | 44,392,848 | – |
| 11th year (1733) | 37,933,743 | – |
| 12th year (1734) | 32,503,428 | – |
| 13th year (1735) | 34,530,485 | – |

*Source*: based on Table B.1 and B.2.
[a] According to the 1775 incentory, the silver figure of the year is 23,711,920 taels.

TABLE B.43 *Inventories of the Silver Treasury during* Qianlong, *1736–1795*

| Year | Year-end inventory | |
|---|---|---|
| | Silver (taels) | Copper coins (strings) |
| 1st year (1736) | 33,959,624 | – |
| 2nd year (1737) | 34,385,138 | – |
| 3rd year (1738) | 34,858,748 | – |
| 4th year (1739) | 32,582,976 | – |
| 5th year (1740) | 30,485,876 | – |
| 6th year (1741) | 31,463,539 | – |
| 7th year (1742) | 32,746,752 | – |
| 8th year (1743) | 29,121,104 | – |
| 9th year (1744) | 31,902,518 | – |

| Year | Year-end inventory | |
|---|---|---|
| | Silver (taels) | Copper coins (strings) |
| 10th year (1745) | 33,170,655 | – |
| 11th year (1746) | 34,633,177 | – |
| 12th year (1747) | 32,363,405 | 5,120 |
| 13th year (1748) | 27,463,645 | 9,044 |
| 14th year (1749) | 28,073,043 | – |
| 15th year (1750) | 30,796,177 | – |
| 16th year (1751) | 32,493,786 | – |
| 17th year (1752) | 38,630,288 | 5,743 |
| 18th year (1753) | 39,870,395 | 7,580 |
| 19th year (1754) | 37,605,423 | 2,316 |
| 20th year (1755) | 42,997,049 | 2,236 |
| 21st year (1756) | 43,222,030 | 10,995 |
| 22nd year (1757) | 40,152,254 | 669 |
| 23rd year (1758) | 36,380,809 | – |
| 24th year (1759) | 36,732,865 | – |
| 25th year (1760) | 35,496,902 | – |
| 26th year (1761) | 36,638,572 | – |
| 27th year (1762) | 41,927,925 | 909 |
| 28th year (1763) | 47,063,611 | 271 |
| 29th year (1764) | 54,273,814 | – |
| 30th year (1765) | 60,336,375 | – |
| 31st year (1766) | 66,613,127 | – |
| 32nd year (1767) | 66,501,052 | – |
| 33rd year (1768) | 71,823,888 | – |
| 34th year (1769) | 76,222,877 | – |
| 35th year (1770) | 77,299,736 | – |
| 36th year (1771) | 78,940,001 | – |
| 37th year (1772) | 78,740,262 | 652 |
| 38th year (1773) | 68,677,071[a] | 646 |
| 39th year (1774) | 73,905,611 | 1,512 |
| 40th year (1775) | 64,957,273 | 2,011 |
| 41st year (1776) | 74,662,671 | 1,517 |
| 42nd year (1777) | 81,824,044 | 1,208 |
| 44th year (1779) | 75,042,231 | 1,596 |
| 45th year (1780) | 75,474,894 | 1,521 |

TABLE B.43 *Inventories of the Silver Treasury during* Qianlong, *1736–1795* (cont.)

| **Year** | **Year–end inventory** | |
|---|---|---|
| | **Silver (taels)** | **Copper coins (strings)** |
| 59th year (1794) | 71,474,458 | 70 |
| 60th year (1795) | 69,391,990 | 38 |

*Source*: based on Tables B.1 and B.3–B.13. The silver figures include the amounts of impure silver, but not those of the old silver seals.

[a] According to the 1775 inventory, the amount of silver of the 38th year is 69,677,071 taels

TABLE B.44 *Inventories of the Silver Treasury during* Jiaqing, *1796–1820*

| **Year** | **Year-end inventory** | |
|---|---|---|
| | **Silver (taels)** | **Copper coins (strings)** |
| 1st year (1796) | 56,584,724 | 77 |
| 2nd year (1797) | 27,919,631 | 17 |
| 3rd year (1798) | 19,185,592 | 132 |
| 6th year (1801) | 16,934,765 | 215 |
| 7th year (1802) | 19,458,973 | 353 |
| 9th year (1804) | 21,645,471 | 3,024 |
| 10th year (1805) | 24,551,905 | 321 |
| 11th year (1806) | 22,928,502 | 86,202 |
| 12th year (1807) | 19,995,570 | 77,831 |
| 15th year (1810) | 22,908,792 | 106,877 |
| 16th year (1811) | 20,784,465 | 106,975 |
| 19th year (1814) | 21,659,563 | 118,943 |
| 20th year (1815) | 24,408,276 | 77074 |
| 21st year (1816) | 23,479,390 | 144,367 |
| 22nd year (1817) | 23,629,605 | 65,182 |
| 23rd year (1818) | 27,669,058 | 109,309 |
| 25th year (1820) | 31,211,102 | 53,411 |

*Source*: based on Tables B.14–B.23.

TABLE B.45 *Inventories of the Silver Treasury during* Daoguang, *1821–1843*

| Year | Year-end inventory | |
|---|---|---|
| | Silver (taels) | Copper coins (strings) |
| 1st year (1821) | 27,489,790 | 51,855 |
| 2nd year (1822) | 23,339,350 | 41,623 |
| 6th year (1826) | 17,580,794 | 65,050 |
| 7th year (1827) | 30,009,706 | 45,017 |
| 8th year (1828) | 33,480,556 | 52,959 |
| 9th year (1829) | 33,325,498 | 124,493 |
| 10th year (1830) | 32,039,315 | 52,684 |
| 12th year (1832) | 25,689,154 | 47,014 |
| 13th year (1833) | 21,963,407 | 48,249 |
| 14th year (1834) | 26,711,918 | 70,886 |
| 22nd year (1842) | 13,006,553 | 49,635 |
| 23rd year (1843) | 9,933,790 | 2,393 |

*Source*: based on Tables B.24–B.31.

TABLE B.46 *Inventories of the Silver Treasury during* Xianfeng, *1853–1861*

| Year | Year-end inventory | |
|---|---|---|
| | Silver (taels) | Coins (strings) |
| 3rd year (1853) | 1,696,895 | 15,891 |
| 4th year (1854) | 1,662,006 | 32,695 |
| 5th year (1855) | 1,496,602 | 118,857 |
| 6th year (1856) | 1,461,275 | 345,803 |
| 8th year (1858) | 2,370,434 | 399,404 |
| 9th year (1859) | 3,025,494 | 3,549,997 |
| 10th year (1860) | 1,175,097 | 454,617 |
| 11th year (1861) | 1,521,784 | 815,115 |

*Source*: based on Tables B.32–B.35.

TABLE B.47 *Inventories of the Silver Treasury during* Guangxu, *1883–1899*

| Year | Year-end inventory | |
|---|---|---|
| | Silver (taels) | Coins (strings) |
| 8th year (1883) | 8,055,470 | 306,849 |
| 9th year (1884) | 9,848,747 | 131,037 |
| 16th year (1890) | 8,231,108 | 957,412 |
| 17th year (1891) | 10,380,382 | 761,676 |
| 22nd year (1896) | 6,825,945 | 687,603 |
| 23rd year (1897) | 5,266,599 | 511,497 |
| 24th year (1898) | 4,866,339 | 325,825 |
| 25th year (1899) | 4,780,492 | 359,482 |

*Source*: based on Tables B.36–B.40. The Zubao silver samples and the inner treasury reserves are not included in the inventory figures.

# References

## Archival Sources

*Daoguang Shiba Nian Zhi Ershiba Nian Suiru Suichu Ce* (道光十八年至二十八年岁入岁出册, Register of Annual Revenues and Expenditures from the 18th to the 28th Year of *Daoguang*), Weng Tonghe (翁同龢) edn. (翁同龢家藏本, now kept by the National Library).

*Daqing Huidian* (大清会典, Administrative Code of the Qing Dynasty), 1690 edn; 1732 edn.; 1764 edn.; 1818 edn.; 1899 edn. [quoted as: *Kangxi Huidian* (1690 edn.); *Yongzheng Huidian* (1732 edn.); *Qianlong Huidian* (1764 edn.); *Jiaqing Huidian* (1818 edn.); *Guangxu Huidian* (1899 edn.)]

*Daqing Huidian Shili* (大清会典事例, Examples of the Administrative Code of the Qing Dynasty), 1899 edn. [quoted as: *Huidian Shili*]

*Daqing Lichao Shilu* (大清历朝实录, Actual Veritable Records of Emperors of the Qing Dynasty). [quoted as: CSL: *Shizu Shilu* (世祖实录, Actual Veritable Record of Emperor Shunzhi); *Shengzu Shilu* (圣祖实录, Actual Veritable Record of Emperor Kangxi); *Shizong Shilu* (世宗实录, Actual Veritable Record of Emperor Yongzheng), etc.]

Daqing Yinhang Shimo Ji (大清银行始末记, Complete Records of Da Qing Bank), Daqing Yinhang Zongqinglichu (大清银行总清理处) comp., 1915 edn.

Guangxu Chao Donghua Lu (光绪朝东华录, Donghua Chronicles of the Reign of *Guangxu*), Zhu Shoupeng(朱寿朋) comp., 1909 edn.

*Guangxu Kuaiji Biao* (光绪会计表, Accounting Tables of Guangxu), by Liu Yueyun (刘岳云), Jiaoyu Shijie She (教育世界社), 1901. [quoted as: *Kuaijibiao*]

*Guangxu Shiyi Nian Gesheng Huibao Churu Kuan Ceshi* (光绪十一年各省汇报出入款册式, Accounting Book Types for reporting revenues/expenditures by provinces, the 11th year of Guangxu), in the library of Institute of Economics, CASS.

Guanxu Zhengyao (光绪政要), Shen Tongsheng 沈桐生comp., 1909 edn.

*Guozhai Jiyao*(国债辑要, Summaries of National Debts), Jiang Shili (蒋士立) comp. (Shanghai: Commercial Press, 1915).

*Haifang Shili* (海防事例, Contribution for coastal defence), Ronglutang (荣禄堂) comp., 1904 edn.

*Huangchao Jingshiwenbian* (皇朝经世文编, A Selection of Statecraft articles), He Changling (贺长龄) et al comp. (Beijing: Zhonghua Book Company (photocopy), 1992).

Hubu Zeli (户部则例, Regulations of the Ministry of Revenue), 1874 ed.

Hubu Yinku Zou'an Jiyao (户部银库奏案辑要, Collected Memorials to the Throne on the Silver Treasury of the Ministry of Revenue), printed by Jingshi Guanshuju (京师官书局, the Capital Official Publishing House) in the late Qing.

*Jnjichu Lufu Zouzhe* (军机处录副奏折, Memorial copies of the Grand Council), in Lufu·Caizheng, FHAC.

*Kang Yong Qian Hubu Yinku Linian Cunyinshu* (康雍乾户部银库历年存银数, Annual Inventories of the Silver Treasury of the Ministry of Revenue during Kangxi, Yongzheng and Qianlong), in *Lishi Dang'an* (历史档案, The Historical Archives), 4 (1984).

*Neige Daku Xiancun Qingdai Hanwen Huangce Mulu* (内阁大库现存清代汉文黄册目录, Catalogue of Extant Chinese Yellow Registers of the Grand Secretariat of the Qing Dynasty), Gugong Wenxian Guan (故宫文献馆, the Documentation Office of the Palace Museum) comp., 1936.

*Qingchao Wenxian Tongkao* (清朝文献通考, Encyclopaedia of Official Documents of the Qing Dynasty) (Shanghai: Commercial Press, 1936).

Qingchao Xu Wenxian Tongkao (清朝续文献通考, Continuation of Encyclopaedia of Official Documents of the Qing Dynasty), by *Liu Jinzao* (刘錦藻) (Shanghai: Commercial Press, 1936).

Qingshi Gao (清史稿, Draft History of the Qing Dynasty), by Zhao Erxun 赵尔巽 et al. (Beijing: Zhonghua Book Company, 1977).

Qingshi Liezhuan (清史列传, Collected Biographies in the Qing Period) (Beijing: Zhonghua Book Company, 1987).

Qing Neige Jiucang Hanwen Huangce Lianhe Mulu (清内阁旧藏汉文黄册联合目录, Union Catalogue of Chinese Yellow Registers of the Grand Secretariat of the Qing Dynasty), Gugong Wenxian Guan (故宫文献馆, the Documentation Office of the Palace Museum), Beijing Daxue Wenke Yanjiusuo (北京大学文科研究所, the Institute of Arts, Peking University) and Zhongyang Yanjiuyuan Lishi Yuyan Yanjiusuo (中央研究院历史语言研究所, the Institute of History and Philology, Academia Sinica) comp., 1947.

Xianfeng Tongzhi Liangchao Shangyu Dang (咸丰同治两朝上谕档, Archives of Imperial Edict during the Reigns of Xianfeng and Tongzhi), FHAC comp. (Guilin: Guangxi Normal University Press, 1998).

Zhongguo Jindai Huobi Shi Ziliao (中国近代货币史资料 (第一辑), Materials on Modern Currency History of China), Zhongguo Renmin Yinhang Zonghang Canshishi Jinrong Shiliao Zu (中国人民银行总行参事室金融史料组) comp. (Beijing: Zhonghua Book Company, 1964). [quoted as: *Huobi Shi Ziliao*]

*Zhongguo Qingdai Waizhai Shi Ziliao* (中国清代外债史资料 (1853 —1911), Historical Materials of Foreign Debts in the Qing Dynasty), Zhongguo Renmin Yinhang (中国人民银行参事室) comp. (Beijing: China Financial Publishing House, 1991).

*Zhong Wai Jiu Yuezhang Huibian* (中外旧约章汇编), Wang Tieya (王铁崖) comp. (Beijing: Sanliangshudian (三联书店), 1957).
*Zhuozeng Changli* (酌增常例, Collected Memorials on Increasing Contributions to Routine Case), 1827ed.
*Zhongguo Hanguan yu Yihetuan Yundong* (中国海关与义和团运动, Chinese Maritime Customs and the Boxer Movement), Beijing: Zhonghua Book Company, 1983).
Zhupi Zouzhe (朱批奏折),in Zhupi·Caizheng (朱批全宗财政类), FHAC.

### Private Notebooks

Far Shishan (法式善), *Taolu Zalu* (陶庐杂录, Reading Notes in Taolu) (Beijing: Zhonghua Book Company, 1959).
He Gangde (何刚德), *Chunming Menglu* (春明梦录) (Shanghai: Shanghai Ancient Books Publishing House, 1983).
Hu Sijing (胡思敬), *Guowen Beicheng* (国闻备乘, Allusions Heard and Seen for Compiling History) (Beijing: Zhonghua Book Company, 2007).
Lingquan Jushi (苓泉居士(杨寿枏)), *Juehua Liao Zaji* (觉花寮杂记, Jottings in Juehualiao Hut), Early Republic edition (民初版本).
Ouyang Yu (欧阳昱), *Jianwen Suolu* (见闻琐录, Trivial Records Heard and Seen) (Changsha: Yuelu Publishing House, 1987).
Wang Kaiyun (王闿运), *Xiangqilou Riji* (湘绮楼日记, Wang Kaiyun's Diary) (Changsha: Yuelu Publishing House, 1997).
Wang Qingyun (王庆云), *Shiqu Yuji* (石渠余纪, Summary Records of Administration Systems of the Imperial Dynasty), 1890 edn.
Wei Yuan (魏源), *Shengwu Ji* (圣武记, Records of Military Accomplishments of the Empire) (Beijing: Zhonghua Book Company, 1984).
Wu Changyuan (吴长元), *Chenyuan Shilue* (宸垣识略, Records of the Imperial Capital) (Beijing: Beijing Ancient Books Publishing House, 1983).
Zhao Liewen (赵烈文), *Nengjingju Riji* (能静居日记, Zhao Liewen's Diary) (Changsha: Yuelu Publishing House, 2013).
Zhao Yi (赵翼), *Yanpu Zaji* (檐曝杂记, Miscellanea during Basking under Eaves) (Beijing: Zhonghua Book Company, 1982).

### Secondary Literature

He Lie (何烈), *Qing Xian Tong Shiqi de Caizheng* (清咸、同时期的财政, The Finance during Xianfeng-Tongzhi of the Qing Dynasty) (Taibei: Guoli Bianyiguan Zhonghua Congshu Bianshen Weiyuanhui (国立编译馆中华丛书编审委员会), 1981).

Jamieson, George, *Zhongguo Duzhi Kao* (中国度支考, Examination of Fiscal Revenues and Expenditures of China), trans. Lin Lezhi (林乐之) (Shanghai: Shanghai Guangxuehui (上海广学会), 1897).

Kishimoto, Mio (岸本美绪), "清代户部黄册について" (Qing Dynasty Silver Treasury "Yellow Registers", Ministry of Revenue and Population), in 石桥秀雄ed., 清代中国の诸问题 (Some problems in the Chinese Qing Dynasty) (Tokyo: Yamakawa Publisher, 1995).

Li Pengnian (李鹏年), "Neige Daku – Qingdai Zuizhongyao de Dang'an Ku" (内阁大库－清代最重要的档案库, Archives of the Grand Secretariat – the Most Important Archives in the Qing Dynasty), *Gugong Bowuyuan Yuankan* (故宫博物院院刊, The Imperial Palace Museum Journal), 3 (1981).

Li Zhenhua (李振华), *Jindai Zhongguo Guoneiwai Dashiji* (近代中国国内外大事记, Domestic and Foreign Memorabilia of Modern China) (Taibei: Wen Hai Press, 1979).

Lu Xun, "Tan Suowei Danei Dang'an" (谈所谓' 大内档案, Talk about the So-called 'Grand Secretariat Archives'), in *Eryi ji* (而已集).

Luo Yudong (罗玉东), *Zhongguo Likin Shi* (中国厘金史, A History of Likin in China), (Shanghai: Commercial Press, 936 ；Taibei: Wen Hai Press, 1986).

Morse, H.B., *The Trade and Administration of the Chinese Empire* (Shanghai: Kelly and Walsh, ltd., 1908).

Peng Zeyi (彭泽益), "Xianfengchao Yinku Shouzhi Pouxi" (咸丰朝银库收支剖析, An Aanalysis of Revenues and Expenditures of the Silver Treasury during the Xianfeng Period), in *Shijiu Shiji Houbanqi de Zhongguo Caizheng yu Jingji* (十九世纪后半期的中国财政与经济, Chinese Finance and Economy in the Second Half of the 19th Century), (Beijing: People's Publishing House, 1983).

Ren Zhiyong (任智勇), "Shishu Wanqing Hubu Yinku Zhidu yu Gengzi Zhihou de Biange" (试述晚清户部银库制度与庚子之后的变革, A Study on the Silver Treasury in the Late Qing and Its Reform after the Boxer Uprising), in *Qingshi Yanjiu* (清史研究), 2 (2005).

Shi Zhihong and Xuyi (史志宏、徐毅), *Wan Qing Caizheng* (晚清财政: 1851~1894, Finance of the Late Qing Dynasty) (Shanghai: Shanghai University of Finance and Economics Press, 2008).

Spector, Stanley, *Li Hung-chang and the Huai Army, A study in nineteenth century Chinese regionalism* (Seattle: University of Washington Press, 1964).

Sun Xiao (孙小), "Daoguang Hubu Yinku Shiqie'an Suolun" (道光户部银库失窃案琐论, A Brief Analysis on the Embezzlement in the Silver Treasury of the Ministry of Revenue during Daoguang), in *Zhongguo Shehui Jingjishi Yanjiu* (中国社会经济史研究, Researches in Chinese Social Economic History), 4 (1985).

Tang Xianglong (汤象龙), *Zhongguo Jindai Haiguan Shuishou he Fenpei Tongji* (中国近代海关税收和分配统计, Statistics on Revenues and Their Distribution of Chinese Modern Martime Customs), (Beijing: Zhonghua Book Company, 1992).

Tang Xianglong (汤象龙), “Daoguang Chao Juanjian zhi Tongji” (道光朝捐监之统计, Statistics of Licentiates-by-purchase during *Daoguang*), in *Shehui kexue zazhi* (社会科学杂志, Jounal of Social Science), 2–4 (1931).

Vries, Peer, “Public Finance in China and Britain in the Long Eighteen Century”, LSE Economic History Working Paper Series, # 167, 2012.

Wu Tingxie (吴廷燮), *Qing Caizheng Kaolue* (清财政考略, An Outline of the Finance of the Qing Dynasty), 1914 edn.

Wu Zhaoxin (吴兆莘), *Zhongguo Shuizhi Shi* (中国税制史, Chinese Tax History) (Shanghai: Commercial Press, 1937).

Xu Daling (许大龄), *Qingdai Juanna Zhidu* (清代捐纳制度, The System of Purchasing Offices by Contributions during the Qing Period), (Taibei: Wen Hai Press, 1984 [photocopy. Originally published by the Harvard Yenching Institute, Yenching University, 1950]).

Xu Zhongshu (徐中舒), “Neige Dang'an zhi Youlai jiqi Zhengli” (内阁档案之由来及其整理, Origin and Rearrangement of the Grand Secretariat Archives), in *Ming Qing Shiliao* (明清史料, Historical Materials of Ming and Qing Dynasties), vol.1.

Xu Zhongshu (徐中舒), “Zhongyang Yanjiuyuan Lishi Yuyan Yanjiusuo Suocang dang'an de Fenxi – zaishu neige daku dang'an zhi youlai jiqi zhengli” (中央研究院历史语言研究所所藏档案的分析－再述内阁大库档案之由来及其整理, An Analysis on the Archives Collected by the Institute of History and Philology of the Academia Sinica – a further discussion on the origin and rearrangement of the Grand Secretariat archives), in *Zhongguo Jindai Jingjishi Yanjiu Jikan* (中国近代经济史研究集刊, Collected Papers of Researches in Chinese Modern Economic History), vol.2–2 (May 1934).

Zhang Xiaotang (张晓堂), “*Qianlong* Nianjian Qing Zhengfu Pingheng Caizheng Zhi Yanjiu” (乾隆年间清政府平衡财政之研究, A Study on the Fiscal Balance of the Central Government during Qianlong), in *Qingshi Yanjiu Ji* (清史研究集, Collected Papers of Studies in Qing History), 7, 1990.

Zhao Jingcheng (赵景澄), “Qingdai Hubu Sanku Shimo” (清代户部三库始末, An account of the Three Stores of the Ministry of Revenue in the Qing Dynasty), in the 53rd historical supplement to *Tienjin Yishi Bao* (天津益世报), May 2, 1937.

Zhou Bodi (周伯棣), *Zhongguo Caizheng Shi* (中国财政史, History of Chinese Finance) (Shanghai: People's Publishing House of Shanghai, 1981).

Zhou Yumin (周育民), *Wanqing Caizheng yu Shehui Bianqian* (晚清财政与社会变迁, Financial and Social Changes in the Late Qing Dynasty), (Shanghai: People's Publishing House of Shanghai, 2000).

# Index